SCHOLAR Study Guide

Higher ESOL

Authored and reviewed by:

Mark Watson

Susan Paton

Heriot-Watt University

Edinburgh EH14 4AS, United Kingdom.

Distributed by the SCHOLAR Forum.

SCHOLAR Study Guide Higher ESOL

Higher ESOL Course Code: C827 76

ISBN 978-1-911057-30-7

Print Production and Fulfilment in UK by Print Trail www.printtrail.com

Acknowledgements

Thanks are due to the members of Heriot-Watt University's SCHOLAR team who planned and created these materials, and to the many colleagues who reviewed the content.

We would like to acknowledge the assistance of the education authorities, colleges, teachers and students who contributed to the SCHOLAR programme and who evaluated these materials.

Grateful acknowledgement is made for permission to use the following material in the SCHOLAR programme:

The Scottish Qualifications Authority for permission to use Past Papers assessments.

The Scottish Government for financial support.

The content of this Study Guide is aligned to the Scottish Qualifications Authority (SQA) curriculum.

Contents

Unit 1: ESOL in Everyday Life

Unit 1 Topic 1

Personal profile

Contents

Learning objective

By the end of this topic you should be able to:

- use present tenses and continuous and perfect aspect, in the context of personal identity

- utilise your knowledge and understanding of compound adjectives

- demonstrate an extended range of vocabulary in the topic area through reading and listening skills practice

- apply your knowledge of writing genre through writing an email.

This topic explores ways of describing ourselves, our personalities and our hobbies. It revises tenses you should already be familiar with at Higher level: *present simple*, *present continuous*, *present perfect simple* and *present perfect continuous*. It introduces advanced vocabulary relevant to the subjects discussed. It includes work on all four skills: speaking, reading, writing, and listening. There are also supplementary pronunciation exercises. Assessment opportunities occur at the end of the topic.

Certain sections contain sound files. You may download these and use them on your mp3 player or equivalent to practise your pronunciation. This may be very useful if there are times when you will not have access to the materials online.

1.1   Grammar: Mixed tenses

Before you start learning new material for ESOL Higher, we will quickly revise some grammar you should already know before you begin.

Using what you have learned from National 5 ESOL or in your own studies, try the following variety of exercises practising tenses you should be familiar with.

Reading: Mixed tenses (10 min)   Go online

Q1: Read the passage and replace the gaps with the most appropriate phrase from the given list.

Phrase list:she has been practising: she has developed: her family is: they never guess: she achieves: she is keeping: she has lived: she has been experiencing: she is thinking:

Keira considers herself to be Scottish, although _____ from overseas. _____ here for the best part of fifteen years and _____ a strong Scottish accent in that time. "When I make new friends, _____ that I was not born here", she says. Keira is currently a student at the Royal Dance Institute and in recent weeks _____ for her final practical exam. She is worried because _____ difficulties with some of the more complicated moves. _____ about specialising in ballet next year and therefore _____ her fingers and toes crossed that _____ the required results in her exams.

Grammar practice: Mixed tenses (10 min)   Go online

For each question select the correct tense from the two choices shown.

Q2: I usually *am eating/eat* a sandwich for lunch at college.

....

Q3: Jonathan *works/is working* in a bank for his work experience placement.

....

Q4: We *have been visiting/have visited* the south coast many times on holiday.

....

Q5: She *is sitting/has been sitting* her dance exam later today.

....

Q6: Vishesh *is waiting/waits* for you at the bus stop.

....

Q7: People *have been becoming/have become* very dependent on their mobile phones.

....

Q8: Jitka *has never failed/is never failing* her English exams.

....

Q9: Wajdi *has always been/is always being* the hardest working student in the class.

....

Q10: Sara, on the other hand, *has never tried/has never been trying* to improve her grades.

....

Q11: I *am revising/have been revising* every day for a month because I am worried about my exam.

Reading: Gayle's story (15 min) Go online

Read the following short passage and answer the questions which follow. The questions should be answered True or False.

Gayle: The English teacher

Gayle has been working as an English teacher for ten years, and she would not swap her job for anything else in the world! To Gayle, teaching is more than an occupation, it is a passion. She studied Accountancy at university, where she gained several distinctions in her studies and found the course an absorbing experience, but she realised that dealing with figures on a day-to-day basis did not appeal to her. She considers herself a social animal and therefore decided to pursue a career in a more people-oriented environment, so she enrolled on a teaching course. The most rewarding part of her job is seeing her students progress over time, from speaking very little English at the outset, to finding jobs or university places, and feeling that she had a part to play in that process. However, she does admit that it is sometimes hard to keep in touch with former students when they leave her class.

Q12: Gayle worked as an accountant before she became a teacher.

a) true
b) false

....

Q13: Teaching is the only job Gayle wants to do.

a) true
b) false

....

Q14: She did not enjoy her accountancy degree.

a) true
b) false

....

Q15: Gayle has an outgoing personality.

a) true
b) false

....

Q16: Gayle never knows what happens to her students once they have left her English class.

a) true
b) false

Vocabulary: Definitions (10 min)   Go online

Q17: Read the passage about Gayle, the English teacher, again.

Gayle: The English Teacher

Gayle has been working as an English teacher for ten years, and she would not swap her job for anything else in the world! To Gayle, teaching is more than an occupation, it is a passion. She studied Accountancy at university, where she gained distinctions in her studies and found the course an absorbing experience, but she realised that dealing with figures on a day to day basis did not appeal to her. She considers herself a social animal and therefore decided to pursue a career in a more people-oriented environment, so she enrolled on a teaching course. The most rewarding part of her job is seeing her students progress over time, from speaking very little English at the outset, to finding jobs or university places, and feeling that she had a part to play in that process. However, she does admit that it has been hard to keep in touch with former students when they leave her class.

Can you highlight a word or expression (no more than three words) which means:

1. Something you enjoy most in life that gives you great pleasure (n.)
2. A sign of excellence; something which shows you have excelled in a subject/situation (n.)
3. Fascinating and interesting (adj.)
4. To go after something that you really want (v.)
5. The beginning of something (n.)

Listening: Follow your dreams (15 min) Go online

For this activity you will need access to the sound file *hg-cesl1-1-1listening.mp3*

Listen to the passage then answer the questions that follow.

Once you have completed this activity, the transcript of the listening is available for you to study in the expected answer.

Q18: Jeremy has been living in Scotland

a) since his childhood
b) since he was three years old
c) for the last three years

....

Q19: Jeremy's father

a) works in the printing trade
b) works as a chef
c) does not work

....

Q20: Jeremy was

a) very successful at school
b) reasonably successful at school
c) an underachiever at school

....

Q21: His choice of university degree was

a) Marketing
b) Law
c) Fine art

....

Q22: These days, Jeremy

a) eats in London
b) owns a hotel in London
c) owns a restaurant in London

1.2 Vocabulary: Physical appearance

The concept of *appearance* includes physical attributes such as height, weight, distinguishing facial features, eye colour, hair colour.

Physical appearance (10 min)   Go online

Look at the descriptions of physical appearance. Which one of these words could NOT be used to describe the attribute shown?

Q23: Height

a) tall
b) short
c) average
d) slender
e) petite

....

Q24: Build

a) pale
b) stocky
c) skinny
d) athletic
e) muscular

....

Q25: Hair colour

a) dark
b) blonde
c) red
d) yellow
e) fair

....

Q26: Hair length

a) waist length
b) shoulder length
c) shaved
d) bald
e) neck length

....

Q27: Hair style

a) curly
b) wavy
c) straight
d) spiky
e) undulating

....

Q28: Eyes

a) brown
b) black
c) green
d) blue
e) hazel

....

Q29: Complexion

a) fair
b) dark
c) sallow
d) pale
e) orange

....

Q30: Clothing

a) casual
b) trendy
c) folded
d) smart
e) scruffy

Physical appearance adjectives (15 min) Go online

Q31: Do you know the meaning of these words? Match the adjective with its meaning:

Adjectives:

1. neutral
2. unflattering
3. flattering
4. polite

Meaning:

A) Praising someone and making them feel pleased
B) Highlighting a negative point
C) Pleasant and following societal rules
D) Politically correct, neither positive nor negative

....

Q32: Look at the following words describing physical appearance and sort them into three columns depending on whether they are flattering, unflattering or polite/neutral. You may wish to use a dictionary.

fat	obese	plump
stocky	overweight	thin
skinny	slim	underweight
slender	ugly	unattractive
plain	muscular	athletic
elderly	old	ancient

flattering	unflattering	polite/neutral

Describing appearance (15 min)   Go online

Complete each question with the most appropriate word(s) from the given list.

Word list: receding hairline: wrinkles: dark complexion: high cheekbones: dimples: fringe: sideburns: freckles: highlights: rosy cheeks.

Q33: If someone has tanned or brown coloured skin, we can describe them as having a
_____.

....

Q34: _____ are the small dents or areas on your cheeks that show when you smile. They are considered attractive.

....

Q35: When people dye small strips of their hair a different colour, these are called
_____

....

Q36: _____ are several light brown coloured spots on your skin, often on the face and arms.

....

Q37: Short hair that hangs over a person's forehead is known as a _____

....

Q38: Models are often chosen because they have _____

....

Q39: The strips of hair that grow down both sides of a man's face are called _____

....

Q40: An early sign of baldness could be a _____ when young.

....

Q41: Most people have a few _____ around their eyes and mouth when they are older.

....

Q42: _____ are an attractive and healthy redness around the centre of the face.

Writing: Appearance (25 min)

Write a short description (approximately 100 words) of yourself or someone you know very well, e.g. a family member or a famous person. Focus on their appearance. You can use some of the adjectives from the previous exercises but also add any other appropriate ones you may already know.

You can check your work against the expected answer.

If you wish feedback, show your work to your teacher or tutor.

1.3   Vocabulary: Idiomatic language

Idioms are expressions which, when taken as one idea, have different meanings from the words that form them. For example, to *burn your bridges* neither refers to fire nor to structures used for crossing. Instead, it is an idiom which has the meaning, *to give yourself no way back or no way of reversing the present situation*.

 Be careful not to confuse idioms with metaphors or similes.

A **simile** compares things by suggesting they are alike.

Example Love is like a rose.

A **metaphor** makes a comparison between two things that are unlike each other in many respects but are implied to have something in common.

Example Life is a dream.

Idioms generally do not make sense if you try to directly translate them word by word to another language, so they must be learned as chunks of language together with their specific meaning.

Idioms using physical features (10 min)	Go online

Q43: Match the idiomatic expression in the first list with its definition in the second list. You may need to use a dictionary.

He is under the thumb.	To tell someone how you feel about something, after a long time of staying quiet
Tracy's new car cost her an arm and a leg.	To give your full attention to something.
Tell me what you know. I am all ears!	To feel nervous about something you are going to do.
Tim resigned after the argument. I think it was a knee jerk reaction.	To make a decision quickly without all the facts, or without thinking properly.
Sean's eyes are bigger than his stomach. He will never manage that!	To disagree about something; to have differing opinions.
I need to speak to my boss. There are a few things I have to get off my chest.	To think you are hungrier than you actually are.
We used to be good friends, but we do not see eye to eye now.	To meet someone socially.
Her dad had a lump in his throat the day she was married.	Something that is very expensive.
The mayor had butterflies in his stomach as he prepared to break the bad news.	To be overcome with emotion and unable to speak.
John always invites himself to parties to try and rub shoulders with celebrities.	To be controlled by another person, often a husband/wife.

1.4   Vocabulary: Compound adjectives

A person's *character* may be defined as a combination of the attributes that make up their personality. It is their behaviour, their manner and their beliefs, and how they react to the world around them.

Compound adjectives are made up of two or more words and are often separated by a hyphen (-).

Examples

1. The adjective and present participle combined

The adjective *hard* and present participle *working* come together to form
hard-working.

. . . .

2. The adjective/adverb and past participle combined

The adjective *absent* and the past participle *minded* come together to form
absent-minded.

Compound adjectives (10 min)   Go online

Q44: Try to make compound adjectives by taking one word from each list.

Hard-	hearted
Absent-	mannered
Well-	minded
Bad-	fashioned
Easy-	going
Hot-	minded
Quick-	witted
Kind-	headed
Old-	tempered
Open-	working

Compound adjective meanings (10 min)   Go online

For each adjective find the sentence from the given list which matches the meaning.

Q45:

Hot-headed	To behave in a polite fashion
Absent-minded	To be able to think of good ideas and responses instantly
Hard-working	To be generous and caring towards others
Old-fashioned	To believe and follow ideas which are no longer relevant, or from the past
Bad-tempered	To do things without thinking about the consequences; to act rashly
Kind-hearted	To be friendly and kind towards people; to be of a relaxed nature
Easy-going	To forget things or be unaware of your surroundings
Quick-witted	To be willing to accept new ideas and other people's opinions
Well-mannered	To become easily angered
Open-minded	To put in a lot of effort into a job or a task

Compound adjectives: Antonyms (10 min)   Go online

In this exercise you are required to match compound adjectives with a corresponding antonym.

Match the antonym (word with the opposite meaning) in the first list to the compound adjective in the second list.

Q46:

Hot-headed	Idle
Absent-minded	Polite
Hard-working	Uptight
Old-fashioned	Ponderous
Bad-tempered	Trendy
Kind-hearted	Intolerant
Easy-going	Mean-spirited
Quick-witted	Cautious
Ill-mannered	Even-tempered
Open-minded	Attentive

1.5 Writing: Describing yourself

Writing: Describing yourself (25 min)

Write a short description of yourself, paying particular attention to describing your personality and giving a description of your physical appearance. You can use some of the adjectives listed in the previous exercises, but you may wish to include other adjectives / information of your own.

You should write around 150 words.

When you are finished show your work to your teacher or tutor. You can also check your work against the expected answer.

1.6 Speaking: The family

Discussion: The family (10 min)

Discuss the following questions with a partner or your teacher.

1. Do you think family life in the UK is similar to family life in your country?

2. Is family life across the world changing because of changes to travel and communication? How?

3. How important is family to you? Why?

Vocabulary review (10 min) Go online

Match the words about family to their definition.

Q47:

Sibling	Attributes or characteristics associated with being a father.
Nuclear family	Woman or man with children but no partner.
Single parent	Describes a couple who have legally separated.
Maternal	Child whose legal parents who are not their original parents.
Adopted	Caring and protective feelings associated with mothers.
Extended family	A brother or sister.
Divorced	Family including parents, children, grandparents, aunts, uncles.
Upbringing	Family including only parents and children.
Childcare	Process in which a child is trained and educated in life.
Paternal	Care and supervision of a child at home or outside.

1.7   Reading: Weddings

The minimum age at which a couple may legally marry in the UK is 16. However many couples wait until they are in their twenties or thirties. You will now read a text about a wedding in Scotland. Before you read, think about your own knowledge and experience of weddings.

Discussion: Weddings (10 min)

Discuss the following questions with a partner or your teacher.

1. At what age do people in your country generally get married?

2. In what ways are weddings celebrated in your country?

3. Who pays for weddings in your country?

4. Are traditional weddings still popular or are younger generations having weddings in a new or different way?

Wedding terms (10 min)   Go online

Q48: Choose from the given list, the role of each person in the wedding image which follows.

- bridesmaid
- best man
- bridegroom
- page boy
- flower girl
- bride

Reading: Wedding

Go online

Read the text which follows and then find words with a similar meaning in the exercise below

Although I have always considered myself to be a very progressive woman, I suppose when it comes to marriage I am quite traditional. We had been dating for around two years and were on holiday in Tuscany when Andy proposed. He got down on one knee when he asked me to marry him and gave me an engagement ring he had chosen for me. Fortunately, we have similar taste!

No sooner had we celebrated the engagement than we began planning the wedding. This involved a great deal of organisation and I had to be uncharacteristically patient and diplomatic! Never before or since have I been offered so much unsolicited advice. As I do not have any sisters, I chose my oldest friend as my bridesmaid. Andy chose his brother as best man and our nephews and nieces were page boys and flower girls.

The ceremony took place in a small local church. I wore a traditional white dress, Andy wore a kilt and my father gave me away. I found this part of the day really nerve-racking. I think it was the gravity and formality of the walk down the aisle. I was worried I might trip or fluff my lines. Andy on the other hand, seemed totally unruffled by the occasion!

I think that the best man has quite a hard job. Not only does he have to ensure things go smoothly on the day but he also has to try and make a humorous speech during the reception when everyone else is eating and drinking!

The reception passed in a flash. It was not until about ten in the evening that I finally let myself go and joined the dancers. Only then did I feel sure that everyone was having a good time. In spite of the nerves, I can honestly say it really was the best day of my life!

Q49: Match the words and phrases with the most appropriate definitions.

Progressive	Worrying
Traditional	Seriousness
Dating	Enlightened
Uncharacteristically	Conventional
Diplomatic	Going out with
Unsolicited	Party
Nerve-racking	Tactful
Gravity	Relaxed
Unruffled	Atypically
Reception	Uninvited

1.8 Reading: Agony Aunt

The letter in the activity which follows was published in the supplement of a national newspaper in the *Ask Maeve* column of the family issues section. Maeve is an *agony aunt* who gives advice to readers. Readers are invited to submit problems to this section, some of which will be published and answered by other readers.

Before you read, discuss the following questions with a partner or your teacher/tutor.

1. Do you / have you ever had disagreements within your family?

2. What kind of issues and problems do you think families tend to have?

3. What kind of problems do you think people would write about to an *agony aunt*?

Reading: Agony Aunt (25 min)

Read the letter and then answer the questions which follow.

Dear Maeve

My parents were divorced three years ago and until recently I lived with my mum and two sisters. My parents' separation was acrimonious. It became particularly unpleasant when my father remarried last year. I used to spend quite a bit of time at my father's house, because my mum and sisters are very close and I often felt left out by them. To be honest my father gave me a lot more freedom than my mother who always nagged about homework and housework. My dad's new wife is now expecting a child and my father has made it quite clear that he has no real interest in seeing my sisters or me. Although I don't think I will miss seeing my dad, I will definitely miss the escape from my mother's regime! I am in my last year at school and plan to go to university next year, hopefully in another city. Meanwhile, I really want to move in with my aunt. She is a great person, has a laid-back approach to life and we get on really well. My mum says I can't move in with my aunt because she has enough on her plate with two children under six and no husband. What should I do?

Christopher

Q50: Christopher's parents had a difficult divorce.

a) true
b) false

....

Q51: Christopher sees his mother as a disciplinarian.

a) true
b) false

....

Q52: Christopher's aunt is uptight and difficult to live with.

a) true
b) false

....

Q53: Christopher's aunt is a single parent.

a) true
b) false

Find phrases in the text with the following meaning:

Q54: Having a strong attachment (1 word)

....

Q55: Not feeling part of something (3 words)

....

Q56: Things with which to deal or cope (3 words)

Vocabulary: Family problems (20 min)   Go online

Below is a summary of the issues raised within the text.

Q57: Fill in the gaps using the most appropriate word from the given list.

Word list: rigid: security: siblings: paternal: insecure: single mother

Christopher is _____ because of his parents' divorce and the closeness of the relationship between his _____ and their mother. His father seems to lack any _____ emotions where Christopher and his sisters are concerned. His mother is trying to provide _____ and boundaries in her son's life which Christopher is desperate to escape. His aunt, a _____ seems to offer a compromise, offering Christopher the security which he needs in a less _____ environment.

1.9   Vocabulary: Collocation

A collocation is where two or more words frequently occur together.

Example 1

One type of collocation is where a verb always occurs with a particular preposition:

Example depend on; disappointed in

Example 2

Another type of collocation is where a verb tends to occur with a particular noun:

Example do the washing up, go dancing

Example 3

A collocation can also be lexical and include nouns, adjectives, verbs and adverbs.

Example bitterly disappointed, blissfully happy.

Making collocations (15 min) Go online

Q58: Create collocations by matching a word from the first list with one from the second list.

1. brought
2. family
3. sibling
4. father
5. bread
6. maternal
7. make
8. have
9. marital
10. single

A) winner
B) up
C) parent
D) a commitment
E) an affair
F) status
G) values
H) figure
I) instinct
J) rivalry

Understanding collocations (5 min) Go online

For this activity you will need access to the sound file *hg-cesl1-1-3listening.mp3*

Listen to Elizabeth. While listening consider the following issues/questions:

Q59: Describe Elizabeth's upbringing:

a) Valuable
b) Supported
c) Traditional

....

Q60: What kind of families did the speaker's friends have when they were children?

a) Similar to hers
b) Different from hers
c) She doesn't mention her friends

....

Q61: Do the speaker's friends and colleagues have two parent families?

a) Mostly yes
b) Mostly no

Collocation meanings (10 min)   Go online

Q62: Match the collocations with the most appropriate definitions.

Sibling rivalry	A person who takes on the role of father in a family or other situation
Bring up	A promise of loyalty and steadfastness
Make a commitment	A desire to protect, nurture and care for others
Maternal instinct	A belief in the moral value of a family
Single parent	To care for and educate
Father figure	A man or woman with children but no partner
Breadwinner	To have a relationship with someone to whom you are not married
Marital status	Description of state of being married or otherwise
Family values	One who earns money in a family
Have an affair	Competitiveness among sisters and brothers

Using collocations (10 min)   Go online

Using the given list of collocations complete the gaps in each question.

List:

bring up: family values: father figure: marital status: breadwinner: having an affair: single parents: sibling rivalry: make a commitment: maternal instinct

Q63: The sisters play competitive tennis but there seems to be no issue with

----

....

Q64: Their marriage broke down because her husband was ---------------

....

Q65: There seems to be no respect for old-fashioned _____ these days.

....

Q66: She often seems exhausted; it's not easy being a single parent and having to _____ the children alone.

....

Q67: He never wanted to _____ to her even after four years of dating, so she married another man.

....

Q68: I find it strange that tabloid newspapers always indicate a person's _____ in reports.

....

Q69: I've always felt that he was more of a _____ than a friend as he is so much older than I am.

....

Q70: He has decided to give up work and look after the children, after all, his wife is the major _____.

....

Q71: She never wanted children; she always said she didn't have much of a _____

....

Q72: It never ceases to amaze me how many of my friends have ended up as _____ .

1.10 Writing: A report

In ESOL assessments and in future study situations, you may be asked to analyse data and produce a report. It is important that you are able to summarise the main points using appropriate language to do so. This activity will provide you with an opportunity to do this.

Writing: A report (30 min)

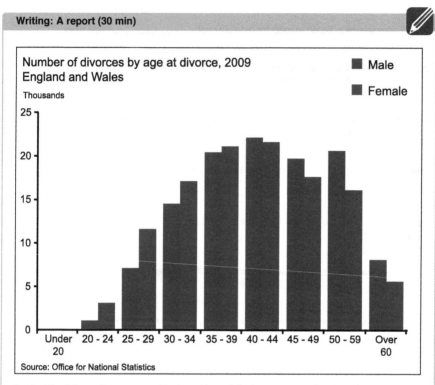

Number of divorces by age at divorce, 2009 England and Wales

Look at the information presented in the table and the language used to describe changes.

The table shows the number of divorces in 2009 by age of divorce in England and Wales.

Write a report for a university professor describing the information in the table.

Write around 150 words.

Before you write your answer to the question consider the following questions:

Q73: Should this be written in formal or informal language?

Q74: Should you attempt to explain the information in the table, i.e. why the divorce rate is changing?

Q75: Should you make recommendations about how the divorce rate could change or what to do next?

When you have written your answer compare what you have written with the model answer given

Use the model to judge your own essay. If you wish feedback, show your work to your teacher or tutor.

1.11 Writing: Email to a friend

Writing: Email to a friend (60 min)

Write an email or letter to a new penfriend in another country. Imagine that you do not know this person and this is the first communication between you.

Write about yourself, giving a description of the following points:

- Personal information: name, age, hometown, nationality etc.
- Your appearance
- Your character
- What you do now (work / study / hobbies)
- Your future plans

Before you begin, consider the following questions.

- What is the purpose of the communication?
- Who is the intended audience of the letter?
- What level of formality (register) would be appropriate?

Make some notes or a mind map to help plan your writing.

Try to write between 200-300 words.

When you are finished ask your teacher or tutor to check your work.

When you have written your answer compare what you have written with the model answer given.

1.12 Reading comprehension: Email to Marie

The following activity is a reading comprehension covering the work of this topic.

Before you begin read the email. Read the email below quickly and try to understand the main ideas before you answer the questions.

Hi Marie

How are you doing? It's been ages since I last heard from you - three weeks at least, where have you been? Haven't even seen you online! I just wanted to check that you are well and catch up with your news. I also wanted to remind you that you are invited to our house as usual for Christmas. Mum and Dad will be delighted to see you. You know they absolutely love the company of our friends. I think because they don't have their parents any more, or grandchildren yet, they feel a bit sorry for themselves.... No pressure!

Anyway, this year Fiona is bringing her new fiancé, Andy. He is really lovely and guess what, he plays the piano really well, so we should be able to do a bit of singing if people are in the mood. He's paying us quite a compliment by coming, because he usually goes to his mother's. Apparently they have an enormous family, spanning four generations. I think Fiona and Andy will get married soon and start a family. They both love kids. However, I can't imagine Fiona being a traditional mum, she's such a high flier at work. I expect she'll keep her job and be the main breadwinner. Not only will Andy have to have to do the cooking, but I'm sure he'll also have to give up his job to look after the offspring. They really are the antithesis of my mum and dad. Anyway, with all of that going on, they are definitely taking the focus away from my single status which is a great relief!

I am really looking forward to Christmas. It'll be fantastic to have a rest as I have been studying really hard for my exams. I'm just doing Sociology at the moment, as you know, but it's more in-depth now that I'm in third year. I'm specialising in the family - it's just so interesting! I've found out lots of fascinating facts. Did you know that in the UK, women tend to instigate divorce far more often than men until about age 40, and then it completely changes and men do the divorcing. How about that? I have also discovered that we are quite normal in not wanting to start a family at the moment, most women in the UK are leaving it later nowadays!

Anyway Marie, let me know if you are coming to stay at Christmas. I want to tell Fiona that I've got a friend coming too. Yes, it's the old sibling rivalry surfacing again!

Take care

Speak soon

Gemma

Reading comprehension: Email to Marie (30 min) Go online

Read the following email once more.

Hi Marie

How are you doing? It's been ages since I last heard from you - three weeks at least, where have you been? Haven't even seen you online! I just wanted to check that you are well and catch up with your news. I also wanted to remind you that you are invited to our house as usual for Christmas. Mum and Dad will be delighted to see you. You know they absolutely love the company of our friends. I think because they don't have their parents any more, or grandchildren yet, they feel a bit sorry for themselves.... No pressure!

Anyway, this year Fiona is bringing her new fiancé, Andy - he is really lovely and guess what, he plays the piano really well, so we should be able to do a bit of singing if people are in the mood. He's paying us quite a complement by coming, because he usually goes to his mother's. Apparently they have an enormous family, spanning four generations. I think Fiona and Andy will get married soon and start a family. They both love kids. However, I can't imagine Fiona being a traditional mum, she's such a high flier at work. I expect she'll keep her job and be the main breadwinner. Not only will Andy have to have to do the cooking, but I'm sure he'll also have to give up his job to look after the offspring. They really are the antithesis of my mum and dad. Anyway, with all of that going on, they are definitely taking the focus away from my single status which is a great relief!

I am really looking forward to Christmas. It'll be fantastic to have a rest as I have been studying really hard for my exams. I'm just doing Sociology at the moment, as you know, but it's more in-depth now that I'm in third year. I'm specialising in the family - it's just so interesting! I've found out lots of fascinating facts. Did you know that in the UK, women tend to instigate divorce far more often than men until about age 40, and then it completely changes and men do the divorcing. How about that? I have also discovered that we are quite normal in not wanting to start a family at the moment, most women in the UK are leaving it later nowadays!

Anyway Marie, let me know if you are coming to stay at Christmas. I want to tell Fiona that I've got a friend coming too. Yes, it's the old sibling rivalry surfacing again!

Take care

Speak soon

Gemma

Q76: Is the email written in informal or formal language? Give examples to support your answer

....

Q77: What is the relationship between Marie and Gemma?

a) They are friends
b) They are mother and daughter
c) They are sisters

....

Q78: What type of family does Gemma have: extended or nuclear?

....

Q79: What type of family does Andy have: extended or nuclear?

Decide whether the following statements are true or false.

Q80: Gemma thinks that Fiona has inherited their mother's parental style.

a) true
b) false

....

Q81: Gemma's parents are keen to fill their house with family and friends.

a) true
b) false

....

Q82: According to Gemma more men than women under forty initiate divorce proceedings.

a) true
b) false

....

Q83: Gemma and her sister have a competitive relationship.

a) true
b) false

1.13   Listening comprehension: Claire and Edwin

You will need access to the sound file *hg-cesl1-1-2listening.mp3* to complete this listening comprehension.

Listen to the following dialogue which contains examples of many of the language areas you have covered within the topic.

Listen to the recording and make short notes about:

- Who is talking
- What they are talking about

Listening comprehension: Claire and Edwin (15 min) Go online

You will need access to the sound file *hg-cesl1-1-2listening.mp3* to complete this listening comprehension.

Listen to the recording again and try to answer the following questions:

Q84: Claire and Edwin met

a) when she was twenty-four
b) while they were working in the hospital
c) when she left England at nineteen

....

Q85: Claire's ex-boyfriend was

a) impatient and smart
b) talkative and smart
c) absent-minded and talkative

....

Q86: Claire describes herself as

a) not having a good attention span
b) being quick-witted
c) not being very intelligent

....

Q87: Barry is tall and good looking.

a) true
b) false

....

Q88: Barry has long, dark hair.

a) true
b) false

....

Q89: Edwin has good taste in clothes.

a) true
b) false

....

Q90: Claire thinks that she is different now compared to when she was younger.

a) true
b) false

. . . .

Q91: The dialogue is mainly about (choose the best answer)

a) Claire and Edwin's wedding plans
b) The stages of life and how people change
c) Claire's relationships past and present

1.14 Vocabulary list

You might find it helpful to have a list of some of the words which have been introduced in this topic.

thesis (noun)	a long essay or piece of writing that is undertaken during academic study
to nag (verb)	to repeatedly ask / tell someone to do sth. they do not want to do
to strengthen (verb)	to make something stronger
to strike sb. (verb)	to have an idea or thought enter your head suddenly
prospects (noun)	chances of achieving something
gradually (adverb)	slowly; stage by stage
to excel (verb)	to do something very well
high-flier (noun)	a person who has achieved a lot
franchise (noun)	a business that has several chains under a central name but each one operates independently
eatery (noun)	another name for a restaurant

Unit 1 Topic 2

Lifestyle

Contents

Learning objective

By the end of this topic you should be able to:

- use a wider range of vocabulary in the topic area

- use passive constructions with greater accuracy

- demonstrate a wider knowledge and understanding of idiomatic phrases

- demonstrate your knowledge of writing genre through writing a report

- demonstrate greater accuracy in pronunciation of topic specific lexis

---

This topic explores the subject of health, including conventional and alternative medicine, through practice in reading, writing, listening and speaking. The grammar sections review and practise passive constructions, and there is a focus on report writing and pronunciation activities. Assessment opportunities occur at the end of the topic.

Certain sections contain sound files. You may download these and use them on your mp3 player or equivalent to practise your pronunciation. This may be very useful if there are times when you will not have access to the materials online.

2.1   Vocabulary: Medical practitioners

Vocabulary: Medical practitioners (20 min)   Go online

You will need access to the following sound files to be able to complete the pronunciation part of this activity.

hg-cesl1-2-1vocab1.mp3 to hg-cesl1-2-1vocab10.mp3

Listen and repeat to practise the pronunciation of the following words.

- surgeon
- pharmacist
- general practitioner
- orthodontist
- anaesthetist
- physiotherapist
- psychiatrist
- cardiologist
- paediatrician
- orthopaedic surgeon

Q1: Match the names of the various different medical practitioners to the definitions.

Definitions:

A) A person who helps with mental health disorders.

B) An expert in medicines and their use.

C) A doctor who specialises in manual or instrumental treatment of the body.

D) A person who treats illness and injury through massage, heat and exercise.

E) A doctor who diagnoses medical problems in the home or in a surgery.

F) A person whose job it is to correct the position of the teeth.

G) A doctor specialising in diagnosis and treatment of conditions affecting the muscular / skeletal system.

H) A doctor who administers drugs and monitors care of patients in surgery.

I) A doctor who specialises in the treatment and care of children.

J) A specialist in the diagnosis and treatment of heart conditions.

Names:

1. paediatrician
2. physiotherapist
3. general practitioner
4. orthodontist
5. surgeon
6. cardiologist
7. orthopaedic surgeon
8. psychiatrist
9. anaesthetist
10. pharmacist

2.2   Reading: A Winter's Tale

Pre-reading activity: A Winter's Tale (10 min)   Go online

Q2:   Find definitions for the words from the text

1. regaling
2. gesticulating
3. concussion
4. overwhelming
5. ramifications
6. protracted
7. fracture
8. humerus
9. plaster cast
10. prevent
11. intimidated
12. atrophy
13. dedication
14. rehabilitate

A) Bandage and hard covering
B) Mild brain injury causing unconsciousness
C) Made to feel small
D) Long bone in the upper arm
E) Commitment
F) Amusing
G) Lengthened
H) Making signs
I) Daunting
J) Restore to previous condition
K) Degenerate
L) Break
M) Impede
N) Consequences

Speaking: Life changing moments (5 min)

Before reading, discuss the following questions with a partner or your tutor, if possible.

1. Have you ever broken a bone in your body?
2. In what ways might breaking a bone change one's life?
3. Have you had moments in your life which you now recognise as pivotal?

Reading: A Winter's Tale (30 min)

Read the text and answer the questions which follow.

A Winter's Tale

1. I broke my arm at the top of a mountain. It was a cold sunny day in December, and the conditions for climbing were good. We had just started to make our descent and I was regaling my friend Drew with an anecdote, gesticulating wildly as I did so. There were only a few small patches of ice at the summit, but unfortunately I managed to slip on one of them, landing backwards on my folded arm as I fell. Since I hit the ground quite forcefully, Drew suspected concussion but in fact I was all too aware of what was happening. I had an overwhelming sense that this moment was going to have long term ramifications.

2. We had ascended the mountain, a Munro of some three thousand feet, in around ninety minutes but our descent was significantly more protracted. I would have appreciated a stretcher, but Drew had no idea that I had a fracture. Throughout the painful trudge downhill I would periodically burst out laughing which belied the reality of the situation. I think this was a consequence of both shock and a heightened adrenalin level.

3. More than three hours had elapsed by the time we reached the foot of the mountain. Drew took me to Accident and Emergency for a check-up where an X-ray revealed a bad fracture of the humerus. In the Orthopaedic ward, the specialist's opinion was that the limb be put in a plaster cast and strapped to my torso. However, the nurses on duty that day argued for a different approach. Christmas was coming and this arrangement would prevent me from dressing up. I did not volunteer an opinion since I was still too stunned and somewhat intimidated by the experts.

4. Several months after the accident, the cast was finally removed. My initial elation gave way to distress as I said hello to my new arm hanging skinny and bent at my side. It seemed that if the specialist had been more resolute the arm would have regained its original shape.

5. After the cast was removed it took several more weeks of physiotherapy to recover any meaningful movement. The muscles had suffered atrophy and my brain had long ago stopped believing that I had a useful left arm. This combination meant that adequate range of movement took some time to be restored. The physiotherapist was inspirational; she really motivated me and instilled me with the confidence to succeed.

6. The experience was life changing and not just because of the transformation in my arm. Six months confinement had given me a lot of time to reflect and I realised that I wanted to change profession. I was so impressed with the care and dedication of the healthcare professionals I met that I decided to train as an occupational therapist. My job is really rewarding, and I have had no cause to look back since my training. Perhaps it was my destiny to lose concentration at the top of that mountain.

Q3:   Given the weather conditions, the writer is not surprised she had an accident.

a) true
b) false

....

Q4: Drew recognised the seriousness of the situation

a) true
b) false

....

Q5: It was a dubious pleasure to have the plaster cast removed

a) true
b) false

....

Q6: The influence of the nursing staff negatively affected the writer's recovery

a) true
b) false

....

Q7: The accident caused degeneration of the arm

a) true
b) false

....

Q8: Range of movement in the arm was restored solely through the perseverance of the physiotherapist

a) true
b) false

....

Q9: The writer is convinced that fate was responsible for the lapse in concentration that caused the accident

a) true
b) false

Q10: Find a word with the following meaning:

Paragraph 4 — *pleasure and excitement*

....

Q11: Find a word with the following meaning:

Paragraph 4 — *severe unhappiness*

....

Q12: Find a word with the following meaning:

Paragraph 5 — *sufficient*

....

Q13: Find a word with the following meaning:

Paragraph 6 — *radical change*

....

Q14: Find a word with the following meaning:

Paragraph 6 — *satisfying*

2.3   Quiz: How healthy are you?

The quiz which follows reflects some of the current recommendations for optimal health.

Try the quiz to see how much you know about being healthy. Then, if possible, discuss the answers to each question and compare your ideas with a partner or your teacher.

How healthy are you? (20 min)   Go online

Q15: The requisite amount of sleep for an average person is

a)   7 - 8 hours
b)   12 - 14 hours
c)   5 - 6 hours

....

Q16: How many caffeine rich drinks (tea, coffee, soft drinks) are prudent on an average day?

a)   5 - 7
b)   8 - 10
c)   1 - 3

....

Q17: You should exercise to the point of perspiration

a)   every day
b)   once a week
c)   three times a week

....

Q18: How much water should you drink every day?

a)   2 litres
b)   1 litre
c)   half a litre

....

Q19: The number of units of alcohol men/women can safely consume each week is?

a) 28 / 21
b) 35 / 28
c) 10 / 10

....

Q20: What are the recommendations on portions of fruit and vegetables one should consume in an average day?

a) ten
b) at least five
c) three or more

....

Q21: Which statement describes a healthy approach to managing stress?

a) I have at least one close friend or family member I can confide in
b) I have a wide network of acquaintances
c) I rely on the internet for advice and support

....

Q22: The best way to maintain a healthy weight is

a) Eat and drink whatever you like and go on a strict diet to lose weight
b) Eat, drink, and exercise in moderation
c) Cut all the fat out of your diet

2.4   Pronunciation: Alternative therapies

Pronunciation: Alternative therapies   Go online

'Alternative' therapy may be defined as any medicinal practice or therapy which is outside the sphere of conventional medicine. Some of these therapies are associated with traditional approaches and have been used for hundreds of years.

For the next exercise you will need access to the sound files:

hg-cesl1-2-2vocab1.mp3 to hg-cesl1-2-2vocab7.mp3

Listen to the correct pronunciation of each of the alternative therapies in the list. Listen and repeat.

Acupuncture
Reiki
Reflexology
Hypnotherapy
Herbalism
Shiatsu
Chiropractic

Alternative therapies (15 min)   Go online

Use the internet or a dictionary to research the following types of alternative therapy and choose the correct answer to match the description.

Q23: Healing based on ancient Japanese system in which energy is directed from the practitioner through touch to meet the needs of the recipient.

a) acupuncture
b) reiki
c) reflexology
d) hypnotherapy
e) herbalism
f) shiatsu
g) chiropractic

....

Q24: Diagnosis and treatment of injuries and disorders associated with the spine and skeletal system. Treatment involves manipulation of the skeletal system and muscles.

a) acupuncture
b) reiki
c) reflexology
d) hypnotherapy
e) herbalism
f) shiatsu
g) chiropractic

....

Q25: A system of healthcare taken from China to Japan which involves using touch, pressure and manipulation to adjust the physical structure of the body. This is thought to enable a person to heal psychologically, physically, emotionally and spiritually.

a) acupuncture
b) reiki
c) reflexology
d) hypnotherapy
e) herbalism
f) shiatsu
g) chiropractic

....

Q26: Treatment thought to have been used thousands of years ago in China and Egypt, based on the idea that there are areas in the feet which correspond to the whole body which can be manipulated to treat the recipient.

a) acupuncture
b) reiki
c) reflexology
d) hypnotherapy
e) herbalism
f) shiatsu
g) chiropractic

....

Q27: Application of techniques inducing a state of deep relaxation to reprogram the unconscious and cure physical and psychological problems.

a) acupuncture
b) reiki
c) reflexology
d) hypnotherapy
e) herbalism
f) shiatsu
g) chiropractic

....

Q28: Based on a Chinese healthcare system around two thousand years old. Looks at illness and pain as an imbalance of vital energy and uses fine needles inserted in the body to re-establish flow.

a) acupuncture
b) reiki
c) reflexology
d) hypnotherapy
e) herbalism
f) shiatsu
g) chiropractic

....

. . . .

Q29: Traditional or folk medicine based on the use of plant extracts to treat ailments.

a) acupuncture
b) reiki
c) reflexology
d) hypnotherapy
e) herbalism
f) shiatsu
g) chiropractic

Therapy synonyms (15 min)

Find synonyms from the text for the following words:

Q30: therapeutic

. . . .

Q31: judgment

. . . .

Q32: structure

. . . .

Q33: match

. . . .

Q34: unevenness

. . . .

Q35: movement

. . . .

Q36: illnesses

2.5   Grammar: Passive constructions

We can use either active or passive constructions in clauses. In active clauses the subject generally tells us what the clause is about and is the agent of action.

Example I went to the doctor.

The doctor diagnosed a virus.

In the first example, **I** is the subject of the clause and the person performing the action. In the second example, **the doctor** is the subject and agent. In both examples the important information is what the subject (I / the doctor) did.

In passive clauses the subject is generally the recipient of the action. We use passive constructions when we want to focus on what happened to the subject and when the agent is unknown or unspecified.

Example I was diagnosed with a virus (by the doctor)

In this example the important information is what happened to the subject.

We also use passive constructions when we want to focus on who was responsible for something or on how it was done.

Example Penicillin was invented by Alexander Fleming. It was discovered almost by accident.

2.5.1 Form of passive

The passive is formed by using:

Verb to be / to get + past participle

Examples

1. I was given a prescription.

....

2. I got stung by a wasp.

2.5.2 Use of passive constructions

We use passives:

A) To describe processes.

Example First the patient is offered an injection.

B) In formal contexts such as when reporting medical facts.

Example Studies have revealed that ...

C) Where the agent is not of immediate importance.

Example He has been awarded a prize for services to medicine.

Recognising passive structures (15 min)

Q37: Read the text below and find **ten** examples of passive structures.

Stress

It is recognised that some stress is a positive thing since it can motivate us to act, increase productivity and improve our performance. However, too much stress can have a very negative impact on our lives in the short term, and can have long term consequences as well.

Sufferers of stress are affected by a range of unpleasant symptoms including insomnia, poor appetite, sweating, and difficulty concentrating. In the long term we are more likely to suffer further health problems such as high blood pressure, strokes, headaches and feelings of anxiety and depression.

A recent study has revealed that there is also a clear link between stress and heart disease. Although this connection has been established, the process by which it occurs is not altogether clear. It is thought that stress may have an indirect link to heart disease because it may lead to an increase in blood pressure and also cause people to overeat, indulge in alcohol or smoke more. High levels of stress mean the body is exposed to unhealthy levels of hormones such as adrenalin and cortisol.

It has been shown that the ability to deal with stress depends upon a range of factors including quality of relationships, emotional intelligence, approach to life and inherited factors. For example, if you have a strong group of friends and family you are likely to be more resilient when under stress.

There are a range of approaches which can be adopted to help tackle stress. Methods which have been found effective in dealing with stress include setting realistic goals, and prioritising tasks. It is believed that finding distractions, and in particular, exercise, can counteract the negative symptoms of stress, as can learning to express emotion and channelling positive thought.

Using passive structures (10 min)

We often use passive structures to make communication more formal, especially in writing.

Change the following sentences to include passive clauses.

Q38: You should take one to two tablets every four to six hours. One to two tablets _____ every four to six hours.

....

Q39: Before you travel you should ensure that the doctor gives you all of the necessary injections. Prior to departure ensure that you _____ all of the necessary injections by your doctor.

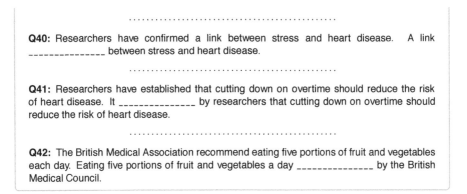

Q40: Researchers have confirmed a link between stress and heart disease. A link _____ between stress and heart disease.

....

Q41: Researchers have established that cutting down on overtime should reduce the risk of heart disease. It _____ by researchers that cutting down on overtime should reduce the risk of heart disease.

....

Q42: The British Medical Association recommend eating five portions of fruit and vegetables each day. Eating five portions of fruit and vegetables a day _____ by the British Medical Council.

2.6 Vocabulary: Idioms and prepositions

Idioms are used frequently in English. The following activities will provide you with practice in using and recognising some of the ones used in connection with the topic of health.

For two of the activities you will need access to the sound files:

hg-cesl1-2-3vocab1.mp3 to hg-cesl1-2-3vocab6.mp3

hg-cesl1-2-4vocab1.mp3 to hg-cesl1-2-4vocab4.mp3

Idiomatic phrases part 1 (10 min) Go online

To do this exercise you need following sound-files:*hg-cesl1-2-3vocab1.mp3 to hg-cesl1-2-3vocab6.mp3*

Q43: Listen to each of the sound files and decide which preposition (from the list provided) you heard to complete the given phrases.

Preposition list:

off: on: under: of (× 2): down:

1. ____ the weather
2. ____ colour
3. clean bill ____ health
4. out ____ sorts
5. run ____
6. ____ the mend

Idiomatic phrases part 2 (10 min)   Go online

To do this exercise you need following sound-files: *hg-cesl1-2-4vocab1.mp3 to hg-cesl1-2-4vocab4.mp3*

Q44: Listen to some more idioms associated with health and this time complete the sentences with the word you hear.

1. As fit as a ____
2. A cast iron ____
3. Pins and ____
4. Recharge my ____

Idiomatic phrases: Match phrases to definitions (10 min)   Go online

Q45:

Which idiomatic expression from the previous exercise has which meaning?

1. To have a strong constitution.
2. To feel unwell.
3. To have an unhealthy pallor.
4. To have a tingling sensation.
5. To feel different from usual in a negative way.
6. Starting to feel better following an illness.
7. A statement of good health.
8. Weakened.
9. To gather strength.
10. To be full of energy and life.

2.7   Writing: A report

Revise the topic before trying this activity.

Q46: Before you begin writing look at the list. Which of the features of writing given are important when producing a report? Choose as many answers as you think are correct.

1. formal language
2. colloquial language
3. contractions
4. paragraph headings

---

5. informal language
6. contractions
7. passive constructions
8. anecdotal evidence
9. use of personal statements
10. objective tone
11. facts
12. opinions

Writing: A report (40 min)

You have been asked to write a report for the head teacher on the quality of food available in your school. Look at the information given below which is based on the observations of 150 pupils surveyed. The results have been collated.

The canteen

- On most days there was a choice of two main courses.
- Pupils found the food filling and reasonably enjoyable but complained that vegetables were often overcooked.
- The desserts were not varied and tended to be quite stodgy.
- On most days fruit was available, although again this was limited to apples, bananas and oranges.
- Homemade soup was available every day and this was well received.
- The water fountain was broken.

The snack shop run by pupils for pupils

- A wide range of cakes and sweets was available in the snack shop.
- There was no fruit for sale.

A van parked outside the school

- Burgers and pastries were always available.
- Soft drinks tended to be of the carbonated type.
- Fresh fruit was not sold.
- Sweets were available.
- Prices were generally cheaper than those in school.

Write a report indicating your findings and your recommendations to improve the quality of the food.

Write approximately 250 - 300 words (excluding headings)

When you are finished show your work to your teacher or tutor.

An model answer is provided in the expected answer section.

2.8   Listening comprehension: Eastern and Western medicines

You will need access to the sound file *hg-cesl1-2-5listening.mp3* to complete this listening comprehension.

Listen to the dialogue.

Listening Comprehension: Eastern and Western medicines (15 min)   Go online

The listening comprehension is available online at this stage. If you do not have access to the internet but are able to listen to the sound file *hg-cesl1-2-5listening.mp3* then you may try the questions which follow.

Listen to the recording again and try to answer the following questions:

Q47: Find a word to complete the sentences based on what you have heard.

1. Where there is pain or illness, the acupuncturist believes there is _____

2. The practice of Chinese Traditional Medicine involves finding out about the nature of illness through _____ and _____.

....

Q48: In five element acupuncture the four areas of interest are: _____

....

Q49: What part of the speaker's course enabled comparison of Eastern and Western medicine?

....

Q50: In acupuncture which physical checks are used to make a diagnosis?

....

Q51: What practices other than needles are used by the acupuncturist?

....

Q52: Which word in the script indicates that the approach addresses mind, body and spirit?

2.9 Reading comprehension: Women's health

The following activity is a reading comprehension covering the work of this topic.

Before you begin, read the passage for gist.

Women in the UK prefer to be thin than healthy, a recent report has revealed. It appears that in the UK, eighty per cent of women are simply not active enough to maintain good health. While the government recommends thirty minutes of moderate exercise around five times a week, according to a survey carried out among thousands of British women, it seems that four out of five women fail to achieve this target. The survey indicated that women's rejection of sport was often based upon body image, the desire to look stylishly thin rather than athletic.

Analysis of trends in schools has revealed that while girls and boys are equally interested in sport up to the age of nine, after this point girls start to lose interest. Factors involved in this defection include: negative experiences of physical instruction at school, a lack of parental encouragement, and a shortage of positive role models. In their early teens, girls tend to be anxious about appearance. The requirement to wear sports clothes and the sporty 'look' are perceived as unfeminine. It seems that young girls are far more likely to emulate wives and girlfriends (WAGS) of sports professionals rather than engage in sporting activities themselves.

The trend is worrying not only because of the links between exercise and health which are acknowledged. Exercise can help to maintain a healthy weight and can protect against heart disease and osteoporosis. It has also been discovered in a study in the United States that even four hours of exercise a week could reduce a teenage girl's chances of developing breast cancer by as much as sixty per cent. However, the statistics are also a cause for concern because women are missing out on a range of other psychological and emotional benefits. Girls who play sport in school are likely to achieve better grades and to have greater confidence and self esteem. They are also less likely to suffer from depression.

Women who have participated in sport are also more likely to do well in a business environment than their more sedentary sisters. Researchers looking into common factors in successful female executives found that a background in athletics is a frequently occurring characteristic. It appears that the competitive environment of sport gives participants grounding in strategies which support them in business. For example, individuals may learn about winning and losing, and as a result are less likely to associate losing with a lack of self worth. Sport also instructs in goal setting and team building. This kind of awareness can be invaluable in the cut and thrust of the business environment.

It has been documented that women's participation in sport increases dramatically during events such as the Olympic Games when television coverage of women in sport is closer to that of men. There is a need to sustain this high profile coverage at other times to show women in powerful and successful sporting roles. There is also an obligation for parents to provide children with opportunities to engage in sport and to encourage them to lead active lives. Help is at hand however, The Women's Sport and Fitness Foundation (WSFF) is a charitable organisation endeavouring to raise the profile of women in sport, addressing leadership and investment issues among others. WSFF has also supported schools and pupils in projects to encourage girls, such as 'feminising' changing rooms, with great success. If girls can begin to enjoy the experience of participation in sport at school, it is hoped that they will continue to do so later in life as well.

Reading comprehension: Women's health (30 min)   Go online

The reading comprehension is available online at this stage. If you do not have access to the internet you may try the questions which follow.

Read the passage once more and answer the questions which follow.

1. Women in the UK prefer to be thin than healthy, a recent report has revealed. It appears that in the UK, eighty per cent of women are simply not active enough to maintain good health. While the government recommends thirty minutes of moderate exercise around five times a week, according to a survey carried out among thousands of British women, it seems that four out of five women fail to achieve this target. The survey indicated that women's rejection of sport was often based upon body image, the desire to look stylishly thin rather than athletic.

2. Analysis of trends in schools has revealed that while girls and boys are equally interested in sport up to the age of nine, after this point girls start to lose interest. Factors involved in this defection include: negative experiences of physical instruction at school, a lack of parental encouragement, and a shortage of positive role models. In their early teens, girls tend to be anxious about appearance. The requirement to wear sports clothes and the sporty 'look' are perceived as unfeminine. It seems that young girls are far more likely to emulate wives and girlfriends (WAGS) of sports professionals rather than engage in sporting activities themselves.

3. The trend is worrying not only because of the links between exercise and health which are acknowledged. Exercise can help to maintain a healthy weight and can protect against heart disease and osteoporosis. It has also been discovered in a study in the United States that even four hours of exercise a week could reduce a teenage girl's chances of developing breast cancer by as much as sixty per cent. However, the statistics are also a cause for concern because women are missing out on a range of other psychological and emotional benefits. Girls who play sport in school are likely to achieve better grades and to have greater confidence and self esteem. They are also less likely to suffer from depression.

4. Women who have participated in sport are also more likely to do well in a business environment than their more sedentary sisters. Researchers looking into common factors in successful female executives found that a background in athletics is a frequently occurring characteristic. It appears that the competitive environment of sport gives participants grounding in strategies which support them in business. For example, individuals may learn about winning and losing, and as a result are less likely to associate losing with a lack of self worth. Sport also instructs in goal setting and team building. This kind of awareness can be invaluable in the cut and thrust of the business environment.

5. It has been documented that women's participation in sport increases dramatically during events such as the Olympic Games when television coverage of women in sport is closer to that of men. There is a need to sustain this high profile coverage at other times to show women in powerful and successful sporting roles. There is also an obligation for parents to provide children with opportunities to engage in sport and to encourage them to lead active lives. Help is at hand however, The Women's Sport and Fitness Foundation (WSFF) is a charitable organisation endeavouring to raise the profile of women in sport, addressing leadership and investment issues among others. WSFF has also supported schools and pupils in projects to encourage girls, such as 'feminising' changing rooms, with great success. If girls can begin to enjoy the experience of participation in sport at school, it is hoped that they will continue to do so later in life as well.

Q53: This text is

a) An extract from a medical journal
b) A publicity document for The Women's Sport and Fitness Foundation
c) A newspaper article about health in the UK
d) An information leaflet published by the British Medical Association

Fill in the gap:

Q54: Women often avoid sport because they want to be _____.
....
Q55: Young women often try to be like _____of sports professionals.
....
Q56: As well as benefitting a woman's physical health, exercise also brings _____benefits.

True or False

Q57: International sporting events influence women's attitudes to sport.
....
Q58: There is nothing parents can do to encourage their children to exercise.

Find words/phrases in the text with the following meaning:

Q59: movement away (paragraph 2)
....
Q60: bone disease (paragraph 3)
....
Q61: knowledge of the basic facts of a subject (paragraph 4)
....
Q62: group giving food, money or other provision where necessary (paragraph 5)

2.10   Vocabulary list

You might find it helpful to have a list of some of the words which have been introduced in this topic.

Adrenalin (noun)	Hormone produced in the body when you are frightened, angry or excited
Anaesthetist (noun)	Doctor who gives anaesthetic to patients in hospitals
Atrophy (verb)	To become weaker
Concussion (noun)	Temporary damage to the brain caused by a fall or a blow to the head
Constitution (noun)	The general state of someone's health
Counteract (verb)	Produce an opposite effect in order to remove the power of something
Dedication (noun)	Giving a lot of time or energy to something
Degeneration (noun)	Process by which something gets worse
Fracture (noun)	Break of a bone
Gesticulate (verb)	Signal, gesture
Humerus (noun)	Long bone in the upper half of your arm
Injection (noun)	Vaccination
Insomnia (noun)	Sleeplessness
Intimidated (adjective)	Nervous or frightened because you are not confident in a situation
Motivate (verb)	Encourage
Overwhelming (adjective)	Awe-inspiring
Pallor (noun)	State of being very pale
Persevere (verb)	To continue to do something in a determined way
Plaster cast (noun)	Protective covering for a broken bone
Practitioner (noun)	Someone involved in a skilled job or activity
Prescription (noun)	Piece of paper on which a doctor writes list of necessary drugs for a patient
Protracted (adjective)	Lasting for a long time
Prudent (adjective)	Careful
Ramifications (noun)	Possible results of an action
Regale (verb)	To entertain with stories or jokes
Rehabilitate (verb)	To return someone or something to a healthy condition
Symptoms (noun)	Physical or mental change caused by disease

Unit 1 Topic 3

Physical environment

Contents

Learning objective

By the end of this topic you should be able to:

- use a wider range of vocabulary in the topic area

- display a greater knowledge and understanding of nouns

- demonstrate your knowledge of writing genre through writing a discursive essay

- demonstrate your knowledge of writing genre through writing an article

- demonstrate greater awareness of syllable stress.

This topic examines habitats, examining life in various countries in both urban and rural environments. It expands on the grammar of the noun, examining its different classifications and relative meanings. Advanced vocabulary relevant to the topic of city and country life is introduced and practised through a variety of activities. The topic includes work on all four skills: speaking, reading, writing, and listening. There are also supplementary pronunciation exercises. Assessment opportunities occur at the end of the topic.

Certain sections contain sound files. You may download these here and use them on your mp3 player or equivalent to practise your pronunciation. This may be very useful if there are times when you will not have access to the materials online.

3.1   Grammar: Nouns

As a student of English, you are learning nouns whenever you learn the name of something new. However, beyond the basic definition of *a naming word*, there are several classifications of nouns in English. Within this topic we will explore the different grammatical categories into which nouns are arranged.

Proper nouns:

These are nouns which do not normally take an article before them. They are generally used to name a particular person, place or thing. Unlike other classes of noun, proper nouns are almost always capitalised.

Examples

1. city names: *Glasgow, London*

    . . . .

2. state and country names: *California, Italy*

    . . . .

3. names of people: *Susan, Murphy*

Common nouns:

These are nouns which are sometimes preceded by an article or other modifier. They are generally used to name a group or class, as opposed to an individual.

Example places, but not exact or unique places: (the/a) *city*; (the) *countryside*

Concrete nouns:

These are nouns which are generally used to name something which is material, physical and visible, and / or non-abstract.

Example Material, physical, non-abstract: *building, mountain, river*

Abstract nouns:

These are nouns which are generally used to name something we cannot necessarily see or touch and / or which are ideas, feelings or qualities. Some are used with an article, and some without.

Example Ideas, feelings, qualities: *(a) dream, love, hate, bravery*

Collective nouns:

These are nouns which are generally used to denote a group of persons or objects, and can be singular or plural in their usage.

Example Groups: *team, community, congregation*

 Standard British English usage is to treat the collective noun as being plural, but you may also see it used in singular form. What is important is to maintain consistency whether using singular or plural (see below):

 Examples

1. Collective noun treated as plural
*The community **are** organising a fundraising event.*
. . . .

2. Collective noun treated as singular
*The community **is** organising a fundraising event.*

Noun categories (15 min)

Go online

Q1: Decide which kind of noun the following is: (proper, collective, common, concrete or abstract)

1. Paris
2. herd
3. committee
4. metropolis
5. danger
6. quiet
7. Asia
8. factory
9. ocean
10. region

Identifying types of noun (15 min)

Go online

Look at the two options for each question and select the correct answer.

Q2: Which is a common noun?

A) district

B) vision

. . . .

Q3: Which is a proper noun?

A) people

B) President

. . . .

Q4: Which is a concrete noun?

A) objective

B) church

. . . .

Q5: Which is an abstract noun?

A) plan

B) crew

. . . .

Q6: Which is a collective noun?

A) population

B) thought

....

Q7: Which is a common noun?

A) nation

B) Queen

....

Q8: Which is a proper noun?

A) country

B) India

....

Q9: Which is a concrete noun?

A) staff

B) roundabout

....

Q10: Which is an abstract noun?

A) network

B) notion

....

Q11: Which is a collective noun?

A) county

B) army

3.2 Speaking: City and country life

(15 min)

Discuss the questions below with a partner or your tutor. You may wish to make notes about your answers to help you with the next exercise.

1. What are the advantages / disadvantages of living in a big city?

2. What are the advantages / disadvantages of living in the countryside?

3. Have you experienced either of these ways of life?

4. Which do you (or would you) prefer? Why?

5. Do you think that country life, as we know it today, will still exist in the future?

3.3 Writing: City life

Writing: City life (60 min)

The advantages of living in a city outweigh the disadvantages.

Write an essay for your tutor discussing this statement with reference to a city that you have either lived in or know very well.

Think about the following areas and include some, or all of them in your essay:

- Lifestyle
- Health
- Crime
- Employment
- Leisure

Use your own knowledge and consult external sources to help you answer the questions.

Before you begin, consider the following questions:

1. What is the purpose of the communication?

2. Who is the intended audience?

3. What level of formality and register would be appropriate?

Make some notes or a mind map to help plan your writing before you begin.

Write an essay between 250-300 words.

When you have finished ask your teacher or tutor to check your work.

An exemplar answer has also been provided for you to compare with your work.

3.4 Vocabulary: The city and the country

The next activities will help you to expand your vocabulary within this subject area.

Vocabulary: The city and the country (15 min) Go online

Q12: Choose a word from the first list which matches a definition taken from the second list.

List:

1. outskirts
2. picturesque
3. suburban
4. quaint
5. bustling
6. inhabitant
7. cultivate
8. commuters
9. amenities
10. infrastructure

Definitions:

A) travellers to and from work
B) the lifestyle of the people who inhabit the area just outside the city
C) busy, crowded and lively
D) the system of public works for a city or town
E) a person who lives in a particular area
F) facilities or conveniences within a town or city
G) old-fashioned and attractive looking (especially when describing a town / village)
H) a view resembling that seen in a painting or photograph
I) a part of town remote from the centre
J) to grow vegetables, or prepare the land for their growth

3.5   Pronunciation: Syllable and word stress

Pronunciation: Syllable and word stress (15 min)   Go online

Q13: Look at the list of words:

1. outskirts
2. picturesque
3. suburban
4. quaint
5. bustling
6. inhabitant
7. cultivate
8. commuters
9. amenities
10. infrastructure

How many syllables does each word have, and where is the word stress in each word?

3.6   Listening: City and country life

Listening: City and country life (25 min)   Go online

You will need access to the sound file *hg-cesl1-3-1listening.mp3* to be able to complete this activity.

You will hear a story told by someone who grew up in the countryside. This person gives their opinion of life in the city and the countryside.

Listen to the recording and answer the questions which follow.

Q14: When the speaker was younger, she felt sorry for her friends.

a) true
b) false

. . . .

Q15: The speaker had never seen a bus until she was 18 years old.

a) true
b) false

. . . .

Q16: Young people from the city fitted into university life more easily than the speaker did.

a) true
b) false

....

Q17: What does the speaker remember about adults and illness from her childhood?

a) Most of the adults he knew were often sick
b) Adults who went to work in the city had more illnesses
c) Adults from the countryside were usually sick

....

Q18: Which of these things does the speaker mention as contributing to poor health in the city?

a) smog, cigarettes and litter
b) mobile phones, laptops and poor water quality
c) chewing gum, drugs and alcohol

....

Q19: Does the speaker ...

a) favour living in the countryside
b) favour living in the city
c) see positives and negatives in both

....

Q20: What is the one thing the speaker sometimes misses about the city?

a) the leisure and nightlife
b) the transport system
c) the people

....

Q21: Where does the speaker live at the moment?

a) we don't know
b) the city
c) the countryside
d) has a home in both

3.7   Reading comprehension: Population control

The following activity is a reading comprehension covering the work of this topic.

Before you begin the activity read the passage quickly for gist.

The imposition of population control methods with a nation is a highly controversial and ethically delicate subject. Population control can be defined as the limitation of population increase, and the methods of limitation can take many forms, from the most basic - improved contraception, to the most morally questionable - increasing the death rate.

Most scholars are familiar with the notorious and well documented case of population control over the last century, that of China's much maligned one-child policy. One in six people in the world today are Chinese, such is the populous mass of the country. To counter the ever increasing drain on economic resources, the one-child policy was introduced in 1979. Dictating how many offspring are allowed is not only highly ethically questionable, but is also all but impossible to enforce. A system of amercement was officially implemented in order to dissuade parents from increasing the size of their family, but stories abound of children being forcibly taken from families and disappearing forever. Equally frequent were tales of forced sterilisation, back alley abortion and infanticide. A trade in child sales was also widely reported, with child brokers being paid by wealthier families to either steal or buy children from poorer couples, to sell on to those who could afford to pay fines to the regime for having more than one child.

Of course, that particular example is population control at its most macabre and least successful. Western nations have long promoted the idea of better access to birth control in the form of contraception. However, studies have shown that easier availability of contraceptives, for example over the counter sales in more developed countries, and through campaigns to generate awareness in less developed nations do not necessarily quell the population increase. Critics point to a lack of education to accompany such schemes as being the key reason for this failure. Furthermore, religious opposition is another obstacle those concerned with overpopulation encounter, for example, with the Pope regularly speaking out against the use of contraception. When the head of the whole Catholic faith is against the idea, it is easy to see the scale of the problem that campaigners face.

Efforts to control populations have not been universally unsuccessful, however. The USA, although still having an increasing population, has a rigid and rigorous immigration policy, which means that the population there is more manageably controlled. Similarly, the UK has also stiffened its regulations regarding the number of foreign students, workers and refugees it accepts annually, in an effort to balance the number of emigrants with the level of immigration. School programmes confronting the issue of teenage pregnancy and raising awareness on this issue have also had some success.

In Iran, a system of free and easy to access birth control has been introduced. To support this move, a drive towards improving literacy rates was also undertaken, and early results have shown that this twofold approach is paying dividends, with family planning becoming more commonplace in the country than it was previously.

The clear answer to the issue of overpopulation is that there is no clear answer, and religious, cultural and economic factors need to be considered on a case by case and nation by nation basis. What is certain, however, is that there will inevitably be more people available in the future to work on finding the solution.

Reading comprehension: Population control (30 min)   Go online

The reading comprehension is available online at this stage. If you do not have access to the internet you may try the questions which follow.

Read the passage once more and answer the questions which follow.

The imposition of population control methods with a nation is a highly controversial and ethically delicate subject. Population control can be defined as the limitation of population increase, and the methods of limitation can take many forms, from the most basic - improved contraception, to the most morally questionable - increasing the death rate.

Most scholars are familiar with the notorious and well documented case of population control over the last century, that of China's much maligned one-child policy. One in six people in the world today are Chinese, such is the populous mass of the country. To counter the ever increasing drain on economic resources, the one-child policy was introduced in 1979. Dictating how many offspring are allowed is not only highly ethically questionable, but is also all but impossible to enforce. A system of amercement was officially implemented in order to dissuade parents from increasing the size of their family, but stories abound of children being forcibly taken from families and disappearing forever. Equally frequent were tales of forced sterilisation, back alley abortion and infanticide. A trade in child sales was also widely reported, with child brokers being paid by wealthier families to either steal or buy children from poorer couples, to sell on to those who could afford to pay fines to the regime for having more than one child.

Of course, that particular example is population control at its most macabre and least successful. Western nations have long promoted the idea of better access to birth control, in the form of contraception. However, studies have shown that easier availability of contraceptives, for example, over the counter in more developed countries, and through campaigns to generate awareness in less developed nations, do not necessarily quell the population increase. Critics point to a lack of education to accompany such schemes as being the key reason for this failure. Furthermore, religious opposition is another obstacle those concerned with overpopulation encounter, for example, with the Pope regularly speaking out against the use of contraception. When the head of the whole Catholic faith is against the idea, it is easy to see the scale of the problem that campaigners face.

Efforts to control populations have not been universally unsuccessful, however. The USA, although still having an increasing population, has a rigid and rigorous immigration policy, which means that the population there is more manageably controlled. Similarly, the UK has also stiffened its regulations regarding the number of foreign students, workers and refugees it accepts annually, in an effort to balance the number of emigrants with the level of immigration. School programmes confronting the issue of teenage pregnancy and raising awareness on this issue have also had some success.

In Iran, a system of free and easy to access birth control has been introduced. To support this move, a drive towards improving literacy rates was also undertaken, and early results have shown that this twofold approach is paying dividends, with family planning becoming more commonplace in the country than it was previously.

The clear answer to the issue of overpopulation is that there is no clear answer, and religious, cultural and economic factors need to be considered on a case by case and nation by nation basis. What is certain, however, is that there will inevitably be more people available in the future to work on finding the solution.

Are the following statements true or false?

Q22: The Chinese one-child policy has received widespread condemnation

a) true
b) false

....

Q23: Western nations are having more success than others with the use of contraception

a) true
b) false

....

Q24: The overall approach to population control has been largely ineffective.

a) true
b) false

For the following questions find a word with the same or similar meaning in the article

Q25: Find a word in the article with the same meaning as 'fine, or forfeit'.

....

Q26: Find a word in the article with the same meaning as 'strict'.

....

Q27: Find a word in the article with the same meaning as 'dreadful, or gruesome'.

....

Q28: Find a word in the article with the same meaning as 'to advise against something'.

....

Q29: The writer of this article:

a) Is in favour of population control
b) Holds a balanced view on the issue of population control
c) Is against population control

3.8   Listening comprehension: The New Atlantis

Now you have completed the topic, listen to the following assessment dialogue. It contains examples of many of the language areas you have covered within the topic.

You will need access to the sound file: *hg-cesl1-3-2listening.mp3* to complete this listening comprehension.

Before you listen, think about the following:

1. Where would you like to live, if you could afford a dream home anywhere?
2. What is the most interesting building project you have heard of?
3. What do you know about Dubai and the developing infrastructure there?

You may wish to take some notes as you listen in order to answer the questions which follow.

Listening comprehension: The New Atlantis (25 min)   Go online

You will need access to the sound file: *hg-cesl1-3-2listening.mp3* to complete this listening comprehension.

Q30: What is the root cause of the problem with the island development in Dubai?:

A) The financial crisis
B) The erosion of the islands
C) The legal action happening against the parent company

....

Q31: Greenland is the only island where nobody is living at present. Is this true or false?

....

Q32: Famous sporting and movie stars have bought islands and have been seen visiting them. Is this true or false?

....

Q33: Many other construction projects in Dubai have been unaffected by the crisis. Is this true or false?

....

Q34: What is the reason that the ferry company are suing?

A) because nobody is buying the islands
B) because the shipping channels are closing up
C) because of the financial crisis damaging their business

....

Q35: The main developer admits that the project has encountered problems. Is this true or false?

....

Q36: The parent company insist that the project can still be a success. Is this true or false ?

....

Q37: The speaker is giving information which is mostly:

A) objective
B) subjective

3.9   Vocabulary list

This is a list of useful vocabulary which is intended to supplement what you have learned. It may also be useful to refer to when attempting the speaking and writing activities within the topic.

architecture (noun)	the practice of designing buildings
blueprint (noun)	a photographic print in white on a blue background used for copying maps and architects' plans
census (noun)	a periodic governmental check of the population
colonist (noun)	a person who settles in a new country
cosmopolitan (adjective)	made up of people or diverse elements from all areas of life
demography (noun)	the study of human populations and how they change over time
density (noun)	the average number of individuals in a particular area, e.g. a city
farmstead (noun)	a farm and its land and buildings
heritage (noun)	property that is passed on through family lines
indigenous (adjective)	describes the people native to a particular region or country
life expectancy (noun)	the average lifespan of a person
locale (noun)	a place viewed in relation to a particular event
meadow (noun)	land that is covered in grass
municipal (adjective)	restricted to one area or locality
parochial (adjective)	of a person limited in range or scope, in terms of their world view
plain (noun)	a large area of flat countryside
provincial (adjective)	of a person with a local or restricted outlook
salad bowl (noun)	the idea of different people not integrating successfully, living separately. The opposite of "melting pot".
sustainability (noun)	relating to a lifestyle involving the use of sustainable methods, particularly when talking about agriculture
urbanite (noun)	someone who lives in the city

Unit 1 Topic 4

Press and media

Contents

Learning objective

By the end of this topic you should be able to:

- use your knowledge and understanding of reported speech in the context of the media

- demonstrate your extended range of vocabulary in the topic area through practice in reading, listening and writing

- outline the features of register through text analysis

- display your increased knowledge of writing genre through writing a letter to the press

- demonstrate your pronunciation across a wider vocabulary

This topic examines the media, including radio, newspapers and television. It offers grammar presentations and activities on the use of reported speech. In addition, advanced vocabulary relevant to the topic of the media is introduced. The topic includes work on all four skills: speaking, reading, writing, and listening. There are supplementary pronunciation exercises. Assessment opportunities occur at the end of the topic.

This topic contains one sound file. You may download this and use it on your mp3 player. This may be very useful if there are times when you will not have access to the materials online.

4.1   1.1 Speaking: Discussing the news

Speaking

Discuss the following questions with a partner or your teacher:

- What different ways do people use to find out about news stories?
- Do you prefer to read the news or watch / listen to it?
- Do you believe the news that you read or hear is always accurate?
- How does watching or reading the news generally make you feel?

4.2   Reading: Analysing register in the press

Discuss the questions below with your partner:

- Do you know the difference between a tabloid newspaper and a broadsheet newspaper?
- Can you think of any examples of tabloid newspapers and broadsheet newspapers in the UK?

A: Local Heroes

A forty-year-old Glasgow man has thanked two local lads who alerted emergency services just after four yesterday afternoon, shortly after they witnessed him falling from the window of a third floor tenement flat. Derek White, separated with two children, is resting in hospital today having broken his leg and collar bone in the dramatic tumble. The local plumber was balancing on the window ledge at the rear of his flat, cleaning windows, when he slipped and fell head first into bushes. Brothers Lee and Jacob Hendry, 7 and 9, ran to White's aid then quickly alerted emergency services. Michael Stewart, 37, a paramedic at the scene, praised the boys' quick-thinking. "Nowadays, good kids are hard to find," he said, adding, "Their parents should be very proud of them." Police also praised the boys. Inspector Tom Murray of Strathclyde Police commented, "They have set a very good example for local children". The boys' mother, Margaret Hendry, 37, a cleaner originally from Thurso, said, "We have always brought them up to be good citizens and to treat others as they would like to be treated themselves. We're ever so proud".

B: Ambulances struggle in severe weather conditions

Recent research into time taken by ambulances to reach emergency callers in Scotland has revealed that response times have dropped noticeably during the winter. It has been acknowledged that this has been one of the worst winters in recent decades. However, it is clear that further monitoring is vital to ascertain whether or not measures should be taken to improve the figures. The Scottish Ambulance Service has a target of reaching three quarters of 'Category A' calls (life threatening emergencies) in under eight minutes. This has not been achieved in recent monitoring (over the last twelve months) which has shown a drop in average response times of 0.03%. Figures which have been revealed as a consequence of freedom of information legislation indicate that the Scottish Ambulance Service reached Category A callers across mainland Scotland within the target time on 72.7% of occasions. Jim Donaldson, local government health service manager, has expressed concern and highlighted the need for careful planning to address the issue and ensure that steps are taken to improve performance regardless of inclement weather conditions.

Analysing register in the press (30 min) Go online

Read the articles below. Which one do you think is from a tabloid newspaper and which one is from a broadsheet newspaper?

A: Local Heroes

A forty-year-old Glasgow man has thanked two local lads who alerted emergency services just after four yesterday afternoon, shortly after they witnessed him falling from the window of a third floor tenement flat. Derek White, separated with two children, is resting in hospital today having broken his leg and collar bone in the dramatic tumble. The local plumber was balancing on the window ledge at the rear of his flat, cleaning windows, when he slipped and fell head first into bushes. Brothers Lee and Jacob Hendry, 7 and 9, ran to White's aid then quickly alerted emergency services. Michael Stewart, 37, a paramedic at the scene, praised the boys' quick-thinking. "Nowadays, good kids are hard to find," he said, adding, "Their parents should be very proud of them." Police also praised the boys. Inspector Tom Murray of Strathclyde Police commented, "They have set a very good example for local children". The boys' mother, Margaret Hendry, 37, a cleaner originally from Thurso, said, "We have always brought them up to be good citizens and to treat others as they would like to be treated themselves. We're ever so proud".

B: Ambulances struggle in severe weather conditions

Recent research into time taken by ambulances to reach emergency callers in Scotland has revealed that response times have dropped noticeably during the winter. It has been acknowledged that this has been one of the worst winters in recent decades. However, it is clear that further monitoring is vital to ascertain whether or not measures should be taken to improve the figures. The Scottish Ambulance Service has a target of reaching three quarters of 'Category A' calls (life threatening emergencies) in under eight minutes. This has not been achieved in recent monitoring (over the last twelve months) which has shown a drop in average response times of 0.03%. Figures which have been revealed as a consequence of freedom of information legislation indicate that the Scottish Ambulance Service reached Category A callers across mainland Scotland within the target time on 72.7% of occasions. Jim Donaldson, local government health service manager, has expressed concern and highlighted the need for careful planning to address the issue and ensure that steps are taken to improve performance regardless of inclement weather conditions.

Q1:   A: Local Heroes

a) Tabloid
b) Broadsheet

....

Q2:   B: Ambulances struggle in severe weather conditions

a) Tabloid
b) Broadsheet

Choose whether these stylistic features are more common in tabloid or broadsheet newspapers

Q3:   Formal language e.g. avoidance of more colloquial phrasal verbs: *avoid* rather than *put off*

a) Tabloid
b) Broadsheet

....

Q4:   Informal language e.g. use of more colloquial phrasal verbs: *pick up*, rather than *collect*

a) Tabloid
b) Broadsheet

....

Q5:   Quotes e.g. "it's not my scene".

a) Tabloid
b) Broadsheet

....

Q6: Long sentences.

a) Tabloid
b) Broadsheet

....

Q7: Age of protagonists.

a) Tabloid
b) Broadsheet

....

Q8: Slang and collocations

a) Tabloid
b) Broadsheet

....

Q9: Passive structures.

a) Tabloid
b) Broadsheet

....

Q10: Contractions

a) Tabloid
b) Broadsheet

Informal synonyms (15 min)   Go online

Look at the examples of formal language from the second text. Match each of them with their corresponding informal synonym.

Q11:

Formal	Informal
recent	answer
ascertain	deal with
response	watch
acknowledge	find out
address	necessary
monitor	but
vital	up to date
indicate	make sure
however	show
ensure	admit

4.3   Newspapers: Vocabulary crossword

Try the following vocabulary activity to test your knowledge about people, ideas and concepts related to the newspaper industry.

Newspapers: Vocabulary review (20 min)   Go online

Q12: Complete the crossword.

Clues Across:

2. opinion piece of writing usually by a senior member of staff

5. collective name of people who write articles for newspapers

7. comic strips to make people laugh

9. newspaper with quality articles and reporting

11. photo journalists

12. report based on discussion with someone

13. area where readers' submissions are published interview (7, 4)

Down:

1. person who writes for a newspaper

3. number of people who read a newspaper or magazine

4. compact newspaper focussing on sensational stories

6. part of a newspaper with stories about celebrities (6, 6)

7. measurement of news content (6, 6)

8. pieces of writing appearing in newspapers

10. the main title of a news story

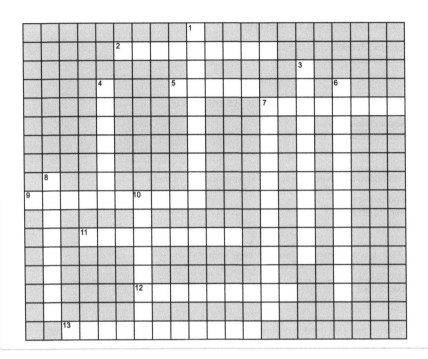

4.4   Grammar: Reported speech

When we repeat words that someone says to us without changing them we use **direct speech**.

We use direct speech to give immediacy or add emphasis to what we say.

When we provide the same information but change the words we heard into our own words we use **reported speech** (reported speech can also be called indirect speech).

Reported speech (10 min)	Go online

Q13: Michael Stewart said that good kids were hard to find.

a) Reported Speech
b) Direct Speech

....

Q14: Nowadays, good kids are hard to find.

a) Reported Speech
b) Direct Speech

....

Q15: Their parents should be very proud of them.

a) Reported Speech
b) Direct Speech

....

Q16: He added that their parents should be very proud of them.

a) Reported Speech
b) Direct Speech

....

Q17: That dog is dangerous! Take him away from me!

a) Reported Speech
b) Direct Speech

....

Q18: The woman said the dog was very dangerous and that he should be taken away.

a) Reported Speech
b) Direct Speech

....

Q19: I'm really tired. I want to lie down.

a) Reported Speech
b) Direct Speech

....

Q20: Steven told me he was tired and that he wanted to lie down.

a) Reported Speech
b) Direct Speech

Direct to reported speech (25 min) Go online

Read the following text.

The actress Brigitta Marzo has been accused of attention-seeking behaviour by fellow travellers, following her heated attack on a young reporter while boarding a plane at Heathrow Airport yesterday afternoon. Marzo, 37, who stars in *Chelsea Flowers*, the directorial debut of Andy Wakeman, was on her way to Cannes when the altercation took place. Nicola Lewis, 27, a journalist for *Sizzle* magazine, travelling to Cannes to cover the film festival, was stunned when Marzo thumped her with her Louis Vuitton handbag. Marzo, known to be both temperamental and terrified of flying, claimed that Lewis was secretly recording her while she queued to board the plane. Lewis insisted that the actress was mistaken. "I took a mobile phone out of my pocket and Marzo went berserk and started hitting me", she said, adding "Clandestine recording? It's not the kind of thing I'd do". The situation was defused by senior flight attendant Jan Bateman, 40, who managed to pour oil on troubled waters, escorting the angry diva to her business class seat while the bruised Lewis made her own way to the rear of the plane. Bateman later told reporters, "I have become used to this kind of thing, it's part of the job". The actress later admitted "I overreacted", and hoped that the journalist might be reconciled by the offer of an exclusive interview. "I've been stung in the past," said Marzo "I am sorry about the misunderstanding. I don't know what came over me but flying affects me very badly". Marzo later admitted, "I had taken tranquillisers and alcohol to try and calm myself down before leaving home. I would like to invite Miss Lewis to visit my hotel room for an exclusive interview tomorrow". John Bishop of Surrey, another passenger, told reporters in Cannes that it was totally unacceptable. "It's a clear PR stunt in my opinion. She is trying to drum up more press coverage, she loves the attention". It is unclear whether Lewis will press charges, the outcome of that may depend on what gossip she can garner from her exclusive, which she confirmed she has arranged with Marzo. "I've got nothing to lose at this stage", she pointed out.

Q21: Examples have been taken from this passage and have partly been changed into reported speech. Complete each example.

1. She said that she _____ a mobile phone out of her pocket and that Marzo _____ berserk and started hitting her.

2. She added that it _____ the kind of thing she would do.

3. Bateman said that she _____ to that kind of thing and that _____ part of the job.

4. The actress claimed that she _____ stung in the past.

5. She said that she _____ about the misunderstanding.

6. Marzo admitted that she _____ tranquillisers and alcohol before leaving home.

7. Marzo _____ Lewis to her hotel room for an interview on _____.

8. John Bishop told reporters that it _____ a PR stunt.

9. Bishop said that Marzo _____ the attention.

10. Lewis pointed out that she _____ nothing to lose.

Speech equivalents (10 min)   Go online

Q22: Match the examples of direct speech in the first list with the corresponding reported speech sentences from the second list.

1. Yes, I suppose you are right. I have caused a lot of trouble.
2. Can I just reiterate the fact that I have apologised for the trouble I have caused.
3. It was the tranquillisers that affected me and made me cause all that trouble.
4. It really is totally out of character.
5. I am sorry for the trouble I have caused.

A) She insisted that it was not the way she normally behaved.
B) She admitted that she had caused a lot of trouble.
C) She claimed that the medication had been at the root of her behaviour.
D) She apologised for the trouble she had caused.
E) She repeated that she had apologised for her behaviour.

4.4.1   Form

When we use reported speech we use a reporting verb. These verbs may be neutral e.g. say, tell, add, ask, reply or they may indicate the attitude of the speaker and suggest interpretation e.g. admit, apologise, claim, mention.

When we use reporting verbs, we have to take care that we use the correct structure after the verb.

Tell is followed by an indirect object and may be followed by a that clause.

Example

He told me (that) the man fell from the window.

Other examples of this type would be persuade, remind.

Say is followed by a that clause.

Example

She said that the man fell from the window.

Other examples of this type would be add, claim, hope, insist

When we use reporting verbs, It is important to learn which clauses are possible and which are not.

Example The doctor recommended that he stay in hospital.

(**Not** The doctor recommended me that he stay in hospital.)

Commas are not necessary after the reporting verb when using reported speech.

4.4.2 Reporting verb tense changes

In general, an understanding of the series of events should clarify the choice of tense necessary. However, it is useful to remember the following as a general guide:

Direct	Reported
Present (including auxiliary verbs)	Past
Past tenses and Present perfect	Past Perfect
Auxiliary verbs in the past	Past Perfect
Auxiliary verbs in the future	Past
Expressions of time and place	Change of word

Examples

1. Direct speech (present tense) to Reported speech (past tense)

I appreciate their kindness

He said that he appreciated their kindness

....

2. They are very kind

He said that they were very kind

3. Direct speech (past tense) to Reported speech (past perfect tense)

I fell from the window

He said that he had fallen from the window

....

4. Direct speech (present perfect tense) to Reported speech (past perfect tense)

I have fallen many times

He said that he had fallen (many times)

5. Direct speech (auxiliary verbs in the past) to Reported speech (past perfect tense)

I was not hurt

He said that he had not been hurt

....

6. Direct speech (auxiliary verbs in the future - will) to Reported speech (past tense - would)

I will go home soon

He said that he would go home soon

....

7. Expressions of time and place
1. here 2. these 3. yesterday 4. tomorrow 5. today
1. there 2. those 3. the day before 4. the following day 5. that day

4.5   Vocabulary: Television programme genres

Television (15 min)   Go online

Q23: A return to the village of Meadowvale where the Sharps are becoming increasingly more annoyed with the MacKays over the street party. Will Jo be able to reconcile herself to playing second fiddle again? Find out in tonight's episode.

a) comedy series
b) documentary
c) drama
d) film
e) reality TV
f) soap opera
g) sport
h) travel

....

Q24: Rom-com starring Kate Dean and Daniel Logan.

a) comedy series
b) documentary
c) drama
d) film
e) reality TV
f) soap opera
g) sport
h) travel

....

Q25: Sleepy villages in Tuscany. We visit six of the most beautiful and invite you to join us.

a) comedy series
b) documentary
c) drama
d) film
e) reality TV
f) soap opera
g) sport
h) travel

. . . .

Q26: Tonight we travel to Yorkshire in search of five stars for our end of year show, to be picked from thirty hopeful candidates.

a) comedy series
b) documentary
c) drama
d) film
e) reality TV
f) soap opera
g) sport
h) travel

. . . .

Q27: 9-5 today: gender and work. Are women still being paid less than men?

a) comedy series
b) documentary
c) drama
d) film
e) reality TV
f) soap opera
g) sport
h) travel

. . . .

Q28: Highlights of today's race in Barcelona.

a) comedy series
b) documentary
c) drama
d) film
e) reality TV
f) soap opera
g) sport
h) travel

. . . .

Q29: Hilarious antics once again as this week Dorothy and Davie find themselves hiding in the cellar as the teenagers take charge of things.

a) comedy series
b) documentary
c) drama
d) film
e) reality TV
f) soap opera
g) sport
h) travel

....

Q30: This week Inspector Foster finds twins' behaviour very suspicious, but can he prove anything?

a) comedy series
b) documentary
c) drama
d) film
e) reality TV
f) soap opera
g) sport
h) travel

Speaking (10 min)

Discuss the questions below with your partner:

- What kind of television shows do you regularly watch?

- Why do you like these genres but not others?

- Which do you think is more entertaining, more informative and more trustworthy: television programming or newspapers?

- Have you ever felt so annoyed or upset about a television programme that you wanted to write a letter or email of complaint? Or maybe you enjoyed a programme so much that you wanted to write to congratulate its makers?

4.6   Reading and writing: Letters to the editor

Language of discussion (15 min)   Go online

When having a discussion or writing a letter or email making a strong point, it is important to maintain appropriate language and not become argumentative or inappropriate. Try the following activity to learn how to use phrases expressing your position clearly but in an appropriate way.

Q31: Use the categories:

Agreeing	Disagreeing	Inviting opinion	Interrupting politely	Stating strong opinions

and decide which category is appropriate for each of the following phrases.

1. That's not quite how I see it
2. What are your feelings on this?
3. I see it a different way
4. Have you considered another way of looking at things
5. That's a good point
6. Exactly!
7. I reject that view entirely
8. Precisely!
9. What do you think?
10. I take your point but. . .
11. What are your views on the matter?
12. You have a point but. . .
13. I agree with you up to a point
14. Do you have any thoughts on this?
15. If I could just make my point
16. Yes I agree with you
17. Could I just say
18. If I could just interject
19. I am quite certain that. . .
20. I really can't agree with you
21. I couldn't agree more.
22. I am convinced
23. I totally disagree
24. I am firmly of the belief

Reading: Letters to the press

Read the following letter to the editor of a national newspaper.

Dear Sir

I am writing to express my concerns over the standard of broadcasting which we are now subjected to on a daily basis. In particular, I would like to state my grave doubts over the director general's decision to present last week's 'Model Conduct' which followed the day-to-day dreariness of six teenagers dreaming of catwalk success .

In an excruciating and apparently interminable 45 minutes we were subjected to inarticulate teenagers discussing their superficial reflections on diet, exercise and trend setting while their apparently uniformly avaricious parents applauded their materialistic aspirations. I was disgusted to hear a description of one girl's daily food intake which could not support a small rodent. Her lack of interest in food was applauded, while others were berated on camera for eating too many 'carbs', the enemy of all mankind it would seem.

The unlikely heroine of the show was Madeleine, a pretty but slightly podgy teenager caught indulging herself in a hot chocolate and croissant in a local cafe when she thought no-one was looking. The one pearl in this otherwise total dross, was her remark as she caught sight of the film crew, "I'm a bit bored now, I'd quite like a day off to do my homework."

In my view, the programme missed an opportunity to explore, in a useful way, the very painful and disturbingly common issue of anorexia in young people. At the same time, there was little, if any, reflection upon the dangers of living our own dreams through our children.

Yours faithfully

Dr. Sally Thompson

Q32: What is the purpose of the letter?

a) To describe a TV programme
b) To complain about a TV programme
c) To warn about the danger of anorexia

. . . .

Q33: What is the tone of the letter?

a) impatient
b) ironic
c) angry

. . . .

Q34: What type of language has been used?

a) formal
b) informal

Synonyms: Letters to the press (10 min)

Go online

Match the following words with their synonyms

Q35:

tedium	berated
agonising	superficial
endless	common
incoherent	dross
shallow	materialistic
greedy	podgy
thoughts	indulging
acquisitive	inarticulate
goals	dullness
rebuked	reflections
treating	interminable
chubby	excruciating
familiar	avaricious
rubbish	aspirations

Writing: Letters page (60 min)

You have been watching 'The Wild Channel' for many years and you are a fan of the channel. Recently you watched a programme about people and their pets.

Write a letter to a newspaper about the programme, saying why you enjoyed / did not enjoy the show .

You may wish to consider the following areas or any of your own ideas about the topic:

- explain why you are writing to the newspaper

- describe the programme you watched and its content

- explain what you particularly liked or disliked the programme and use phrases you have learned to express or support your points of argument

You should write approximately 300-350 words.

When you have finished show your work to your teacher or tutor. An exemplar answer is also provided.

4.7   Listening comprehension: Media

You will need access to the sound file: *hg-cesl1-4-1listening.mp3* to complete this listening comprehension.

Listen to the dialogue.

Listening comprehension: Media (15 min)   Go online

Listen to the recording again and try to answer the following questions:

Q36: What is the **main** topic of conversation?

a) How the speakers spent the weekend
b) How the speakers find out what is happening in the world
c) Comparing paper and online information sources

....

Q37: How do the speakers know each other?

a) The speakers are flatmates
b) The speakers are colleagues
c) The speakers are married

....

Q38: Jocelyn stayed at home because

a) She prefers to be indoors
b) The football was cancelled
c) She was inhibited from going out
d) She wanted to read the newspapers

....

Q39: Gary thinks that the most important source of news is

a) News agencies
b) Newspapers online
c) Ordinary people
d) Journalists

....

Q40: Jocelyn says that newspapers offer news which is

a) More up to date
b) More in-depth
c) More interesting
d) More visual

....

Q41: Which **three** of these statements reflect Gary's views:

A) People nowadays are more proactive

B) People expect more from journalists

C) Journalists are often economical with the truth

D) Journalists have less power nowadays

E) People have the opportunity nowadays to question reporting

F) Only journalists have the insights we need to keep up with current affairs

. . . .

Q42: How would you describe Jocelyn's attitude to online news

a) Sceptical

b) Positive

c) Negative

d) Open-minded

. . . .

Q43: Which of the following best describes the tone of the conversation between Gary and Jocelyn

a) Antagonistic

b) Friendly chat

c) Polite discussion

d) Heated debate

4.8 Reading comprehension: Media

The following activity is a reading comprehension covering the work of this topic.

Before you begin read the passage.

Press Freedom

1.The quality and quantity of news information which we have exposure to is, in many ways, contingent upon location. In some parts of the world, governments impose strict controls over the media, and have power over various elements of content. For example, in autocratic regimes governments tend to restrict access to information which they consider to be against the public interest, or which is immoral or harmful, or indeed threatens the country's stability. Decisions about what constitutes 'public interest' in such countries are made by government bodies.

2. Freedom of information is generally considered an intrinsic feature of democratic countries. Arguments in favour of this include the right of individuals to access information, in order to make informed choices about issues, especially those which directly affect them. Without media scrutiny it becomes difficult to uphold accountability. Similarly, there have been many cases in which it has been the work of investigative journalists which has brought to light miscarriages of justice.

3.   Some would argue that in a free market economy it is really not possible to have unfettered broadcast media. In order to maintain good circulation, newspapers, magazines and journals are constrained by the need to interest, amuse and entertain. Similarly, where survival is dependent upon advertising revenue, broadcast media cannot challenge messages of advertisers who have financial power over them.

4. In recent years, the internet has provided us with news from around the globe. This has been a cause for alarm among governments who wish to maintain power over what citizens access. In today's climate of widespread technological access, some authorities attempt to retain control by forcing users to register blogs and websites and by blocking, or even systematically jamming online news sources.   Nevertheless, social media technologies can provide journalists and individuals with a platform which circumvents controls and enables transfer of news information.

5.   The attempts of superpowers to keep sensitive information secret has been further undermined by the appearance of organisations such as Wikileaks. Wikileaks is a website which publishes anonymous contributions from news sources and whistleblowers in order to expose what is described, in their view, as unethical behaviour by governments and corporations. With respect to the verification of the 'leaks' themselves, Wikileaks are said to have a team of five experts, specialising in particular areas, who vet information prior to publishing.

6. The ability to maintain control over published data is becoming more of a challenge as news becomes less dependent upon traditional media. The stricter the government concerned, the more assiduous it will require to be in quashing rebellious movements. All of this is good news for freedom of information lobbyists.

Reading comprehension: Media   Go online

Read the passage once more and answer the questions which follow.

Press Freedom

1.The quality and quantity of news information which we have exposure to is, in many ways, contingent upon location. In some parts of the world, governments impose strict controls over the media, and have power over various elements of content. For example, in autocratic regimes governments tend to restrict access to information which they consider to be against the public interest, or which is immoral or harmful, or indeed threatens the country's stability. Decisions about what constitutes 'public interest' in such countries are made by government bodies.

2.   Freedom of information is generally considered an intrinsic feature of democratic countries.   Arguments in favour of this include the right of individuals to access information, in order to make informed choices about issues, especially those which directly affect them. Without media scrutiny it becomes difficult to uphold accountability. Similarly, there have been many cases in which it has been the work of investigative journalists which has brought to light miscarriages of justice.

3.   Some would argue that in a free market economy it is really not possible to have unfettered broadcast media.   In order to maintain good circulation, newspapers, magazines and journals are constrained by the need to interest, amuse and entertain. Similarly, where survival is dependent upon advertising revenue, broadcast media cannot challenge messages of advertisers who have financial power over them.

---

4. In recent years, the internet has provided us with news from around the globe. This has been a cause for alarm among governments who wish to maintain power over what citizens access. In today's climate of widespread technological access, some authorities attempt to retain control by forcing users to register blogs and websites and by blocking, or even systematically jamming online news sources. Nevertheless, social media technologies can provide journalists and individuals with a platform which circumvents controls and enables transfer of news information.

5. The attempts of superpowers to keep sensitive information secret has been further undermined by the appearance of organisations such as Wikileaks. Wikileaks is a website which publishes anonymous contributions from news sources and whistleblowers in order to expose what is described, in their view, as unethical behaviour by governments and corporations. With respect to the verification of the 'leaks' themselves, Wikileaks are said to have a team of five experts, specialising in particular areas, who vet information prior to publishing.

6. The ability to maintain control over published data is becoming more of a challenge as news becomes less dependent upon traditional media. The stricter the government concerned, the more assiduous it will require to be in quashing rebellious movements. All of this is good news for freedom of information lobbyists.

Q44: Match the headings in the list to the paragraph numbers.

A) Future dissent
B) Organised subversion
C) Controlling governments
D) Speaking freely
E) Limiting factors
F) Modern media

....

Q45: In paragraph 1, in the sentence "Decisions about what constitutes 'public interest' in such countries are made by government bodies", what **two-word phrase** does the word 'such' refer to?

....

Q46: In paragraph 2, in the sentence "Arguments in favour of this include the right of individuals to access information, in order to make informed choices about issues, especially those which directly affect them", what **three-word phrase** does the word 'this' refer to?

Q47: In countries in which there are dictatorships, publishing decisions are made by the press.

a) true
b) false

....

Q48: One purpose of a relatively free press is to ensure that people may be forced to explain their actions.

a) true
b) false

....

Q49: In the future, governments should find it easier to control news sources.

a) true
b) false

....

Q50: This text is most likely to have come from

a) A newspaper article about press limitation
b) An essay about freedom of information for students
c) An internet information site

....

Q51: Which of the following subjects are not discussed in the text? (choose one)

a) Dissemination of information in different countries
b) Technologies which evade press controls
c) Rights of the individual to privacy
d) Impediments to press freedom

4.9 Vocabulary list

You might find it helpful to have a list of some of the words which have been introduced in this topic.

accountability (adjective)	responsibility
altercation (noun)	argument
anorexia (noun)	illness resulting in serious weight loss in which individual will not eat
antics (noun)	funny, silly or strange behaviour
autocratic (adjective)	dictatorial
berserk (adjective)	very angry, out of control
clandestine (adjective)	secret, covert
contingent (adjective)	dependent
debut (noun)	first appearance
to defuse (verb)	to make calm; to control
dissemination (noun)	distribution
dissent (noun)	disagreement
diva (noun)	very successful and famous female singer
to evade (verb)	to avoid
exclusive (noun)	limited to only one person or group of people
exposure (noun)	publicity
grave (noun)	serious
to garner (verb)	to gather
impediment (noun)	obstacle
interminable (adjective)	continuing for too long
insight (noun)	clear deep understanding
intrinsic (adjective)	important or basic characteristic of something
ironic (adjective)	interesting or funny because different from expected
journalist (noun)	writer for newspaper or magazine
open minded (adjective)	willing to consider ideas that are new or different
proactive (adjective)	take action by causing change not just reacting to change
protagonist (noun)	important supporter of idea or political system
sceptical (adjective)	doubting that something is true or useful
scrutiny (noun)	close examination
to sting (verb)	to cheat
to subject (verb)	to force someone to put up with something
subversion (noun)	destruction or damage to something such as a political system
systematically (adverb)	methodically
temperamental (adjective)	someone whose mood often changes quite suddenly
unethical (adjective)	not based on moral belief (not ethical)
unfettered (adjective)	free, not limited by rules or other constraints /influences

Unit 1 Topic 5

Technology

Contents

Learning objective

By the end of this topic you should be able to:

- demonstrate your knowledge and understanding of defining and non-defining relative clauses in the context of technology

- use your extended range of vocabulary in the topic area through practice in reading, listening and writing

- demonstrate your increased knowledge of writing genre through writing a discursive essay

- demonstrate your pronunciation and your awareness of syllable stress

This topic examines technology, exploring the areas of computing, the internet, robotics and electronics, and how these impact upon people's lives. It also offers grammar presentations and activities on defining and non-defining relative clauses and adverbs of degree. In addition, advanced vocabulary relevant to the topic of technology is introduced. The topic includes work on all four skills: speaking, reading, writing, and listening. There are also supplementary pronunciation exercises. Assessment opportunities occur at the end of the topic.

Learning objective

By the end of this topic you should be able to:

- demonstrate your knowledge and understanding of defining and non-defining relative clauses in the context of technology

- use your extended range of vocabulary in the topic area through practice in reading, listening and writing

- demonstrate your increased knowledge of writing genre through writing a discursive essay

- demonstrate your pronunciation and your awareness of syllable stress

---

5.1   Vocabulary: Technology acronyms and initialisms

An **acronym** is an abbreviation which consists of the initial letters of more than one word pronounced together as a new word.

Example ROM, PIN, LASER

(Read Only Memory, Personal Identification Number, Light Amplification by Stimulated Emission of Radiation)

An **initialism** is an abbreviation which consists of the initial letters of more than one word pronounced separately.

Example CD, CPU, ATM

(Compact Disc, Central Processing Unit, Automated Teller Machine)

Acronyms and initialisms (20 min) Go online

Q1: Look at the following acronyms and initialisms relating to technology:

SMS, HDTV, USB, RAM, GPS, JPEG, CPU, PDF, LCD, DVD, ISP

Do you know where they are used?

Try to guess as many as you can and complete a table with these headings:

Computer Hardware	File Extensions	Internet	Television / Video	Other

....

Q2: Do you know what any of them mean? Match the acronym or initialism with what it is used for:

1. This is a company that provides access to the internet
2. This is a device often used by drivers to display live maps, helping them find locations
3. This is the standard format of photographs as used by most digital devices
4. This is a file format which resembles a printed document but is an electronic image of the text and graphics

---

 Note: It is often not necessary to understand the individual words in an acronym or an initialism in English in order to understand the meaning of the object or idea under consideration. If you are curious about the expanded meanings of the acronyms or initialisms covered, look them up on the internet, in your dictionary or in the expected answer.

5.2 Reading: Is cyberspace still open?

Reading: Cyberspace (40 min) Go online

Read the passage if you need to and answer the questions which follow.

If you're old enough to remember cyberspace, then your internal CPU is probably in need of a refresher course in techno speak. According to the famous quote, which is attributed to Benjamin Franklin, death and taxes are the two certainties in life, but there is another certainty, at some point in your late twenties or early thirties, you'll lose touch with all that is hip and trendy about society and become something of an outsider looking in on all things 'cool'. The language you use is by no means excepted from this phenomenon and, in fact, buzzwords that once made you sound "of the moment" will now make you sound, well, frankly, past it. Technological language is particularly susceptible to obsolescence. As new technologies supersede old ones, so does the corresponding terminology. The phraseology which is used today will, in the future, prove a giveaway that you are no longer part of the it, or indeed

---

IT crowd. Here's a rundown of what not to say when talking computers to your friends, colleagues and kids:

Surfing the web - Does anyone 'surf' any more? Ask the average fourteen-year-old if they have surfed the 'net lately and they'll very probably stare blankly at you, before returning to their IPad to 'Google' the latest mobile phone apps. 'Surfing' has been reclaimed by wetsuit-clad, camper-van driving college dropouts, and once again should only be attempted by those with a board and a penchant for racing sharks at the backstroke, so don't risk the embarrassment of saying you actually do it on your home computer.

Intranet and Extranet - Intrawhat? Extrawho? Once a staple part of the company handbook, references to either of these terms these days will show you up in business as the kind of person who probably still thinks a filofax and a pinstripe suit are this year's "must have" fashion accessories. 'Virtual Private Network' is the lingo this century.

PDA - Remember PDAs? The Personal Digital Assistant? Yes? Well, try to forget them. And erase the terms 'bleeper' and 'pager' from your lexicon while you're at it. The way things are heading we may no longer even be talking about the 'mobile' before too long, as 'smartphone' is fast becoming the word on everyone's lips.

Long-distance calls - "Operator, could you reverse the charges on this long-distance call?" If you find yourself still uttering these words, then it's time to extinguish that torch and re-emerge from your cave. With the advent of Voice over Internet Protocol services such as Skype, and the prevalence and relative inexpensiveness of calling from mobiles all over the world, the days of the number of miles between receivers determining the price of your call are long gone. Besides, the widespread automation of telephony systems makes you wonder if there are even any operators out there to call any more?!

Weblog - First we had home pages, then we had websites, then everyone and their dog became a freelance journalist with the arrival of weblogs, or 'blogs' for short. Blogging was ubiquitous not so long ago, but mention it today and people will then realise why you don't respond to their tweets or Facebook messages - you've yet to discover social networking, or this decade.

World Wide Web, the Information Superhighway and Cyberspace - These were the biggies when the internet first came to be such a huge part of our lives. There's nothing wrong with using any of these terms today either, so long as you are writing a historical essay. Such references were consigned to the annals years ago, so stick with 'internet' and try to avoid the temptation to shorten it to 'net' or 'web' - such terms are best left with curtains and spiders.

Q3: The author's opinion on people who use outdated technological terminology is:

a)   sarcastic and patronising.
b)   angry and annoyed.
c)   conceited and smug.

....

Q4: The article comes from:

a)   a broadsheet newspaper.
b)   a lifestyle column in a magazine.
c)   a guidebook to the internet.

. . . .

Q5: Technological terms are more likely to become extinct from a language quicker than other linguistic terms.

a) True
b) False

. . . .

Q6: Fourteen-year-olds are not interested in using the internet any more.

a) True
b) False

. . . .

Q7: The term, 'World Wide Web', is still commonly used by people today.

a) True
b) False

. . . .

Q8: Find the word in the passage which means *The state of being out of date, or no longer relevant (n.)*

. . . .

Q9: Find the word in the passage which means *To replace with something newer (v.)*

. . . .

Q10: Find the word in the passage which means *Without emotion or expression (adv.)*

. . . .

Q11: Find the word in the passage which means *Available for hire, working without a contract (adj.)*

. . . .

Q12: Find the word in the passage which means *Disposed of permanently (v.)*

. . . .

Q13: Find the word in the passage which means *The arrival of something (n.)*

5.3 Grammar: Defining and non-defining relative clauses

Relative clauses: Grammar presentation

Relative clauses add information to a sentence. The function of a relative clause is similar to that of an **adjectival** or **prepositional** phrase .

Examples

1. Adjectival phrase

The flat screen television.

....

2. Prepositional phrase

The television with the flat screen.

....

3. Relative clause

The television which has a flat screen.

We can use relative clauses to avoid repetition.

Example I have just bought a new television. The television has a flat screen.

I have just bought a new television which has a flat screen.

We can make a distinction between **defining** and **non-defining** relative clauses.

Defining relative clauses are *crucial* to the understanding of the sentence and therefore cannot be left out.

Example The television which I gave to my mother has stopped working (the relative clause *which I gave to my mother* indicates which television we are talking about).

Non-defining relative clauses provide extra information in a sentence and therefore can be left out.

Example The television, which I only bought last year, has stopped working.

The following relative pronouns can be used to introduce relative clauses:

- that
- which
- who
- what
- whom
- whose
- when
- why

5.3.1   Defining relative clauses

The following forms are most common when using defining relative clauses:

Where the relative clause defines the **subject** and is **a person** we use *who, whom* or *that.*

Example   The teacher *who* taught us most about technology was Mrs Lamb

When the relative clause defines the **subject** and is **a thing** we use *that* or *which.*

Example   The lessons *that* taught us most about technology were the practical computing sessions

Where the relative clause defines the **object** and is **a person or a thing** we use *that.*

Examples

1. The teacher *that* I liked best was Mrs Lamb

   . . . .

2. The lesson *that* I liked the best was the practical computing session

---

 *When the relative clause defines the **object** we can leave out the relative pronoun*

Example   The teacher *that* I liked the best was Mrs Lamb.

The teacher I liked best was Mrs Lamb.

5.3.2   Non-defining relative clauses

The following forms are most common when using **non-defining** relative clauses:

Where the relative clause refers to the **subject** and is **a person** we use *who.*

Example   My brother, *who* is a computer technician, lives in Edinburgh.

Where the relative clause refers to the **subject** and is **a thing** we use *which.*

Example   My brother's favourite computer is his palmtop, *which* he uses when he is travelling.

Where the relative clause defines the **object** and is **a person** we use *who* or *whom.*

Example   My brother, *who (whom)* I have just visited, is a computer technician.

Where the relative clause refers to the **object** and is **a thing** we use *which*.

Example My brother's computer, *which* he bought last week, is fantastic.

Relative clauses (20 min)   Go online

Q14:
Look at the highlighted phrases in extracts adapted from the reading activity.

a) ...the famous quote, **which is attributed to Benjamin Franklin**, suggests there are two certainties in life...

b) The phraseology **which is used today** will, in the future, prove a giveaway...

Which of the highlighted phrases shows:

1. information that is crucial to the meaning of the phrase (defining).
2. information that is not crucial to the meaning of the phrase (non-defining).

Q15: Steve Jobs was credited with democratising the computer. He co-founded Apple technology with Steve Wozniak.

....

Q16: Social networking sites give us more information than journalists. They have arguably transformed the way we access news.

....

Q17: External hard drives are now essential in most organisations. They prevent computers from losing processing time.

....

Q18: A local bus driver has been suspended. He was using a mobile phone behind the wheel.

....

Q19: Mark Zuckerberg still uses his social networking site. He is the founder of Facebook.

....

Q20: Bill Gates is still the richest man in America. He is the creator of Microsoft.

Forming relative clauses (15 min)

Write sentences using defining relative clauses to describe the following items or people from the field of technology.

Example : mp3 player

This is a device which allows you to play downloaded music.

Ask your teacher to check your answers or look at the exemplar answer to see some suggestions.

Q21: Computer programmer

....

Q22: Blu-Ray player

....

Q23: Interactive whiteboard

....

Q24: Web designer

....

Q25: Digital camera

5.4 Reading: Questionnaire 'Can you live without technology?'

Answer the survey in the next activity and find out what kind of technology user you are.

Questionnaire 'Can you live without technology?' (20 min) Go online

Survey: Answer the questions and note your results (how many A,B and Cs you select)

1. How large is your television screen ?

   A) Over 32 inches. I need it to watch my favourite movies, soaps and sport in glorious high resolution with surround sound! Get the popcorn out! Wow, this is 3D. . . !

   B) Under 32 inches. I do enjoy watching TV but I also value the tranquillity of my living room. I prefer to have a nice painting as the centrepiece of my room.

   C) TV? I hate TV. I'd rather spend time with real people who I can actually speak and listen to, rather than just look at.

2. Do you have a wireless internet connection in your home or on a mobile phone?

   A) Yes, of course I do. It's my lifeblood. I have wireless on pretty much all my electronic devices, e-book reader, mobile, tablet. . .

   B) I have the internet, but it's not wireless. I'm thinking about upgrading though as most of my friends use Wi-Fi and it seems pretty good.

   C) The interwhat? I've got the Encyclopaedia Britannica, who needs that new-fangled nonsense?

---

3. How often do you check your email or update your status on social networking sites?

   A) I need to orchestrate my social life effectively, so I do this a lot. It makes everything so much easier than using the phone.

   B) I'll periodically check my messages during the week, after all, it's nice to hear from friends and occasionally check up on what they've been doing.

   C) I'd rather call my friends or meet up with them face-to-face. Social networkers always pretend to have more friends than they really do anyway. . . it's all a bit of a circus.

4. Do you download music, movies, films or books from the internet?

   A) My whole music and movie collection is practically digital these days. I can access it anywhere and it is all streamed from one device to another. It's amazing!

   B) Sometimes, but I still buy DVDs, enjoy a trip to the cinema and appreciate the feel and sound of the pages turning in an old-fashioned paperback.

   C) Never. I've heard if you use Y-tunes or whatever it's called, or download anything from the internet you get a computer virus or instantly go to jail. Anyway, I don't know how to and wouldn't be interested in trying.

5. How often do you buy a new, or upgrade your existing, mobile phone?

   A) I wouldn't be seen dead with last year's model. I consider myself something of a trend-setter. A high Megapixel camera, lots of memory and great apps are vital.

   B) I might get a new one, but only if my old one is really out of date or doesn't work any more. I suppose if I saw one I really liked, or one that had some nice features, I could be tempted.

   C) I can think of four hundred better ways to spend four hundred pounds than on a telephone. People walk around with these things glued to their ears, ignoring the people they are actually with, in the belief that something more important is occurring elsewhere.

Look at your results and what they say about your view on technology. Do you agree?

If you answered **mostly A)** you are probably a **Digital Native** - you have been brought up with technology throughout your life and see it as being of paramount importance in both work and play. It would be difficult for you to cope if it all disappeared tomorrow.

If you answered **mostly B)** you are likely to be a **Digital Immigrant** - you have some reservations about the use of technology, possibly because you remember what life was like in pre-internet times, so although you might have adopted the use of some technological equipment, and even buy some of the flashy newer gadgets, you still realise there is an outside world.

If you answered **mostly C)** there's every chance you are a **Technophobe**. You really don't see the point in all these electronic gizmos, you still think tweets are the sounds that birds make and Facebook is some sort of accident that happens when you fall over in a library.

5.5 Writing: Discursive essay on technology

Writing: Discursive essay on technology (60 min)

Consider your answers to the previous activity, and think about the variety of viewpoints that different people have on technology.

Write a discursive essay for your class tutor, describing the following areas of technology and their relative merits and drawbacks. Think about how these inventions have made people's lives easier as well as how they may have had a negative impact upon society.

- Digital cameras

- Social networking sites

- Video games

Before you begin, consider the following questions:

- What is the purpose of the communication?

- Who is the intended audience of the essay?

- What level of formality and register would be appropriate?

Make some notes or a mind map to help plan your writing before you begin.

Try to write between **300 - 350** words.

When you have finished, ask your teacher or tutor to check your work.

There is an exemplar answer given in the expected answers.

5.6 Pronunciation: Technology

Many words in the field of technology may be unfamiliar. The next activity will give you practice in how to pronounce some of these words.

Pronunciation: Technology (10 min) Go online

You need access to the sound files: *hg-cesl1-5-1vocab1.mp3 to hg-cesl1-5-1vocab10.mp3*

Q26: Listen to the pronunciation of the following words.

How many syllables does the word have?

Where is the main stress in the word?

1. Technological
2. Capacity
3. Prototype
4. Expansion
5. Laboratory
6. Integration
7. Supersede
8. Interconnectivity
9. Obsolescence
10. Telephony

5.7   Writing: Future technology

Revise the topic before trying the next activity in which you will be asked to write an article about your **interpretation** of what the town or city you live in will be like, twenty years in the future.

Writing: Future technology (60 min)

Your local newspaper has approached you to write an article about your interpretation of what the town or city you live in will be like, twenty years in the future.

Include all of the following points (not necessarily in the following order):

- Discussion of what your town / city looks like today

- How it has changed over recent years

- What the major changes will be, and how technological advances will shape this change

- Your opinion of the town / city today

- Your view on how advances in technology will affect people's daily lives, working habits and free time within your town / city.

Before you begin, consider the following questions:

- What is the purpose of the communication?

- Who is intended the audience of the article?

- What level of formality and register would be appropriate?

Make some notes or a mind map to help plan your writing before you begin.

Try to write between **300-350** words.

Ask your teacher to check your work.

There is also an exemplar answer for you to look at when you have finished.

5.8 Reading comprehension: The internet

The following activity is a reading comprehension covering the work of this topic.

Reading comprehension: The internet (30 min)   Go online

Before you begin, read the passage for gist.

The internet — what an invention! Arguably it has been the most important technological advancement of our generation, if not the last century. Nowadays it is omnipresent, and most of us have become so accustomed to its place in our daily lives that when we cannot get online due to a power outage, or worse yet, being in a Wi-Fi 'not-spot', we wonder how we will accomplish anything that day.

Yes, the wonderful internet has boundless possibilities. The world's greatest repository of encyclopaedic knowledge is at our fingertips. My question to you is this, Are we maximising its potential? Many people in the developed world have had high speed access for over a decade, so where are the medical breakthroughs and miracle cures that international networks of medical specialists should bring? Where are the solutions to global warming and economic imbalance? Where does the problem lie here? Are we not using the internet enough?

Well, in fact, we **are** using it enough... too much, in fact. It seems we do not have the ability to prioritise what is important, and therefore instead of species advancement, procrastination and evasion are the chief uses of the internet, and causes of the proliferation of a new form of mental illness, namely 'internet addiction'.

A simple search on the misused tool itself reveals in excess of a million hits for internet addiction disorder (IAD), otherwise known as web dependency syndrome. The General Medical Council recognises it as a mental illness in the UK, although in some countries battle still rages to achieve this classification, for example in the USA, where antiquated government documentation still infers that people can only be addicted to harmful substances and not actions.

Instead of harnessing the limitless potential of the internet, we are allowing it to subjugate us. IAD regularly leads to neglect of work or parental obligation, and in its most extreme guises has seen individuals charged with murder over unpaid online auction fees and deaths from sleep deprivation due to online gaming addictions. What is more, it has been linked to several thousand cases of violent assault and it makes gambling, pornography and infidelity instantly accessible from your own home.

Internet policing, internet service provider pricing policies and government censoring can all lessen these harmful effects, but they are no substitute for self-discipline and self-regulation. Is it not time that we started using, as opposed to misusing, the gift of the internet?

Q27: The most appropriate title for the article is:

A) Most people don't understand the internet

B) There must be more to the internet than this

C) The internet breeds mental illness

D) The internet is used too much

....

Q28: The author's view on the internet itself is:

a) Generally positive and optimistic

b) Generally negative and pessimistic

c) Neither positive nor negative

....

Q29: It is now universally accepted that internet addiction disorder or IAD is a mental illness.

a) true

b) false

....

Q30: The author says that the internet is controlling us rather than the other way around.

a) true

b) false

....

Q31: The author thinks the key to management of IAD is more effective government strategies.

a) true

b) false

....

Q32: Find a word in the text which means *everywhere*

....

Q33: Find a word in the text which means *time wasting* or *delaying something*

....

Q34: Find a word in the text which means *faithlessness*

5.9 Listening comprehension: Technology

The following activity is a listening comprehension covering the work of this topic.

You will need access to the sound file *hg-cesl1-5-2listening* to continue with this activity.

Before you begin, listen to the speakers to establish the gist of the conversation.

Listening comprehension: Technology Go online

Listen to the recording again.

You will need access to the sound file *hg-cesl1-5-2listening* to continue with this activity.

Q35: The main topic under discussion in this recording is

a) Innovative technologies
b) A technology conference
c) Assistive technology
d) The impact of technology in today's society

. . . .

Q36: Which of the following does Katy say you can find at the Techware conference? Pick three answers

A) New inventions
B) Stands selling new devices
C) Information about computers
D) Presentations
E) Technology fans
F) International speakers

. . . .

Q37: Listen for the missing word
According to Martin when using the mobile phone, numbers are found in terms of their _____ to number five.

. . . .

Q38: Listen for the missing word
According to Martin when using the mobile phone users can get spoken _____.

. . . .

Q39: There are five stages in using the Penfriend. Number the stages into the correct order.

Stages

- Attach a label to an object
- Point the scanner at the object
- Play back your message
- Register it with an optical scanner
- Record your voice

....

Q40: Martin thinks that the innovative assistive technology has been sufficiently supported by the IT industry.

a) true
b) false

....

Q41: Martin thinks that the market for assistive technologies is likely to grow in the future.

a) true
b) false

....

Q42: Martin is positive about the future of assistive technologies.

a) true
b) false

5.10 Vocabulary list

This is a list of related vocabulary which is intended to supplement what you have learned. It may also be useful to refer to when attempting the speaking and writing activities within the topic.

application (noun)	a piece of software with a particular purpose, often used in conjunction with smart phones
to augment (verb)	to make something bigger or better by adding more to it
to automate (verb)	to convert something to automatic operation
blueprint (noun)	a design plan for a new concept, often in the form of a technical drawing
Bluetooth (noun)	a low cost, short-range wireless system for transferring data
component (noun)	a part of a larger thing, very often machinery
digital divide (noun phrase)	the gap between the amount of internet access in developed nations and less developed nations
to discontinue (verb)	to stop making or producing a product
ergonomics (noun)	the study of design efficiency relating to equipment
to evolve (verb)	to develop to a more complex state
firewall (noun)	part of a computer system which prevents unwanted access to a network
frontier (noun)	the extreme limit of knowledge and understanding in a particular area
groundbreaking (adjective)	pioneering, a new and potentially important idea not seen before
to mechanise (verb)	to equip with machinery
megapixels (noun)	one million pixels. The resolution or quality by which digital images are measured
podcast (noun)	an audio file available for download
productivity (noun)	the level of efficiency of a person, machine or company
streaming video (noun phrase)	video transmission over the internet
vision (noun)	the ability to plan the future with a sense of perception or foresight
Wiki (noun)	a website developed by a community of people with a common aim

Unit 1 Topic 6

Planning a trip

Contents

Learning objective

By the end of this topic you should be able to:

- use a wider range of vocabulary in the topic area

- use separable and inseparable phrasal verbs with greater accuracy

- demonstrate wider knowledge and understanding of punctuation through practice

- demonstrate a knowledge of writing genre by writing an informal email

- demonstrate greater awareness of word stress

Learning objective

By the end of this topic you should be able to:

- use a wider range of vocabulary in the topic area
- use separable and inseparable phrasal verbs with greater accuracy
- demonstrate wider knowledge and understanding of punctuation through practice
- demonstrate a knowledge of writing genre by writing an informal email
- demonstrate greater awareness of word stress

This topic examines transport and travel, exploring methods of transportation, types of holidays and accommodation, local and world travel and its effects on the economy and the environment. It introduces grammar points covering separable and inseparable phrasal verbs with literal and idiomatic meanings. Advanced vocabulary relevant to the topic of transport and travel is introduced and practised through a variety of activities. The topic includes work on all four skills: speaking, reading, writing, and listening. There are also supplementary pronunciation exercises. Assessment opportunities occur at the end of the topic.

Certain sections contain sound files. You may download these and use them on your mp3 player or equivalent to practise your pronunciation. This may be very useful if there are times when you will not have access to the materials online.

6.1   Vocabulary: Transport

People use several different methods of transport nowadays. This section's activities will provide you with common terms associated with forms of transport.

Types of vehicle (10 min)   Go online

Q1:   Do you know if these types of vehicle travel on roads, by rail, air or sea?

Organise them into categories: Road / overland, Rail / on track, Air, Sea

1. HGV
2. freight train
3. tram
4. hot air balloon
5. hovercraft
6. underground / subway
7. moped
8. yacht
9. cruise liner

---

10. quad bike
11. trawler
12. glider

Methods of transport (10 min)   Go online

Choose the correct word from the list provided to identify the method of transport described.

List: HGV: freight train: tram: hot air balloon: hovercraft: underground / subway: moped: yacht: cruise liner: trawler: glider: quad bike

You may need to make some words plural.

Q2:

1. I didn't think there were many _____ around these days, but there are still several in use on the south coast of England. It's an exciting alternative to travelling by boat, and the kids love the idea that they are floating on a bed of air!

2. So, let me get this straight. . . in a _____ it's just you up in the air in a plane with no engine? Sounds dangerous to me.

3. I'm just back from Rome. You should see the streets there - crazy traffic! Everyone is riding around on _____.

4. Scotland used to be famous for its _____ but they were replaced with buses many years ago, and the rails have long since been removed.

5. Personally, I think that _____ should only be used off-road for sporting activities. They are too slow and the driver is too exposed to be on the road.

Parts of a vehicle (15 min)   Go online

Look at the pictures of two of the most common types of vehicle: the aeroplane and the car. Can you identify and label the following parts of these vehicles?

You may wish to use a dictionary to help you.

Q3:

1. bonnet, bumper, boot, flaps, landing gear, nose-cone, windscreen, tail fin, cockpit, headlight

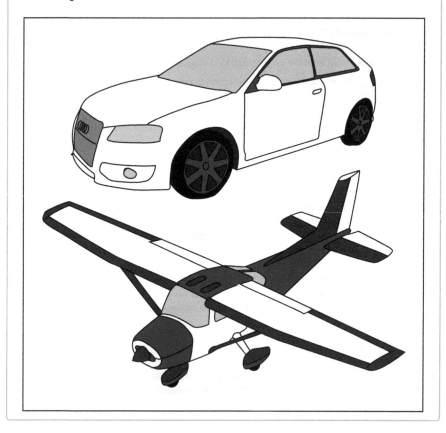

6.2   Punctuation

Punctuation is used to help clarify the meaning of a passage of text.

- full stops
- commas
- capital letters

- inverted commas
- parentheses
- apostrophes

Punctuation (5 min)   Go online

Can you match the correct name to each punctuation mark?

Q4:

full stops	()
commas	A
capital letters	,
inverted commas	.
parentheses	;
apostrophes	" "

Reading: punctuation (20 min)   Go online

Q5:

Rewrite the following text to include appropriate punctuation where necessary: full stops, commas, capital letters, inverted commas, parentheses and apostrophes.

Ask your teacher or tutor to check your work or compare it with the model answer when you have finished.

Strike action threatens to ruin festive period

Almost a million anyplace airways passengers face christmas travel chaos after the airlines cabin crew voted yesterday to back a twelve-day strike that will ground its planes beyond the new year the unprecedented walkout over staffing and salary cuts which will last from the 22nd december next tuesday to 2nd january has left many customers scrambling to book on other airlines or trying to make alternative arrangements via crowded express trains anyplace airways sheer size as a long-haul carrier would make it difficult for other carriers to accommodate its passengers according to observers within our industry if these strikes go ahead a huge number of people will be stranded said tom westland aviation author and former pilot i cannot think of any route where flights would not have been fully booked so there are going to be a lot of angry anyplace airways customers, and possibly a lot of legal battles in the coming months

---

6.3   Reading: Airline strike

Reading: Airline strike (20 min)   Go online

Read an expanded version of the text and answer the questions that follow.

Almost a million Anyplace Airways passengers face Christmas travel chaos, after the airline's cabin crew voted yesterday to back a twelve-day strike that will ground its planes beyond the New Year. The unprecedented walkout over staffing and salary cuts, which will last from the 22nd December (next Tuesday) to 2nd January, has left many customers scrambling to book on other airlines or trying to make alternative arrangements via crowded express trains. Anyplace Airways' sheer size as a long-haul carrier would make it difficult for other carriers to accommodate its passengers, according to observers within our industry. "If these strikes go ahead, a huge number of people will be stranded", said Tom Westland, aviation author and former pilot. "I cannot think of any route where flights would not have been fully booked, so there are going to be a lot of angry Anyplace Airways customers, and possibly a lot of legal battles in the coming months."

Representatives from Anyplace Airways were conspicuous by their absence at their management offices, and were initially unavailable for comment, later issuing a terse press release downplaying the consequences of any mooted strike action. Rival firms have been more forthcoming with their statements, with budget carrier ByronAir stating that they have more than doubled their regular schedule of flights and will be more than happy to assist, they claim, all of the stranded passengers on their journeys home. Air US have also indicated a willingness to come to the aid of beleaguered flyers, and were unable to resist a sly dig at their competitor's predicament, stating the following on their website, "Air US - the airline that looks after our crew, so they turn up for work to look after you".

Q6:   Where does this article come from?

a)   An aviation industry magazine
b)   A tabloid newspaper
c)   A broadsheet newspaper

....

Q7:   A strike of this size and length has never been seen before in the industry.

a)   true
b)   false

....

Q8:   Although inconvenient, the planned industrial action is not expected to cause too much upheaval.

a)   true
b)   false

....

Q9: There is a concern that other carriers may find it difficult to accommodate Anyplace Airways passengers.

a) true
b) false

. . . .

Q10: The Anyplace Airways board of management refused to comment on the matter.

a) true
b) false

Synonyms (10 min) Go online

Q11: The first list contains words which are taken from the reading passage. Match them with their corresponding synonym from the second list.

Words from passage:

1. unprecedented
2. sheer
3. accommodate
4. aviation
5. former
6. conspicuous
7. mooted
8. forthcoming
9. beleaguered
10. predicament

Synonym list:

A) flying
B) harassed
C) apparent
D) suggested, proposed
E) communicative
F) enormous, unrestricted
G) (difficult) situation
H) unique
I) one-time
J) cater for

Word stress (15 min)   Go online

You will need access to sound files *hg-cesl1-6-2vocab1.mp3 to hg-cesl1-6-2vocab10.mp3*.

Look at the words below, taken from the previous exercises.

How do you pronounce each word?

Listen to the recordings and repeat the words, then guess how many syllables are in each word and where the primary stress lies.

Q12: Number of syllables

a) two
b) three
c) four
d) five

....

Q13: Syllable with stress

a) first
b) second
c) third

Q14: Number of syllables

a) two
b) three
c) four
d) five

....

Q15: Syllable with stress

a) first
b) second
c) third
d) fourth
e) fifth

Q16: Number of syllables

a) two
b) three
c) four
d) five

....

Q17: Syllable with stress

a) first
b) second
c) third
d) fourth
e) fifth

Q18: Number of syllables

a) two
b) three
c) four

....

Q19: Syllable with stress

a) first
b) second
c) third
d) fourth
e) fifth

Q20: Number of syllables

a) two
b) three
c) four
d) five

....

Q21: Syllable with stress

a) first
b) second
c) third
d) fourth
e) fifth

Q22: Number of syllables

a) two
b) three
c) four
d) five

....

Q23: Syllable with stress

a) first
b) second
c) third
d) fourth
e) fifth

Q24: Number of syllables

a) two
b) three
c) four
d) five

. . . .

Q25: Syllable with stress

a) first
b) second
c) third
d) fourth
e) fifth

Q26: Number of syllables

a) two
b) three
c) four
d) five

. . . .

Q27: Syllable with stress

a) first
b) second
c) third
d) fourth
e) fifth

Q28: Number of syllables

a) two
b) three
c) four

. . . .

Q29: Syllable with stress

a) first
b) second
c) third
d) fourth
e) fifth

Q30: Number of syllables

a) two
b) three
c) four
d) five

....

Q31: Syllable with stress

a) first
b) second
c) third
d) fourth
e) fifth

6.4   Vocabulary: Holiday accommodation

This section will explore holiday accommodation and the vocabulary that you can use to describe these types.

Vocabulary: Holiday accommodation (15 min)   Go online

Q32: Match the following items of vocabulary describing holiday accommodation from the first list with their respective descriptions taken from the second list.

Items of vocabulary:

1. Campsite
2. Self-catering apartment
3. Youth hostel
4. Hotel
5. Chalet
6. Timeshare
7. House swap
8. Bed and Breakfast (B & B)
9. Retreat
10. Caravan site

Descriptions:

A) A place where people park caravans or motorhomes for use as holiday homes

B) A building with many private rooms, dining and leisure facilities for guests

C) A smaller building which offers boarding accommodation and typically one meal included in the price

D) A very basic type of shared accommodation, usually with an upper age limit

E) A wooden cabin often found in ski resorts or forested areas

F) A holiday property jointly owned by several people who take turns occupying it

G) An outdoor area where several people can pitch tents

H) A quiet and tranquil place of religious or spiritual healing

I) A purpose built holiday home where the holiday makers do their own cooking, cleaning etc

J) An exchange of homes between two families in different countries for an agreed period of time

---

Choice of accommodation (10 min) Go online

Decide which accommodation would be most appropriate for each holidaymaker and then drag and drop the items of vocabulary to the appropriate place.

Q33: Think back to the previous activity. Which type of accommodation from the given list would be most suitable for the following people?

List: Campsite: Self-catering apartment: Youth hostel: Hotel: Chalet: Timeshare: House swap: B & B: Retreat: Caravan site

1. An elderly couple who enjoy having everything in one place, but don't have time to cook for themselves

2. Two young and single friends for whom budget is the uppermost concern when booking a city break

3. A middle-aged couple who crave both adventure and privacy from the same holiday

4. A family of five on a fly-drive holiday who want to base themselves near the tourist attractions, but not on the main strip of hotels

5. A young couple seeking outdoor escape from the hustle and bustle of the big smoke

6.5 Listening: Tourist haven?

Listening: Tourist haven? (25 min) Go online

For this activity you will need access to the sound file: *hg-cesl1-6-1listening.mp3*

Read the following text which has words/phrases missing. Next listen to a recording of the script and try complete the gaps by typing in the appropriate vocabulary. You may have to listen more than once.

Q34:

What price a tourist haven?

Mallorca is the biggest of the Balearic Islands. It used to be one of the most _____ parts of Europe and farming was the main source of employment. Forty years ago, however, things started to change, and nowadays Mallorca is one of Europe's _____ package holiday destinations, specialising in family holidays. Millions of visitors _____ to the island, swelling the off-season _____ population of just seven hundred thousand. These visitors bring with them jobs and money, but at what cost?

One of the biggest problems caused by such a high level of tourism is the impact on the environment. A _____ amount of building has taken place to accommodate tourists without much consideration for the environment. In many areas the coastline has been destroyed. Mass tourism has also brought traffic _____ issues and pollution. Mallorca has the highest level of car _____ per capita in Europe. Another major problem facing Mallorca is that of waste, which is increasing by 10 - 15% per year. Something _____ would have to be done to solve this problem. There is also the issue of water shortage. At times, fresh drinking water has had to be shipped in from the mainland.

Many tourists are not interested in the environment or the culture of the country they are visiting. Indeed even those who buy property and become resident in the country often form ghettos of their own nationalities, failing to _____ or show an interest in local culture and traditions. The purchase of property by foreign visitors causes property prices to _____, making it more difficult for young locals to buy homes. This _____ the division between local people and the thirty thousand Europeans who have chosen to migrate to Mallorca. While the attitude of some tourists is _____, since they seem to _____ the sensitivities of local people, they do bring employment and much needed cash to the community.

The economic impact of tourism in Mallorca has been _____, because tourism has all but put an end to farming. People have abandoned farming for easier jobs in the tourist industry. This has led to a critical loss of independence and has had a damaging effect on the culture of the island, as generic forms of entertainment replace more _____ ones, once again to meet tourist needs. The people of Mallorca find themselves in an unenviable position - where once they craved the _____ of tourists and their spending power, now they are a necessary evil for the economic stability of the island.

....

When you have completed the gapfill activity, listen to the recording again taking notes in order to answer the questions which follow:

Q35: What are the main advantages and disadvantages of tourism on the island of Mallorca?

6.6   Grammar: Phrasal verbs

A phrasal verb (also known as a multi-part or multi-word verb) is a combination of either:

1. a verb + a particle

   Example take off

2. a verb + an adverb + a preposition / particle

   Example run out of

3. a verb + a particle + a preposition

   Example break away from

Phrasal verbs have their own semantic meaning. The grouping of words forms one particular meaning, often very different from its individual parts. For this reason, phrasal verbs are difficult for non-native speakers to grasp, and therefore they are best learned according to

1. topic (e.g. transport)

2. the root verb (all phrasal verbs beginning with *put*: put up with, put on, put out, put through)

   Example The plane *ran out of* fuel and had to make an emergency landing.

Here, the phrasal verb to *run out of* expresses the idea that the fuel had all been used, and it therefore has no relation to the verb *to run*, the adverb *out*, or the preposition *of*.

Phrasal verbs have an infinitive and can be fully conjugated, as with any one word verb:

Example : Run out of

run out of: infinitive
ran out of: past simple
will have run out of: future perfect

6.6.1   Separable and inseparable phrasal verbs

There are rules governing the word order of phrasal verbs within sentences.

Phrasal verbs can either be inseparable or separable.

6.6.1.1   Inseparable phrasal verbs

In this type of phrasal verb, the individual words must remain adjacent to one another in the sentence, and can never be separated. When using inseparable phrasal verbs, it is also necessary for the object of the sentence to come after the particle:

Example The passengers *got off* the flight in Dublin.

It is NOT possible to say: The passengers *got* the flight *off* in Dublin.

6.6.1.2   Separable phrasal verbs

This type of phrasal verb can remain together, or, as the name suggests, may be separated in some instances. With many separable phrasal verbs, the object of the sentence can come before or after the particle:

Object before the particle (phrasal verb is separated):

Example *Turn* the engine *off.*

Similarly, an object pronoun can be placed before the particle:

Example *Turn* it *off.*

The object can also be placed after the particle (phrasal verb remains together):

Example *Turn off* the engine.

6.6.2   Phrasal verbs: Literal and idiomatic meanings

Phrasal verbs can either be literal in meaning, or can have a figurative or idiomatic meaning.

Phrasal verbs with **literal** meanings are typically easy to understand, as they mean exactly what one would expect them to mean:

Example The pilot took off his jacket at the start of the flight.

In this instance, to take off means to remove, as in to take an item of clothing off one's body.

Phrasal verbs with **idiomatic** meanings can be more complex, and depend on an implicit understanding of their use. They generally have to be taught / learned to acquire this understanding:

Example The plane took off from runway five.

Here, nobody removed the plane. To take off, when referring to aircraft, means for an aeroplane to become airborne.

 A common misconception is that phrasal verbs are informal, and, as such, are not found in formal texts. Many phrasal verbs are in fact neutral in register, and are perfectly acceptable in most types of written communication. If in doubt, check with a grammar reference book or your tutor.

6.6.3 Phrasal verbs practice

The two activities which follow will give you practice with these types of verb.

Phrasal verbs in context (10 min)   Go online

Read the sentences which contain phrasal verbs in context and then try to work out the meaning of the phrasal verbs.

1. Karl, you've overslept again! Get up before the hotel charges us for an extra night for not checking out in time!

2. We, at Gator Tours, recommend buying an all-day 'Snapper' ticket. Folks, it not only saves you money on your bus fare, it makes getting around the city so much easier.

3. Jenny and Colin are at the airport seeing Antonia off. The week she spent in Scotland flew by. I can't believe she's going back to Italy so soon. . .

4. As a child, David used to enjoy watching the aeroplanes touch down through his binoculars from the attic window.

5. Every item of luggage is accounted for. You can close the doors and prepare for take off.

6. Wow, taxis in this country are tiny! It'll be a bit of a squash, but I'm sure the six of us will be able to clamber in somehow!

7. You're two hours too early to check in. There's a good diner round the corner if you want to get a bite to eat while we make up the room? You can leave your bags here in the meantime.

8. If we're taking the hire car back today, I don't think it's worth our while filling the tank up all the way.

9. We'll need to set off early if we're going to hike to the campsite by sundown.

10. Driver, I'm sorry, I think I've left my passport in the hotel room. Could you double back so I can go and check?

Q36: Match the phrasal verbs in the first list with their meaning from the second list.

Phrasal verbs

1. check out
2. get around
3. set off
4. fill up
5. check in
6. see off
7. touch down
8. account for
9. clamber in
10. double back

Meanings

A) to return from the direction you came
B) to leave a place and pay the bill after staying there (typically some kind of accommodation)
C) to land (when describing a plane)
D) to depart on a trip; to begin travelling
E) to take a total; to ensure everything is in order
F) to replenish
G) to arrive in a place and confirm your stay (typically some kind of accommodation)
H) to climb or move awkwardly
I) to wish friends or family members a safe departure, usually on a holiday or a move
J) to sightsee; to travel

Phrasal verb synonyms (10 min)   Go online

Q37: Match the phrasal verbs in the first list with a synonymous one word verb or phrase from the second list.

Phrasal verbs

1. check out
2. get around
3. set off
4. fill up
5. check in
6. see off

7. touch down

8. account for

9. clamber in

10. double back

Meanings

A) travel

B) make/form a total

C) say goodbye (to someone)

D) vacate (the premises)

E) start

F) climb across or into (somewhere with difficulty)

G) replenish

H) retrace

I) land

J) arrive (at a hotel or airport desk)

 Synonymous (adj.) - from Synonym (n.): Having the same meaning.

6.7   Writing: Informal email

Revise this topic and its vocabulary before trying the following activity.

Writing: Informal email (60 min)

Your friend from overseas has just contacted you to ask you to visit him. You have known each other a long time, but you have never been to his country before, and you have a number of concerns about the political situation, the climate and the food over there. You are also quite unfamiliar with the sightseeing opportunities where he lives.

Write an email to your friend, asking advice about the following things:

- What method of transport you should use to get there
- What you need to plan before you leave: visa, immunisation, language tips
- What you should take with you: clothes, money, documents, medicine etc
- What you can do when you arrive.

Before you begin, consider the following questions:

What is the purpose of the communication?
Who is the intended audience of the article?
What level of formality and register would be appropriate?

Make some notes or a mind map to help plan your writing before you begin.

Try to write between 200 and 300 words.

Ask your teacher to check your work.

6.8   Reading comprehension: Holidays

The following activity is a reading comprehension covering the work of this topic.

Before you begin read the passage for gist.

Holiday Advice

Booking a holiday has become an activity that anyone with a computer and internet connection can do in a matter of minutes. However, with the widespread availability of package holidays being merely clicks away, there is a definite requirement to become a more discerning consumer to ensure the 'holiday from hell' scenario is not one you will be enduring on your next getaway.

What steps can you take? Well, package holidays have not always had the best of reputations, in no small part due to the fly-by-night travel agents who pushed dodgy accommodation in underdeveloped resorts on thousands of unsuspecting travellers in the 1980s and '90s. Things have changed considerably since then though, so don't allow the negative connotations you may automatically associate with the term to be the overriding factor when making your decision over which kind of holiday to go on. In fact, package holidays have never been easier to tweak or tailor than they are now. Want to fly with an alternative carrier? No problem, deselect the allotted flight and opt for an alternative. Three star self-catering not really your idea of relaxation? A click here and a click there and you can soon be in the care of luxury hoteliers instead, without adjusting your two-centre break, having to change the duration, or forego the drop-top Corvette that you wanted to hire for the drive.

Whether your preference is for a package deal or a bespoke vacation, the key to a successful holiday is in the planning. Before you start booking and augmenting your holiday with niceties, you need to diligently research your destination, ferreting out all the little secrets about the city which, in pre-internet days, only the locals knew about.

You must also consider the length of the journey there, as this can make or break your trip. If it takes more than five or six hours to arrive, you may lose the best part of a day of your stay due to fatigue or jet lag, and chances are you'll still be tired and grumpy the next day... and if you're not, your other half will be. Bear in mind that budget airlines often mislead holiday makers by flying to airports in locales which could not be considered in close proximity to the destination by any measure, leaving you several hours and more money away from where you actually wanted to be. London, Scotland anyone?

Recent studies have shown that European destinations are increasing in popularity as people crave the extra hours of sunlight offered by the northern hemisphere, but remember that *sunlight* does not always equate to *sunshine*. As for what to take, well, appropriate clothes and money go without saying. Traveller's cheques are becoming a thing of the past and can often be more of a hindrance these days, so steer clear of those and just use plastic. If you are going further afield to a less frequented country, remember to take a note of the embassy phone number, and for added peace of mind, leave a copy of your itinerary and your passport with friends or family back home.

Reading comprehension: Holidays (30 min) Go online

Read the passage once more and answer the questions which follow.

Holiday Advice

Booking a holiday has become an activity that anyone with a computer and internet connection can do in a matter of minutes. However, with the widespread availability of package holidays being merely clicks away, there is a definite requirement to become a more discerning consumer to ensure the 'holiday from hell' scenario is not one you will be enduring on your next getaway.

What steps can you take? Well, package holidays have not always had the best of reputations, in no small part due to the fly-by-night travel agents who pushed dodgy accommodation in underdeveloped resorts on thousands of unsuspecting travellers in the 1980s and '90s. Things have changed considerably since then though, so don't allow the negative connotations you may automatically associate with the term to be the overriding factor when making your decision over which kind of holiday to go on. In fact, package holidays have never been easier to tweak or tailor than they are now. Want to fly with an alternative carrier? No problem, deselect the allotted flight and opt for an alternative. Three star self-catering not really your idea of relaxation? A click here and a click there and you can soon be in the care of luxury hoteliers instead, without adjusting your two-centre break, having to change the duration, or forego the drop-top Corvette that you wanted to hire for the drive.

Whether your preference is for a package deal or a bespoke vacation, the key to a successful holiday is in the planning. Before you start booking and augmenting your holiday with niceties, you need to diligently research your destination, ferreting out all the little secrets about the city which, in pre-internet days, only the locals knew about.

You must also consider the length of the journey there, as this can make or break your trip. If it takes more than five or six hours to arrive, you may lose the best part of a day of your stay due to fatigue or jet lag, and chances are you'll still be tired and grumpy the next day... and if you're not, your other half will be. Bear in mind that budget airlines often mislead holiday makers by flying to airports in locales which could not be considered in close proximity to the destination by any measure, leaving you several hours and more money away from where you actually wanted to be. London, Scotland anyone?

Recent studies have shown that European destinations are increasing in popularity as people crave the extra hours of sunlight offered by the northern hemisphere, but remember that *sunlight* does not always equate to *sunshine*. As for what to take, well, appropriate clothes and money go without saying. Traveller's cheques are becoming a thing of the past and can often be more of a hindrance these days, so steer clear of those and just use plastic. If you are going further afield to a less frequented country, remember to take a note of the embassy phone number, and for added peace of mind, leave a copy of your itinerary and your passport with friends or family back home.

Q38: Who is the intended audience for this article?

a) First-time travellers
b) Potential holiday makers
c) Veteran travellers

....

Q39: Where would you find this article?

a) In a tabloid newspaper supplement
b) In a broadsheet newspaper supplement
c) In a specialist magazine for travellers

....

Q40: Decide, from reading the passage, if the following statements are

• true
• false

1. Package holidays still have a bad reputation with many people today.
2. Adding extra options to your trip is not the most important thing to do when booking a holiday.
3. More holiday makers are travelling to Europe for the better weather.

....

Q41: Find a word which means *feelings or associations* in the article

....

Q42: Find a word which means *very carefully* in the article

....

Q43: Find a word which means *places or areas* in the article

....

Q44: What does *it* refer to in the sentence beginning:
If it takes more than five or six hours to arrive . . .

....

Q45: What does *those* refer to in the sentence ending :
. . . so steer clear of those and just use plastic.

6.9 Listening comprehension: Holidays

Now you have completed the topic, listen to the following assessment dialogue. It contains examples of many of the language areas you have covered within the topic.

Before listening think about the following:

1. What do you like doing on holiday?
2. Which of the following types of holiday appeal to you most and why?
   a) An activity holiday
   b) A working trip
   c) An educational holiday
   d) A beach holiday
   e) A city break
   f) A retreat
3. What is the best, most interesting or most unusual holiday that you have ever had?

Listen to three speakers, Ross, Alison and Sue, answering question three. You may wish to take some notes as you listen.

Listening comprehension: Holidays (25 min)   Go online

You will need access to the sound file *hg-cesl1-6-3listening.mp3* to complete this listening comprehension.

Listen to the recording again and try to answer the following questions:

Q46: Decide whether Ross, Alison or Sue made the following statements.

1. I don't generally enjoy holidays
2. I felt a bit let down by my holiday
3. I felt emotionally revitalised
4. The holiday was not what I expected
5. The holiday helped me cope with life
6. I didn't plan the trip. It just happened
7. I find it difficult to relax

....

Answer the following questions either **true** or **false**

Q47:

1. Ross finds it difficult to get any work done.
2. Ross thinks that his interest in hill-walking prompted him to start climbing.
3. Ross believes that the appeal of climbing lies entirely in its capacity to absorb the mind.
4. Alison's art teacher at home helped her if she became hesitant.
5. Alison found the challenge of her painting holiday worthwhile.
6. Alison and the other participants supported each other during the course.
7. Sue's choice of holiday was entirely based on a need to restore her physical health.
8. Sue is generally a bit of a livewire when on holiday.
9. Sue was disappointed in the food offered on her holiday

6.10 Vocabulary list

This is a list of useful vocabulary which is intended to supplement what you have learned. It may also be useful to refer to when attempting the speaking and writing activities within the topic.

agritourism (noun)	a type of tourism which involves the act of visiting or touring farms, ranches and other natural areas to support local people and produce
all-inclusive (adjective)	a holiday where everything is included in the price paid up-front
amenities (noun)	the facilities and equipment in a hotel or a town
to collide (verb)	to crash into something
to commute (verb)	to travel to and from work
congestion (noun)	a problem with traffic circulation; a traffic jam
diversion (noun)	an alternative route, necessary because the main route is not available
domestic (adjective)	an internal flight within country borders
to embark / disembark (verb)	to get on / off a vehicle, e.g. an aeroplane, boat, train
to emit (verb)	to give out or discharge, e.g. fumes
excursion (noun)	a short journey taken for pleasure; an outing; a trip
gangway (noun)	an opening in a ship where passengers board
to hitch-hike (verb)	to travel for free by taking a lift from the driver of a vehicle
peak-time (noun)	periods of the year or day when travel is busier and more expensive, e.g. summer holidays
to pedestrianise (verb)	to convert a road into a pedestrian (person) only area for walking / shopping etc
quay (noun)	a platform next to water where ships can dock and passengers embark / disembark
season ticket (noun)	a ticket valid for a period of travel, e.g. a month, which is typically cheaper than purchasing several individual tickets
stopover (noun)	a break in a journey or a flight, e.g. The flight from London to Sydney had a four-hour stopover in Dubai
to stow (verb)	to place or store an item in a neat and careful way
turnstile (noun)	a mechanical gate which is used to control the flow of people by allowing only one to pass at a time e.g. between different areas in a train station

Unit 1 Topic 7

Current affairs

Contents

Learning objective

By the end of this topic you should be able to:

- use a wider range of vocabulary in the topic area
- use compound adjectives with greater accuracy
- use cleft and pseudo-cleft sentences with greater accuracy
- demonstrate your knowledge of writing genre through writing a film review
- demonstrate greater awareness of sentence stress

This topic explores the area of entertainment, including Art, Music, Literature, Theatre, Cinema, Dance, and Sport.

It revises the use of cleft sentences, pseudo-cleft sentences and compound adjectives and introduces advanced vocabulary relevant to the subjects discussed. It includes work on all four skills: speaking, reading, writing, and listening. There are also supplementary pronunciation exercises. Assessment opportunities occur at the end of the topic.

Certain sections contain sound files. You may download these here and use them on your mp3 player or equivalent to practise your pronunciation. This may be very useful if there are times when you will not have access to the materials online.

7.1   Entertainment and leisure

Vocabulary Review: Entertainment and leisure   Go online

You will now have an opportunity to revise some vocabulary associated with entertainment and leisure activities.

Q1:   Decide on the category for each item listed. (Note: some may apply to more than one category).

Categories: theatre: music: art: dance: film: literature: sport

Items:

spectator: flamenco: poetry: feature: racquet: installation: winter: blues: still life: classical: animation: play: ballet: water: expressionist: autobiography: watercolour: crime: hip-hop: choral: romantic: musical: ballroom: comedy: jazz: team: rap: tango: drama: sculpture: war: non-fiction:

Speaking: Talking about entertainment (15 min)

Choose six of the words from the activity above and write a question based on each word, for example:

Novel — What was the last novel you read?

Installation — Do you like to visit art galleries or museums and look at art installations?

Work with a partner or your tutor. Ask and answer each other's questions.

Entertainment Vocabulary in context Go online

Q2: Complete each of the sentences below by selecting the correct word from the choices offered:

1. The play was marvellous, at the end the actors got a standing **applause/ovation**
2. The lighting really added to the atmosphere in the theatre, the stage was lit only by **footlights/headlights**
3. I didn't really enjoy the film but it got really good**reviews/critics**
4. We understood the film perfectly because there were **subtitles/supratitles** in our language
5. We were late for the concert and had to run down the **aisle/corridor** in the dark to find our seats
6. My favourite type of films are **romantic/romance** comedies
7. I love the Christmas carol concert. The **composer/conductor** gets the orchestra to wear Christmas hats
8. We have just been to the Museum of Modern Art to see an **instalment/installation**
9. The dancers were amazing! Their **acting/performances** were first class
10. My mother is an actress and she used to let me watch the performance **backstage/ front of house**

7.2 Grammar: Cleft sentences

In general new and/or important information is placed at the end of a clause.

Example Keira Knightley starred in Pirates of the Caribbean.

However, in cleft sentences we change the usual order of information and place the new or important information after *it* and a form of the verb *to be* .

Example It was Keira Knightley who starred in Pirates of the Caribbean.

In this example the subject of the sentence is highlighted and thereby the information that it was Keira Knightley, as opposed to any other actress, who starred in the film.

Various other elements of a sentence can be highlighted in the same way.

Example It was in 2003 that Keira Knightley starred in Pirates of the Caribbean.

In this example the adverbial clause *in 2003* is highlighted.

Pseudo-clefting refers to the process in which a word (generally a question word) is used at the start of a clause and again the new and/or important information is placed after a form of the verb to be

---

Example   What I enjoyed about Pirates of the Caribbean was the performance of Keira Knightley

   It is usually possible to reverse the order of a pseudo-cleft sentence

Example   What I found really amusing was the character played by Johnny Depp.

The character played by Johnny Depp was what I found really amusing.

Cleft and pseudo-cleft sentences (20 min)

Rewrite the following sentences using the word given so that the meaning remains the same.

Q3:   In the end we decided to go the cinema rather than stay at home. What...

....

Q4:   The reviews must have put people off going to see the play. It ...

....

Q5:   We tended to go to the theatre more often when we lived in London. It ...

....

Q6:   I have never understood why people rave about opera. What ...

....

Q7:   I wish people would refrain from consuming chips and crisps in the cinema. What ...

....

Q8:   Finding out about far-flung and exotic locations is what attracts me to travel writing. What ...

....

Q9:   I didn't start painting until I was in my thirties! It ...

....

Q10:   One of my favourite forms of entertainment is the joy of reading a good book. It...

Word emphasis (20 min)

Use a form of the verb *to be* and *it* to rewrite the following sentences so that emphasis is given to the words in italics.

Q11: *John likes eating in restaurants*, but Sally doesn't.

....

Q12: Films didn't become really popular *until they were produced with sound.*

....

Q13: She wanted to focus on *ballet*, not tap.

....

Q14: I don't think it's practice that makes one a perfect musician, *it's talent*!

....

Q15: She is aspiring to *celebrity status*, not self-fulfilment.

....

Q16: He has written several novels about crime but he is more famous for *the novel he wrote last year.*

7.3   Reading: Film recommendations

Reading: Film recommendations (40 min)

Before Reading consider the following questions

1. What kind of films do you like to watch?
2. Do you have a favourite film?
3. What sources of information would you refer to for film recommendations?

Now read the text and answer the questions which follow.

For a highly entertaining movie with intoxicating plot, witty dialogue and compelling performances, Erin Brockovich, directed by Steven Soderbergh and starring Julia Roberts, is certainly worth a watch. What makes it even more compelling is the fact that it is based on a true story.

Julia Roberts plays the eponymous heroine, a bright but brash, unemployed, single mother of three. By practically stalking a lawyer she hired to defend her after a car accident, Erin manages to get an administrative job in a legal firm. What starts off as a lowly office job metamorphosises into a high stakes legal battle, with Erin in the driving seat, as the firm takes on a multimillion dollar energy corporation (PG&E) accused of poisoning the water, and therefore the residents, of the small Californian town of Hinkley.

It is Ed Masry, played by Albert Finney, who is the legal 'expert', but it is Erin who wins the confidence of the people of Hinkley, browbeating the opposition with her razor-sharp wit and ultimately emerging triumphant.

In terms of her employment prospects, we end the film convinced that Erin will succeed. However, it is the future of her relationship with her new boyfriend about which we are left uncertain. Aaron Eckhart stars as George, Erin's neighbour turned friend, babysitter and eventually, boyfriend. What happens between them is a kind of reversal of traditional gender roles. Erin becomes increasingly more immersed in the case against PG&E and starts confronting highly qualified lawyers with great success, and as a result her confidence increases. This leads her to devote further time away from home in pursuit of evidence for the case. Unfortunately, this impacts very negatively on her relationship with George. It is a sense of feeling neglected and taken for granted, more often attributed to female roles, which prompts George to ask her to give up her job.

It is perhaps in the role of Brockovich that we see Roberts fully engaged with a character for the first time. The witty one liners strike a fine balance between aggression and humour. As the jaded Masry, Finney's understated performance is perfect. In Erin Brockovich, Soderbergh steers carefully, avoiding cliché and over-sentimentality with resounding success.

Q17: What kind of text is this?

a) A research report
b) A film review
c) A newspaper story

....

Q18: Where would you be likely to find this kind of text?

a) A journal
b) A news website
c) A magazine or online entertainment site

....

Q19: Find seven examples of cleft or pseudo-cleft sentences in the text.

....

Q20: In the sentence beginning *What happens between them* . . . to which people does the word *them* refer?

Find words with the following definitions in the text

Q21: Making one feel drunk / lightheaded

....

Q22: Strong (argument for something)

....

Q23: When the name of the hero / heroine is the same as the book / film etc

....

Q24: Describes a person showing a lot of confidence but a lack of respect

....

Q25: In a position of no respect

....

Q26: Completely changes

....

Q27: Extremely sharp

....

Q28: To have an effect

....

Q29: When a person is able to use words in a clever and humorous way

....

Q30: Without trying to attract attention

7.4   Writing: Film review

Writing: Film review (60 min)

You have been asked to write a film review for your school/college magazine. You should discuss some of the following aspects of the film:

- plot
- characters / performances / costumes
- soundtrack
- scenery / location
- costumes
- location
- your opinion —whether or not you would recommend the film

Write between 300 - 350 words

Before you begin, consider the following questions:

- What is the purpose of the communication?
- Who is the intended audience ?
- What level of formality and register would be appropriate?

Look back at the example film review from the previous exercise to help generate ideas. Ask your teacher or tutor to check your work when you finish.

7.5   Listening: Music and emotions

Speaking: Music and emotions (10 min)

Discuss the following questions with a partner or your tutor.

- How do you feel when you listen to music?
- Do you listen to different kinds of music at different times in your life or different times in the day / week?
- Do different types of music make you feel different emotions?

- Can you give examples of how these kinds of music make you feel: classical music, heavy metal, folk music, pop music? e.g. relaxed, sleepy, happy etc.

Listening: Music and emotions (30 min)   Go online

You will need access to the following sound file *hg-cesl1-7-1listening.mp3* to try this activity.

Listen to the speakers discussing their feelings when listening to various types of music and then answer the questions which follow.

Q31: Who is obsessive about the music they describe?

....

Q32: Who says that the music they enjoy mirrors different emotions that they have?

....

Q33: Who suggests that the music brings about reflection?

....

Q34: Who expresses extreme admiration and wonder for a type of music?

....

Q35: Who finds that their favourite music perks them up?

....

Q36: Who feels a sense of gloom or sadness when listening to their chosen music?

....

Q37: Who has empathy with the music?

....

Q38: Who has found that music caused them a problem?

The following words are all synonyms of words you heard in the recording. Listen again to the recording and type in the words you hear which have the same meanings as those below. You may need to use a dictionary to help you with the spelling of some words. If you are stuck, you may read the listening transcript here to help you. (Start with capital letter in text box)

Q39: Reduced

....

Q40: Connection

....

Q41: Angry

....

Q42: Mixture

....

Q43: Suggest

....

Q44: Sluggish

....

Q45: Reverie

....

Q46: Replicate

7.6   Grammar: Prepositions

Grammar: Prepositions   Go online

Read the following text about one of Britain's most famous authors and type in the missing prepositions:

Q47: In the following text there is a preposition missing in some of the lines. Decide where a word is missing and type the word in the space.

The novelist Jane Austen is known worldwide ____ her popular novels describing the society of pre-industrial England. She was born ____ Hampshire, England in 1775 and was one of eight children. Apart ____ three years at a school in Oxford, Jane received most ____ her education at home. She began writing seriously ____ the late eighteenth century and is credited ____ giving the novel its modern character through her treatment of everyday life. She focussed particularly ____ the rituals of courtship which she observed in her own family and ____ the professional and upper classes. Since writing was not considered an appropriate preoccupation _____ a woman Jane disguised her identity at the start ____ her literary career. Although the preoccupation of most of her heroines is courtship and marriage, she herself never married. She is thought ____ have had ____ least one proposal which she rejected because she would not marry someone she did not love. She spent the last eight years ____ her life ____ Chawton in a 17th century house which is now owned by the National Trust and preserved in her memory. She wrote some ____ her best and most popular works ____ this house.

7.7 Listening comprehension: Leisure

Now you have completed the topic, listen to the following assessment dialogue. It contains examples of many of the language areas you have covered within the topic.

You will need access to the sound file*hg-cesl1-7-2listening.mp3* to complete this listening comprehension.

Listen to the passage before you try the activity.

The listening comprehension is available online at this stage. If you do not have access to the internet but are able to listen to the sound file 2-listening-hg-esl3-3et1.mp3 then you may try the questions which follow.

Listen to the recording again and try to answer the following questions:

Q48: The broadcast is primarily concerned with

a) Describing outdoor activities
b) Promoting holidays in Scotland
c) Describing a mountain biking centre

....

Q49: Complete the following sentences with no more than four words

1. The men interviewed by Miranda at Glentress said that mountain biking was _____ to work.
2. Another interviewee said that he enjoyed _____.

....

Q50: What has made Glentress better than other destinations for mountain biking?

a) Investment and varied landscape at Glentress.
b) Popularity and better equipment at Glentress.
c) Higher mountains and good instructors at Glentress.

....

Q51: Which features of the black trail make it the most challenging?

a) It is hard to find and it is dangerous.
b) It is long and it is a gruelling, difficult climb.
c) It is short but very high in the mountains.

Decide whether the following statements are **true**, **false**.

Q52: The interviewer is dubious about the need to travel to places like Glentress to do mountain biking.

a) True
b) False

....

Q53: Some of the cyclists get involved in contests about their cycling equipment.

a) True
b) False

....

Q54: Miranda took the conversation in the hub seriously.

a) True
b) False

....

Q55: Miranda recommended forward planning because trails are often booked up in advance.

a) True
b) False

7.8   Reading Comprehension: Jane Austen Critique

The following activity is a reading comprehension covering the work of this topic.

Before you begin read the passage. Read the passage quickly to grasp the gist of it.

"Human nature is so well disposed towards those who are in interesting situations, that a young person, who either marries or dies, is sure of being kindly spoken of" (p194) It is significant that Austen should open a chapter of Emma with this comment since analysis of human nature would appear to be the major concern of the novel. The focus is upon human character and motivation within a small, enclosed society. In the context of the novel occasions such as birth, marriage and death are of paramount importance and all social interaction is vital. Thus the prospective marriage of Mr Elton at this point in the novel is of particular consequence to Emma. In an attempt to 'match' Mr Elton and Harriet, Emma unwittingly encouraged a proposal to herself. The latter's temporary departure from Highbury alleviated the embarrassment of this situation. In Mr Elton's return however, Emma senses "a source of profitable humiliation to her own mind" (p195) The marriage of Mr Elton is a key issue in the novel in the sense that it is a yardstick by which we are able to measure the development of Emma's character within a moral framework.

The focus in Emma is upon a small, enclosed society. The world outside Highbury is a means by which we can gain perspective and gain some understanding of the values prevalent in the town. Mr Elton's departure symbolises this idea. Mr Elton had gone away "rejected and mortified" (p194) but the influence of the outside world gives him a new outlook and he returns "gay and self-satisfied" (p194) Austen's use of language at this point emphasises the indignation in Mr Elton's departure which is in stark contrast to the triumph of his return. The phrase 'he had gone' is supported with adjectives indicating low mood 'rejected, mortified, disappointed'. In contrast to this is the effect of the sentence beginning 'he came back' full of adjectives suggesting vigour such as gay, eager, busy.

The soon to be Mrs Elton, as a product of the world outside Highbury, is used in this chapter as a means by which we gain understanding of Emma. It is clear that Emma does not feel in any way inferior to the prospective Mrs Elton. Although the latter might be materially comfortable, Emma feels that there is more involved in determining social class than money. 'As to connection, there Emma was perfectly easy' (p195) Emma's view of Mr Elton's fiancée is held in focus by the narrator's comments. Mr Elton has become engaged "to another as superior, of course, to the first as under such circumstances what is gained always is to what is lost" (p.194) This technique is used by Jane Austen throughout the novel and the narrator's criticisms of the marriage are both explicit and implicit. Description of the courtship makes it obvious that the marriage is one of speed and convenience. It is pointed out that Miss Hawkins money is a 'point of some dignity as well as some convenience' (p194) The courtship is described in one paragraph, indeed in one sentence, with the use of short clauses and dashes. As a result the idea of speed is given a more subtle emphasis.

In consequence of the enclosed quality of Highbury a great deal of importance is placed upon social interaction at all levels. There is an intricate structure of protocol to which all members of the society must adhere. A town voice has developed against which all behaviour must be gauged. This becomes very clear in references to 'a certain glance of Mrs Coles' and ' by some means or other discovered' (p194)

Elegance of language is a major stylistic feature throughout the novel and reflects the formality of the society with which the author is concerned. Austen has confined her interest to a small society and has developed specific techniques of contrast and narration in order to illuminate it.

Reading Comprehension: Jane Austen Critique (30 min)   Go online

The reading comprehension is available online at this stage. If you do not have access to the internet you may try the questions which follow.

Read the passage once more and answer the questions which follow.

"Human nature is so well disposed towards those who are in interesting situations, that a young person, who either marries or dies, is sure of being kindly spoken of" (p194) It is significant that Austen should open a chapter of Emma with this comment since analysis of human nature would appear to be the major concern of the novel. The focus is upon human character and motivation within a small, enclosed society. In the context of the novel occasions such as birth, marriage and death are of paramount importance and all social interaction is vital. Thus the prospective marriage of Mr Elton at this point in the novel is of particular consequence to Emma. In an attempt to 'match' Mr Elton and Harriet, Emma unwittingly encouraged a proposal to herself. The latter's temporary departure from Highbury alleviated the embarrassment of this situation. In Mr Elton's return however, Emma senses "a source of profitable humiliation to her own mind" (p195) The marriage of Mr Elton is a key issue in the novel in the sense that it is a yardstick by which we are able to measure the development of Emma's character within a moral framework.

The focus in Emma is upon a small, enclosed society. The world outside Highbury is a means by which we can gain perspective and gain some understanding of the values prevalent in the town. Mr Elton's departure symbolises this idea. Mr Elton had gone away "rejected and mortified" (p194) but the influence of the outside world gives him a new outlook and he returns "gay and self-satisfied" (p194) Austen's use of language at this point emphasises the indignation in Mr Elton's departure which is in stark contrast to the triumph of his return. The phrase 'he had gone' is supported with adjectives indicating low mood 'rejected, mortified, disappointed'. In contrast to this is the effect of the sentence beginning 'he came back' full of adjectives suggesting vigour such as gay, eager, busy.

The soon to be Mrs Elton, as a product of the world outside Highbury, is used in this chapter as a means by which we gain understanding of Emma. It is clear that Emma does not feel in any way inferior to the prospective Mrs Elton. Although the latter might be materially comfortable, Emma feels that there is more involved in determining social class than money. 'As to connection, there Emma was perfectly easy' (p195) Emma's view of Mr Elton's fiancée is held in focus by the narrator's comments. Mr Elton has become engaged "to another as superior, of course, to the first as under such circumstances what is gained always is to what is lost" (p.194) This technique is used by Jane Austen throughout the novel and the narrator's criticisms of the marriage are both explicit and implicit. Description of the courtship makes it obvious that the marriage is one of speed and convenience. It is pointed out that Miss Hawkins money is a 'point of some dignity as well as some convenience' (p194) The courtship is described in one paragraph, indeed in one sentence, with the use of short clauses and dashes. As a result the idea of speed is given a more subtle emphasis.

In consequence of the enclosed quality of Highbury a great deal of importance is placed upon social interaction at all levels. There is an intricate structure of protocol to which all members of the society must adhere. A town voice has developed against which all behaviour must be gauged. This becomes very clear in references to 'a certain glance of Mrs Coles' and ' by some means or other discovered' (p194)

Elegance of language is a major stylistic feature throughout the novel and reflects the formality of the society with which the author is concerned. Austen has confined her interest to a small society and has developed specific techniques of contrast and narration in order to illuminate it.

Q56: What kind of writing is this?

a) A book review
b) A critical essay of a novel
c) An article
d) A report

....

Q57: The opening quote is a comment on

a) Birth, marriage and death
b) Gossip
c) Interesting situations
d) Human nature

Decide, from reading the passage, if the following statements are **true** or **false**.

Q58: Emma is embarrassed by Mr Elton's return to Highbury because he had rejected her.

a) True
b) False

....

Q59: The writer suggests that Mr Elton's contact with a wider world than Highbury rejuvenated him.

a) True
b) False

....

Q60: The narrator's view of the forthcoming marriage conflicts with that of Emma.

a) True
b) False

....

Q61: The writer suggests that Miss Haughton is superior to Emma only in the sense that she has agreed to marry Mr Elton.

a) True
b) False

....

Q62: In what way does the language of the novel support the notion of a speedy courtship? (two answers)?

....

Q63: On what basis is behaviour judged within the town?

....

Q64: What methods does the author employ in order to reflect the correctness of the society she describes?

....

Q65: What methods does Austen employ to demonstrate small town issues?

7.9   Vocabulary list

This is a list of useful vocabulary which is intended to supplement what you have learned. It may also be useful to refer to when attempting the speaking and writing activities within the topic.

browbeat (verb)	badger
hardship (noun)	privation
installation (noun)	modern sculpture where artist uses space, sound, movement for example to make an often temporary exhibit
jaded (adjective)	lacking interest in things in general or particular
ovation (noun)	appreciation shown through prolonged applause
preoccupied (adjective)	worried / absorbed in something
prompt (verb)	encourage
rave (verb)	enthuse
refrain (verb)	stop doing something
therapeutic (adjective)	causing someone to feel happier and more relaxed

Unit 1 Topic 8

Cultural awareness

Contents

Learning objective

By the end of this topic you should be able to:

- use your extended knowledge and understanding of narrative tenses in the context of cultural awareness;

- demonstrate your knowledge and understanding of discourse markers;

- use an extended range of vocabulary in the topic area through practice in word transformation;

- use an extended range of vocabulary in the topic area more accurately through practice in reading, listening and writing;

- demonstrate your awareness of features of register: field, tenor and mode;

- apply your increased knowledge of writing genre through writing an article;

- demonstrate your enhanced pronunciation skills through greater awareness of intonation.

This topic explores the differences in culture and behaviour between different countries, by listening to people talking about their experiences of living in a new country. There will be opportunities to extend vocabulary in the topic area and to focus on the use of narrative tenses.

It includes work on all four skills: reading, writing, speaking and listening. There are also supplementary pronunciation exercises. Assessment opportunities occur at the end of the topic.

Certain sections contain sound files. You may download these and use them on your mp3 player or equivalent to practise your pronunciation. This may be very useful if there are times when you will not have access to the materials online.

8.1 Listening: Cultural differences

You are going to listen to Christina, Paul and Gosia talking about their experiences of living abroad. Before you listen, think about a country that you have visited and think about the ways it differs from your home country.

You can write down some notes to help you later.

Christina, Paul and Gosia (15 min) Go online

Christina, Paul and Gosia were all asked the same five questions.

Reorder the sentences below to make the questions that were asked, using a capital letter to begin the question.

Q1: country did you live a in decide why to different?

. . . .

Q2: difficulty did new your environment any to adapting have you?

. . . .

Q3: you between your and differences find did country home your what new?

. . . .

Q4: you homesickness suffer did from?

. . . .

Q5: advantages living and of a were what disadvantages the different in country?

What they said (25 min)   Go online

You will need access to the following sound files to complete this activity:

hg-cesl1-8-1listening1.mp3
hg-cesl1-8-1listening2.mp3
hg-cesl1-8-1listening3.mp3

Listen to Christina and answer the questions which follow.

Christina

Q6: Which country is Christina from?

a) Italy
b) The UK
c) Ireland

....

Q7: Which country did Christina travel to?

a) Italy
b) The UK
c) Ireland

....

Q8: Christina knew the language before she went to her new country.

a) true
b) false

....

Q9: In her home country, teachers might socialise by going to bars after evening classes.

a) true
b) false

....

Q10: Christina did not use email when she lived abroad because she didn't understand computers.

a) true
b) false

....

Q11: Christina thinks the dramatic and emotional nature of the local people was not an entirely positive feature.

a) true
b) false

© HERIOT-WATT UNIVERSITY

Paul

Listen to Paul and answer the questions which follow.

Q12: Which country is Paul from?

a) Japan
b) Australia
c) The UK

....

Q13: Which country did Paul travel to?

a) Japan
b) Australia
c) The UK

....

Q14: Paul did not have any difficulty with the new language.

a) true
b) false

....

Q15: Paul had some difficulties in finding food to suit his taste.

a) true
b) false

....

Q16: Paul earned a good living in Japan.

a) true
b) false

....

Q17: Paul says that in his host country people rarely made decisions independently.

a) true
b) false

Gosia

Listen to Gosia and then answer the questions which follow.

Q18: Which country is Gosia from?

a) The UK
b) Holland
c) Poland

....

Q19: Which country did Gosia travel to?

a) The UK
b) Holland
c) Poland

....

Q20: Gosia decided to leave her home country because of a perceived lack of opportunity.

a) true
b) false

....

Q21: Gosia found life in her new country easy from the start.

a) true
b) false

....

Q22: Gosia thinks that Scotland is a more diverse country, in terms of nationalities, than Poland.

a) true
b) false

....

Q23: Gosia feels that there are only advantages for her in living in the UK.

a) true
b) false

Adjectives: Synonyms (15 min)   Go online

The words below all come from the recording you just listened to. Match the adjectives in the first list to their synonyms from the second list.

Q24:

1. gregarious
2. expressive
3. chaotic
4. displaced
5. clichéd
6. radical
7. prospects
8. cope
9. empathy
10. stressed

A) outlook
B) communicative
C) exiled
D) understanding
E) outgoing
F) unoriginal
G) drastic
H) manage
I) disorganised
J) anxious

8.2   Grammar: Narrative tenses

Past perfect simple tense is used to focus on the fact that an event took place and finished before another event in the past.

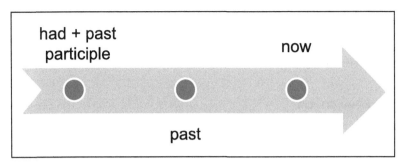

Past perfect continuous tense is used when describing an event which was repeated or took place over a period of time or an activity which took place before a particular time in the past.

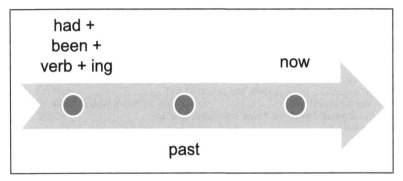

Past simple tense is used to describe an action, event or state completed in the past.

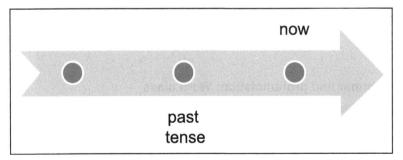

Check your understanding by examining the following sentences. Which tense is being used in each sentence?

Q25: When I took on a full-time job, I had learned a bit of the language

. . . .

Q26: I went to stay with friends

. . . .

Q27: I had been working in Scotland

Narrative tenses (20 min)   Go online ❄

Complete the sentences in the correct tense and aspect using the words and phrases in the given list.

List: had not been prepared: had been encouraged: had not visited: travelled: was: had been practising: had packed: felt: had done: had convinced: decided: had ever seen: slept: did not find: had never been: covered: had: proved: arrived: had also crammed:

Q28: When I _____ in Chile for a visit a few years ago, I _____ really excited and also a bit nervous. I _____ South America before but _____ some research on the country and I _____ Spanish for a few months prior to leaving the UK. I _____ lots of summer clothes but _____ in some waterproof layers and some thermals, for visiting the south of the country. I _____ quite well prepared and _____ myself that there would be few surprises! We _____ to visit one of Chile's beautiful national parks close to the famous Torres del Paine mountains and we _____ to follow this recommendation. We _____ for three hours through the most magnificent scenery I _____ to reach our accommodation, a hostel in a log cabin. Unfortunately, as a vegetarian, I _____ much to eat at dinner time. We _____ in bunks in small rooms with other hikers. I _____ so cold in my life and went to bed wearing all of my clothes, including my hat and gloves! The distances we _____ were immense and I simply _____ for the incredible cold. However, despite this, we _____ had a fantastic trip, the scenery _____ spectacular and the people very friendly.

8.3   Grammar and pronunciation: Word class

Word class refers to a group of words such as nouns, verbs or adjectives that behave in the same way grammatically

Sometimes another class of a word can be created by using the stem (basic form), and changing the ending.

Example : to recommend (verb)

to recommend (verb) + ation = Recommendation (noun)

to recommend (verb) + ed = Recommended (adjective)

Word class Go online

Q29: Complete the table by adding the appropriate word class.

Noun	Verb	Adjective
		sociable
	offend	
	express	
perception		
		adaptable
	identify	
culture	**no verb**	

Syllable stress (15 min) Go online

Look at the words in the table and find the stressed syllable. Listen to the recording of each word and practise saying these words.

Noun	Verb	Adjective
relaxation	to relax	relaxing
decision	to decide	decisive
frustration	to frustrate	frustrating
acceptance	to accept	acceptable
surprise	to surprise	surprising
influence	to influence	influential
accommodation	to accommodate	accommodating

8.4 Reading: Polite behaviour

This section will explore polite behaviour in the UK and consider what that means today. This will be achieved through a reading activity. An analysis of writing genre and a focus on features of writing style is also included.

Pre-reading activity: Polite behaviour (10 min)

Before you read, discuss the following questions with your partner or tutor and make some notes about your answers:

1. What kinds of polite behaviour did you learn when you were growing up?

2. What kinds of behaviour do you consider very rude?

3. Are there rules of polite behaviour between men and women in your country?

4. Are there rules of polite behaviour which are unique to your country?

Polite behaviour (25 min)

The text below is divided into five paragraphs. The headings are in a random order. Read the headings and the text. Choose the most suitable heading for each paragraph. Note that one heading is not required.

1. Don't stand too close

2. Don't call me I'll call you

3. Equal rights to good manners

4. Technology is not polite

5. Excuse me, I can't hear myself think!

6. No surprises please

A) Changes over the last ten to twenty years, including the exponential rise in technologies have been dramatic and exciting yet I think it's fair to say that in the UK, many of us feel a little disgruntled by the consequences of their use. I wouldn't describe myself as technophobic; in fact I'm quite addicted to my mobile phone and use a laptop every day. However, I am fully aware of many drawbacks associated with communications technologies. They have totally transformed the ways we connect with other people but in my view we haven't spent enough time deciding how to make all this new technology polite. It has all happened too fast - and, as a result, it often offends.

B) Much of what we experience, but react so furiously against, is nothing more than bad manners. The outrage felt by many toward current behaviour is summed up by the letters of protest in newspapers from commuters. Travellers are incensed by mobile phones and other devices on trains, with someone next to them in the carriage yelling "I'm on the train!" or pumping music through headphones which don't quite contain the sounds. In many ways, we Brits are old-fashioned. We still like the order of queues, we really don't expect anyone to skip them, and we don't like anyone trying to cut into the front of a lane of waiting traffic from an empty filter lane going another route. If you do break these taboos however, we're far more likely to give you a cold stare than actually shout at you.

C) Perhaps what it is that people like me are disenchanted with is essentially an issue of space, or, to be more precise, a lack of it. Maybe the rules of polite behaviour are based upon a primitive need to protect and control our territory. Whatever the roots of manners might be, and clearly they lack universality; generally, in the UK we don't like uninvited guests. Dropping in unannounced is not considered de rigueur, in fact it can often be awkward for the host. Arriving without forewarning is likely to force your intended host to hide behind curtains or assume other undignified positions of refuge until you have safely departed. On the other hand, perversely, if you have been invited to dinner at seven o'clock then that's pretty much when we expect to see you.

D) We extend this distaste for the uninvited to cold calling and leaflet distribution. We particularly detest unsolicited telephone calls. Traditionally we had rules around acceptable times to make a call. In the UK, the family evening meal took place around 6-7pm. Nowadays this is apparently the perfect time to call up and ask if it would be okay to have a quick chat about your bank balance. Chirpy telesales staff routinely invade our homes nowadays, with an overly familiar approach where they immediately adopt our first names. First names are for friends, family and maybe colleagues! Perhaps the family and regular meal times are outmoded concepts, but surely it's never polite to call someone up out of the blue to enquire about their need for a bank loan? Talking about money and disclosing personal information to a stranger is very questionable.

E) In the field of sexual politics, technology has simply muddied the waters. Much of what is perceived of as 'cool' is simply bad manners in disguise. With film stars ending their relationships via text, announcing breakups and revealing personal information about ex-partners on social media sites it looks as though standards of polite behaviour may have disappeared forever. The speed of new technology brings many welcome changes but this speed can be dangerous in personal relationships. A hastily fired text often fails to get the desired response. In texting, as in most of our new technologies, it really only takes a little bit of consideration to improve things!

Check the expected answer for the correct order before answering the next three questions.

Q30: This piece of writing is most likely to be found in

a) a newspaper or magazine
b) a textbook
c) a tourist information guide
d) a guide to manners in the UK

. . . .

Q31: Which adjective best reflects the writer's intended tone?

a) angry
b) friendly
c) humorous
d) irritated

Find one word in each paragraph that indicates the following views:

Q32: (Paragraph one) The writer is not content with the changes brought about by technology.

. . . .

Q33: (Paragraph two) The writer thinks mobile phones really annoy people on trains.

. . . .

Q34: (Paragraph three) The idea that things are the same all over the world.

. . . .

Q35: (Paragraph four) The idea of something being obsolete or no longer relevant.

8.5   Grammar: Discourse markers

We use discourse markers (sometimes called linkers or conjuncts) as signposts in our writing and speaking, to show how pieces of information relate to each other. We also use discourse markers to indicate our opinion of what we are saying or writing and to prepare the audience.

Example It had been raining heavily all day. However, we still went out for a long walk.

However indicates to the reader that the information to follow may surprise, i.e. we do not expect people to take a long walk in the rain.

Discourse markers   Go online

Q36: Put the given discourse markers from the text into the correct category.

Discourse markers: nevertheless, and, as a result, however, on the other hand, similarly, but, what is more, consequently.

Categories

1. Additive: giving more information
2. Contrastive: introducing a point of contrast
3. Concessive: concedes an unexpected point
4. Resultative: introducing an outcome

8.6   Writing: Field, tenor and mode

When we speak or write, we have to ensure that the language we use is appropriate. Appropriate language takes into consideration the context; this includes the cultural context, and the expectations of the people we are communicating with. We need to think about the following:

a) What is the purpose of the communication?

b) Who is communicating with whom and what is the relationship between them?

c) What type of language is being used i.e. spoken or written?

Analysing writing (15 min)

Look at the language in the following paragraph and answer the questions.

Mick
Won't be home till eight - will grab a bite at the gym with Carol - remember to pay the window cleaner -Txt you later?
Sarah xx

Q37: What is the purpose of the communication?

....

Q38: Who is communicating with whom and what is the relationship between them?

....

Q39: What type of language is being used i.e. spoken or written?

Understanding style (15 min) Go online

Q40: Think about the ways that the three elements identified in the last activity affect the language.

Select features from the list which indicate an appropriate style for a written note or text message between a couple talking about plans for the evening.

- informal language
- formal language
- colloquial expressions (e.g .to *chat* = to *speak*)
- abbreviations
- formal linkers (e.g. *nevertheless* is a formal linker)
- informal linkers (e.g. *but* is an informal linker)
- headings
- subheadings
- titles
- introduction
- conclusion
- formal vocabulary
- long complex sentences
- contractions.

8.7   Writing

You have been asked to write an article for your school / college magazine about a trip you took to a city in another country.

Q41: Before you begin consider the following questions:

1. What is the purpose of the communication?
2. Who is communicating with whom and what is the relationship between them?
3. What type of language is being used i.e. spoken or written?

....

Q42: Select from the list of language features to ensure that the language you use is appropriate.

Language features:

- informal language
- formal language
- neutral
- colloquial expressions (e.g. to *chat* = to *speak*)
- abbreviations
- formal linkers (e.g. *nevertheless* is a formal linker)
- informal linkers (e.g. *but* is an informal linker)
- headings
- subheadings
- titles
- introduction
- conclusion
- formal vocabulary
- long complex sentences
- contractions.

Features of writing: A visit to a foreign city

Look at the question below and then read a model answer in order to focus on features of writing.

You have been asked to write an article for your school / college magazine about a trip you took to a city in another country. Describe the trip, say what you enjoyed / did not enjoy.

Discuss some of the cultural aspects of the country you visited.

Write around 200 words.

Q43: Now read the model answer again, this time with paragraph numbers, and try to match the paragraph numbers to the paragraph titles below:

Model answer

1. When my friend emailed an invitation to Perugia, she told me to give it some thought, sixty seconds later, I emailed her back to accept. I couldn't resist!

2. Anna had said the architecture in Perugia was amazing, and that it was full of incredibly famous paintings. Perfect for art lovers! For foodies, it's full of wonderful Italian delicacies. What's not to like?

3. I flew to Florence in July, and caught a train to Perugia. The trains seemed old-fashioned, the people lively and exuberant. Due to the sizzling heat, passengers were leaning out of open windows chatting to others. I found the singsong of the Italian accents and the strong smell of ground coffee in the air intoxicating.

4. Perugia is the capital of Umbria and a centre of medieval art. It's full of amazing structures, like the San Lorenzo Cathedral in the city centre and a Roman aqueduct which connects two of the city's hills.

5. In the surrounding area, Assissi is worth a visit. The countryside is a pleasant contrast to the hustle and bustle of the city.

6. Umbria hosts a jazz festival every year in July. The city was buzzing with visitors and we were spoiled for choice in terms of musical entertainment.

7. I can't recommend Perugia enough for a visit. For me, the scenery, architecture, food and entertainment all deserve ten out of ten!

A) The hostess

B) The surrounding area

C) Conclusion

D) Entertainment

E) The city of Perugia

F) Introduction

G) First impressions

Appropriate language (15 min) Go online

Read the text and then answer the questions which follow.

When my friend emailed an invitation to Perugia, she told me to give it some thought, sixty seconds later, I emailed her back to accept. I couldn't resist!

Anna had said the architecture in Perugia was amazing, and that it was full of incredibly famous paintings. Perfect for art lovers! For foodies, it's full of wonderful Italian delicacies. What's not to like?

I flew to Florence in July, and caught a train to Perugia. The trains seemed old-fashioned, the people lively and exuberant. Due to the sizzling heat, passengers were leaning out of open windows chatting to others. I found the singsong of the Italian accents and the strong smell

---

of ground coffee in the air intoxicating.

Perugia is the capital of Umbria and a centre of medieval art. It's full of amazing structures, like the San Lorenzo Cathedral in the city centre and a Roman aqueduct which connects two of the city's hills.

In the surrounding area, Assissi is worth a visit. The countryside is a pleasant contrast to the hustle and bustle of the city.

Umbria hosts a jazz festival every year in July. The city was buzzing with visitors and we were spoiled for choice in terms of musical entertainment.

I can't recommend Perugia enough for a visit. For me, the scenery, architecture, food and entertainment all deserve ten out of ten!

Q44: Find four examples of contractions

An example is provided.

Example couldn't, it's, what's, can't

Writing: School magazine article (60 min)

Write an answer to the following question.

You have been asked to write an article for your school / college magazine about a city which you have visited, explaining why it is different from your home town.

You may give the article a title if you wish.

Write around 350 words.

Show your work to your teacher or tutor when you are finished.

There is an exemplar answer provided.

8.8   Pronunciation: Intonation

You will need access to the following sound files to complete this section.

hg-cesl1-8-3listening1.mp3
hg-cesl1-8-3listening2.mp3
hg-cesl1-8-4intonation1.mp3 to hg-cesl1-8-4intonation6.mp3

When we wish to appear polite it is important to make sure that the tone of our voice is working with us and not against us!

When we are speaking, the pitch of our voice goes up and down. This is referred to as *intonation*. Intonation helps us to express ourselves more effectively and to understand better what others say to us. Our choice of rising or falling intonation can change the meaning of what we say.

Listen to the following examples. The first speaker is interested and second speaker is not.

Examples

1. Interested

hg-cesl1-8-3listening1.mp3

rising intonation

. . . .

2. Not interested

hg-cesl1-8-3listening2.mp3

falling intonation

Intonation (10 min)   Go online

You will need sound files *hg-cesl1-8-4intonation1.mp3* to *hg-cesl1-8-4intonation6.mp3* to do this activity

Q45: How exciting

a) Rising
b) Falling

. . . .

Q46: How exciting

a) Rising
b) Falling

. . . .

Q47: Terrific

a) Rising
b) Falling

. . . .

Q48: Terrific

a) Rising
b) Falling

. . . .

Q49: That's amazing

a) Rising
b) Falling

....

Q50: That's amazing

a) Rising
b) Falling

Intonation in a dialogue (15 min)   Go online

You will need access to the sound file*hg-cesl1-8-5listening.mp3* to complete this activity.

This activity is a pronunciation activity and is best done with a partner. Each person should take on one of the roles.

Q51:
Listen to the script and mark the patterns of intonation on your copy of the script.

Check your markings with the answer.

With your partner practise using rising and falling intonation with the marked up script (corrected if necessary). Remember you can listen to the dialogue to compare.

Script

Julie - Hello Carol! How are you?

Carol - I'm fine thanks ...you?

Julie - Oh I'm all right

Carol - You don't sound it! Is there something wrong?

Julie - Not really it's just that I was supposed to be going to the cinema tonight and I was so looking forward to it but John just cancelled!

Carol - Oh that's a shame

Julie - Yes I know I haven't been out for two weeks - I've been studying really hard.

Carol - Look I don't have any plans for tonight I'll come with you!

Julie - Really!

Carol - Yes I'd love to come

Julie - Great! Let's do that!

8.9   Listening comprehension: Paula and Jamie

A listening comprehension follows to test your understanding of this topic.

You will need access to the sound files:*hg-cesl1-8et1-listening.mp3, hg-cesl1-8et1-listening1.mp3*

---

to hg-cesl1-8et1-listening2.mp3 to complete this listening comprehension.

Before you begin, listen to Paula and Jamie and familiarise yourself with their conversation

---

Listening comprehension: Paula and Jamie   Go online

Listen to Paula and Jamie and then answer the questions.

You will need access to the sound files:*hg-cesl1-8et1-listening.mp3, hg-cesl1-8et1-listening1.mp3 to hg-cesl1-8et1-listening2.mp3* to complete this listening comprehension.

Q52: Which country is Paula from?

....

Q53: Which country did Paula visit?

....

Q54: Paula found her new life quite frantic.

a) true
b) false

....

Q55: Paula never worried about what she might be missing at home.

a) true
b) false

....

Q56: Paula says people in the UK are generally quite averse to smoking nowadays.

a) true
b) false

....

Q57: People in Scotland are more _____ than people in Spain.

....

Q58: People in Spain _____ differently because the weather is better.

....

Q59: In the UK people are expected to accept or decline invitations. It would be _____ as rude not to respond.

....

Q60: Which country is Jamie from?

....

Q61: Which country did Jamie visit?

....

Q62: Jamie had initial reservations about the move to a new country.

a) true
b) false

....

Q63: Jamie thinks that sense of humour is influenced by cultural factors.

a) true
b) false

....

Q64: Jamie really only enjoyed the new country because he was a student

a) true
b) false

....

Q65: Jamie made the most of the study opportunity because he had had to work very hard to get into the university.

a) true
b) false

....

Q66: Sense of humour is often best where people have shared _____.

....

Q67: At universities in the UK not all students _____ on the opportunities they have.

8.10   Reading comprehension: Natalie

A reading comprehension follows to test your understanding of this topic.

Before you begin read the passage and check that you understand it.

Hi Mum and Dad

Well, I've now been here for a week and a half, so I hope that you are getting ready for my return! As I said, Gabriella is really nice... we hit it off immediately and I am sure that you will like her as much as I do. Her family have made me really welcome so I hope that we can do the same for her.

Gabriella is vegetarian like me, so we shouldn't have too much trouble feeding her. She is not as fussy about eating as I am mum, so am sure you will manage to cope with the extra guest for a week —please don't get stressed! I expect her to adapt really easily to our home as she is also very used to big families. Mind you, Gabriella's family are all very gregarious. Mealtimes are a bit chaotic! I thought we were bad!

When we arrive I'd like to take her on a city tour. I think we'll take the open top bus around the city. It is June, so hopefully we'll get a dry day but of course there are no guarantees in the west of Scotland. I also want to take her to Loch Lomond and the Trossachs. Gabby is very keen on the idea of castles, so I thought we could go to Stirling Castle one day and Edinburgh another.

I've been telling them all about cultural behaviour in the UK. I've told them that it's important to be on time, stand in queues and say sorry constantly! I have also explained to Gabriella that she will struggle to understand and be understood, as my Scottish accent is mild by comparison with some!

I am really enjoying my time here and would be happy to stay longer. It's nice that I can bring an Italian person back at least — it's a bit like holding on to Italy. I think it will be interesting to find out what Gabriella's first impressions of Scotland are. I can't wait to introduce her to all my friends. I really think they'll get on well. Gabriella's really great, I feel like I've always known her she's really perceptive and seems to really understand me already.

Anyway I should go and get some more sun before returning to chilly Scotland! See you soon and thanks again for letting me do this!!!

Love Natalie x

Reading comprehension: Natalie   Go online

Q68: Natalie is in Italy because

a) she has friends there
b) she is on an exchange visit
c) she is learning Italian

....

Q69: Compared to Natalie,

a) Gabriella is easily pleased where food is concerned
b) Gabriella is very particular about food
c) Gabriella has a similar approach to food

....

Q70: Compared to Natalie's family, Gabriella's family

a) are less gregarious
b) are quiet and retiring
c) are louder but just as friendly

....

Q71: Natalie thinks Gabriella will struggle to fit in with Natalie's family.

a) true
b) false

....

Q72: The weather in Scotland is unpredictable.

a) true
b) false

....

Q73: People in the UK appear apologetic.

a) true
b) false

....

Q74: Natalie thinks Gabriella lacks intuition.

a) true
b) false

....

Q75: Natalie plans to extend her stay in Italy.

a) true
b) false

8.11 Vocabulary list

You might find it helpful to have a list of some of the words which have been introduced in this topic.

acceptable (adjective)	satisfactory
to acclimatise (verb)	to become used to something
to accommodate (verb)	to adapt
to adapt (verb)	to modify
buzzing (adjective)	lively
chaotic (adjective)	disorganised
to chill out (verb)	to relax
clichéd (adjective)	unoriginal
culture (noun)	traditions /mores
disenchanted (adjective)	disillusioned /disappointed
disgruntled (adjective)	annoyed /dissatisfied
displaced (adjective)	exiled

to drop in (verb)	to visit
empathy (noun)	understanding
exponential (adverb)	describing an increase
expressive (adjective)	communicative
frustrating (adjective)	annoying
fussy (adjective)	choosy/ selective
genre (noun)	style/ type
gregarious (adjective)	outgoing
immense (adjective)	very big
incensed (adjective)	enraged
influential (adjective)	one able to exert power or influence
intuition (noun)	instinct
intoxicating (adjective)	enthralling

invariably (adjective)	usually
to offend (verb)	to upset
particular (adjective)	picky/selective
perceived (adjective)	apparent
prospects (noun)	chances
radical (adjective)	drastic
relaxing (adjective)	calming
retiring (adjective)	introverted
to sample (verb)	to try
shake up (noun)	change
to socialise (verb)	to meet people
taboo (noun)	restriction
technophobe (noun)	one who fears /dislikes technology

Unit 2: ESOL in Context (Work)

Unit 2 Topic 1

Personal ambition

Contents

Learning objective

By the end of this topic you should be able to:

- demonstrate your knowledge and understanding of ways of talking about the future including tense and aspect in the context of personal ambition

- use your extended range of vocabulary in the topic area through practice in reading, listening and writing

- demonstrate your increased knowledge of writing genre through writing an article

- demonstrate an extended range of pronunciation and your awareness of word stress

This topic explores the subject of personal ambition, including ideas about dreams, aspirations and hopes in people of all ages and from all areas of society. It revises the various grammatical structures used to discuss the future, focusing on tense and aspect. At Higher level you should already be familiar with these forms. In addition, advanced vocabulary relevant to the topic of personal ambition is introduced. The topic includes work on all four skills: speaking, reading, writing and listening. There are also supplementary pronunciation exercises. Assessment opportunities occur at the end of the topic.

Certain sections contain sound files. You may download these and use them on your mp3 player or equivalent to practise your pronunciation. This may be very useful if there are times when you will not have access to the materials online.

1.1   Grammar (revision): Future forms: 'Be going to'

In English we may express the future in a variety of different ways. The first we shall examine is the use of *'be going to'.* We use *'be going to'*:

1. with a base from to describe future events or activities

   Example

   I'm going to travel to Barcelona this summer

2. for future predictions which are based on evidence at, or before, the time of speaking

   Example

   It's going to snow this afternoon

Uses of the be going to future tense (10 min)   Go online

Q1:   For each sentence decide whether it is an example of:

- Planned future event
- Prediction based on evidence

A) Susan is so tired of my cooking, she's going to enrol on a cookery course herself.

B) I need to do well in this project. Tom says management are going to give me more responsibility in their next venture.

C) Sally is so greedy, I'm sure she's not going to share any of that money with you.

D) Norma is going to quit her job because she cannot continue working with that horrible woman.

E) I'm not going to apply for that job. I know what I want to do next year already.

1.1.1   Future forms: Structure: be going to

1. In all persons the **affirmative** is formed using

   Subject + verb 'to be' + going to + infinitive

   Example I am going to live in Paris one day; She is going to start a new job soon.

2. The negative is formed in a similar way, the verb *to be* being the only change:

   Subject + verb 'to be' (negative) + going to + infinitive

   Example They aren't going to succeed in business with that attitude.

3. Questions using auxiliary verbs are formed by:

   inverting the subject and verb 'to be'

   Example Is she (She ⇆ is) going to become famous?

4. Questions using other verbs are formed using

   question word + verb 'to be' + subject + going to + infinitive

   Example Where are they going to visit next?

1.2   Grammar (revision): Future forms: Present tenses

Example *I'm going to go to Australia for my gap year (going to future)*

I'm going to Australia for my gap year (present continuous)

Some native speakers prefer to avoid repetition of the verb. This is a matter of personal choice.

Present tenses to talk about the future. When we are talking about a future arrangement or a timetabled /scheduled event in the future, we may use present tenses.

Example *I leave for Australia on Sunday.*

I am seeing some friends on Saturday to say goodbye.

1.3   Grammar (revision): Future forms: 'Will'

We use *will*:

1. To describe an action or event which is unplanned or spontaneous

   Example That sounds fun. I think I'll come along to the audition too.

2. For predictions that are not based on evidence, but instead on opinion or belief.

   Example He'll go far in this company because I've heard he has got great people skills.

Uses of the will future tense (10 min)   Go online

Decide whether each of the sentences is an example of:

- Unplanned action or event
- Prediction based on opinion or belief

Q2:   Janice has all the qualities to succeed. I think she'll do well.

a) Unplanned action or event
b) Prediction based on opinion or belief

....

Q3:   I'll learn to swim easily because all my family are strong swimmers.

a) Unplanned action or event
b) Prediction based on opinion or belief

....

Q4:   Joseph will play guitar at tonight's gig. He answered an SOS from his old band mates.

a) Unplanned action or event
b) Prediction based on opinion or belief

....

Q5:   I'll take the dogs to the park. You continue with your studies.

a) Unplanned action or event
b) Prediction based on opinion or belief

....

Q6:   The company won't stay afloat making decisions like that.

a) Unplanned action or event
b) Prediction based on opinion or belief

1.3.1 Future forms: Structure: will

1. In all persons the affirmative is formed using:
   Subject + will + infinitive

   Example I will buy us some champagne to celebrate your news!

2. Negatives are formed using:
   Subject + will not (won't) + infinitive

   Example I won't continue with Spanish next year as I just don't understand it

3. Questions are formed by:
   inverting the subject and will

   Example Will you (you ⇋ will) continue with Spanish next year?

1.4   Reading: A little girl with big dreams

The next activity will provide practice in deciding which form of future should be used.

Going to and will forms (15 min)	Go online

Q7: In the text choose whether the *italicised* verbs should be in the 'be going to' or 'will' future form

A little girl with big dreams

My daughter Morgan is only six years old, but she has more ideas, opinions and plans than most of my adult friends. She knows what secondary school and university she *will/'s going to attend*, which boy from her class *is going to/will* be her future husband and how much money she is *going to/will* earn when she's thirty! Yes, it seems I as a parent *am going to/will* have little input because Morgan has already got it all figured out. "*I am going to/will* wear my red dress today because I want to look pretty for singing class", she says, and in restaurants she assumes control, "I think I *am going to/will* have the fillet of sole, but not too much sauce". Times have changed since I was young, and it's hard to stop your kids behaving this way when all their friends are doing likewise. Compared to some of her playmates, Morgan isn't that bad, in fact. I've heard stories of credit cards being used, "I *am going to/will* buy Barbie a new car" and holidays plans being ruined, "I *won't/am not going to* stay at gran's house because it's boring, so you *are going to/will* have to cancel your holiday to France", all because of spoiled and petulant children. Will our kids, or our children's children, ever enjoy the naïve innocence of childhood that we once had? I *won't/am not going to* put money on society reverting back to how it was, put it that way. Morgan *will/is going to* be an adult before she knows it and only then will she realise how much she has missed out on. Having said that, she tells me she *will/is going to* be a princess with six palaces by the time she's twelve, and I've been promised one of them, so perhaps it's not all bad news!

1.5   Vocabulary: Career ambitions

This section provides a series of activities which focus on the vocabulary that you might use when talking about ambition.

How ambitious are you?	Go online

Q8: Look at the following words which describe varying levels of ambition.

Can you sort them into two groups, **ambitious** or **unambitious**, depending on their meaning? You may wish to use a dictionary to help you.

A) determined

B) listless

C) indifferent

D) disciplined

E) apathetic

F) passive

G) aimless

H) resolute

I) dedicated

J) eager

K) shiftless

L) driven

Word class   Go online

Q9: Look again at the adjectives describing ambition. Change the word class (eg. noun, verb, adjective, adverb) to make the noun and adverbial form.

Note: Three of the words have no adverbial form. Leave these blank.

Noun	Adjective	Adverb
	determined	
	dedicated	
	driven	
	listless	
	shiftless	
	indifferent	
	apathetic	
	passive	
	eager	
	aimless	
	disciplined	
	resolute	

Pronunciation: Syllables and stress (15 min)   Go online

To be able to do this activity you will need access to *hg-cesl2-1-1wordstress1.mp3* to *hg-cesl2-1-1wordstress13.mp3*

Q10: Can you categorise the following words into three, four or five syllable words and also place them into the correct word stress pattern?

oOo	$ooOoo$	$oooOo$	Ooo

Ooo
disciplined

Try to do the same with these words:

1. apathetically:
2. determination:
3. apathy:
4. passiveness:
5. indifferent:
6. eagerness:
7. shiftlessness:
8. determined:
9. dedicated:
10. dedicatedly:
11. indifferently:
12. resolutely:

Reading: Ambition in the workplace (10 min)

Go online

Q11: The sentences below are taken from a conversation about ambition in the workplace. Read what the employees are saying and choose the appropriate expression to fill the gap in the conversation.

Expressions:career ladder, overlooked, fast track, demoted, perks, glass ceiling

Did you hear about Brian, the new flight attendant? He's only been here a few months but I've heard gossip that the directors have an eye on him because they want to _____ him to a management post.

Not another person to get promoted ahead of me! I'm starting to tire of being _____. I'll have been here nine years next month and I'm standing still.

You'll get that promotion one day. I think it is just the luck of the draw, I really don't think there is a _____ for female employees at this company.

Try telling that to Suzy. I've heard that she's being _____ from her position, probably so that Brian can be moved up.

That's not what I heard. Suzy will have been flying for twenty years soon, so she's going part-time because she wants to spend more time with her family. They're letting her cash in part of her pension now as well, it's one of the _____ of having our job.

Oh, I didn't realise. That's not so bad. Well, good luck to Brian then - he's a nice guy and I suppose he deserves to move up the _____. I just hope I'll be next!

Definitions (10 min)   Go online

Q12: Match the expressions in the first list with the most appropriate meaning from the second list.

A) to demote

B) glass ceiling

C) perk

D) to overlook

E) career ladder

F) to fast track

1. To rapidly advance a person's career

2. To ignore or fail to notice

3. An invisible barrier to promotion, often based on unspoken prejudice

4. To reduce status or position to a less important level

5. A benefit or advantage in a job

6. The progression route from entry in a company to the top

1.6 Speaking: Ambition

Speaking: Ambition (25 min)

Talk to your partner or teacher about your ambitions and hopes for the future. You should take 15 minutes to prepare to discuss the topic, making some short notes.

Consider the following questions and have a conversation using them and your own ideas (8-10 minutes):

- Are you ambitious?

- Do you think ambition is a positive or negative characteristic in a person? Why?

- What is your greatest achievement —personal and working/studying achievement?

- What are your hopes and dreams for the future?

- "Hard work breeds success". What do you think this statement means and to what extent do you agree with it?

1.7   Grammar: Future forms: Future continuous

Going to and will future tenses also have continuous forms.

The future continuous tense is used:

1. To describe future events in progress

    Example I'm going to be working at that time

2. To refer to the future in a neutral way, often to reassure, or prior to making a request

    Example Will you be needing any more help?

1.7.1   Forming the future continuous tense

In the continuous form, there is no **perceived** difference in meaning between the use of *going to, will* or *shall* before the verb.

1. We form the future continuous using:

    Subject + will/shall/be going to + be + -ing form of the verb

    Examples

    1. They will be making changes to their house for the new baby soon

        . . . .

    2. They are going to be moving to a bigger house next month

---

Understanding the future continuous tense (15 min)   Go online

Q13: Check your understanding of the future continuous tense by rearranging the following sentences, and then matching them with the corresponding answer:

Rearrange:

1. next are production They theatrical month a be Citizen's the to performing going new at
2. be your week Will you car tomorrow? a using
3. be with it's shall sure okay anyway, I'm at Linda John's staying house her. so

---

1.8 Grammar: Future perfect simple tense

The future perfect simple tense is used:

1. to make a prediction that an action or event will be finished by a particular point in time in the future

   Example I will have finished all my essays by Christmas.

2. to make a prediction about a situation in the present time

   Example It's okay to enter the boardroom. They will have finished their meeting by now.

1.8.1 Forming the future perfect simple tense

To form the future perfect simple:

1. In affirmative sentences use
   Subject + will + have + past participle of the verb

2. In negative sentences use
   Subject + will not (won't) + have + past participle of the verb

3. In questions
   Invert the subject and will/won't

 The future perfect simple can be used with shall instead of will. This does not change the meaning, although shall is considered to be more formal and old-fashioned than will.

Use of the future perfect simple tense (10 min) Go online

Change the verb form (in brackets) to the future perfect simple, to help you make the full sentence:

Joe (spend) all his wages by tomorrow

Q14: Joe _ _ _ _ _ _ _ _ _ _ all his wages by tomorrow

....

Sheila (take) the credit as usual

Q15: Sheila _ _ _ _ _ _ _ _ _ _ the credit as usual

....

They (finish) band practice by now

Q16: They _____ band practice by now

....

We (graduate) from university by/in November

Q17: We _____ from university by/in November

....

Harry (leave) the house by now

Q18: Harry _____ the house by now

1.9   Grammar: Future perfect continuous tense

We use the future perfect continuous to show how long an event or action has been in progress by a particular point in the future. The action is likely to continue beyond that point.

Example I will have been living in Edinburgh for ten years by 2018.

 We often use the prepositions for and by with the future perfect continuous

    1. to indicate the duration of the action,

        Example *for ten years,* **for** *a month*

    2. and to mark the future point we are referring to

        Example *by next week,* **by** *the time I am fifty*

1.9.1   Forming the future perfect continuous tense

To form the future perfect continuous we use

Subject + will + have + been + -*ing* form of the verb

Example In August Joe will have been studying for four years.

Use of the future perfect continuous tense (15 min)   Go online

Combine the following to make sentences in future perfect continuous

Example I work in London. 2015 will be my 5th year working there.
I will have been working in London for five years by 2015.

Q19: Shannon is thirty next year. She has ridden horses since she was five.

....

Q20: James is improving his German. Next month it will be two years since he started learning.

....

Q21: My sister is coming to see us in January, five years since we moved in together.

....

Q22: Jill still isn't finished that song she started writing in June. She says it will be ready by Christmas.

1.10   Reading: A driving ambition

The next activity will provide practice in reading and understanding passages containing the tenses explained in this topic.

Reading: A driving ambition (25 min)   Go online

Read the following short passage and answer the questions which follow.

A driving ambition

Paul Duncan is a thirty-five year old, self-employed driving instructor. Paul had been an architect, but he was laid off unexpectedly in the housing crisis and found himself urgently seeking an alternative means of gainful employment. Paul will have been doing this job for three years come Easter. Initially he worked for BMS instructors and then, seeing the opportunity for increased earnings, he parted company with the national instruction firm and, of his own volition, set up under his own name. Later this week, the seventieth pupil Paul has been tutoring will have sat, and hopefully passed, their driving test. "That's what I'm in it for", he says. "I earn a decent living, but I will probably never take home anything approaching what I did as an architect. It wasn't a bad line of employment, financially speaking, but it wasn't really emotionally rewarding. "Contrasting that with what I do now, well, I will never tire of seeing happy pupils re-emerge from the test centre to give me the good news. It's an uplifting experience on each and every occasion."

Paul will have been together with his wife Veronica for twelve years next month, and she has always been a supporter of his plans. "Paul tends to be quite spontaneous. His goals are always changing. When he was made redundant from the housing business, he didn't hesitate in refocusing his ambition on another project. "I, however, lack commitment to the professional aspect of my own life. "I've always been a homebody, so I think that's how we maintain the equilibrium."

Q23: Paul chose to leave his job as an architect.

a) true
b) false

....

Q24: Paul has been working for BMS instructors for three years.

a) true
b) false

....

Q25: Paul earns less now than he did as an architect.

a) true
b) false

....

Q26: Paul's wife thinks that Paul is too quick to make decisions and that he should take more time to think.

a) true
b) false

....

Q27: Paul's wife has more interest in her domestic and family life than in her career.

a) true
b) false

Read the passage about Paul, the driving instructor, again.

A driving ambition

Paul Duncan is a thirty-five year old, self-employed driving instructor. Paul had been an architect, but he was laid off unexpectedly in the housing crisis and found himself urgently seeking an alternative means of gainful employment. Paul will have been doing this job for three years come Easter. Initially he worked for BMS instructors and then, seeing the opportunity for increased earnings, he parted company with the national instruction firm and, of his own volition, set up under his own name. Later this week, the seventieth pupil Paul has been tutoring will have sat, and hopefully passed, their driving test. "That's what I'm in it for", he says. "I earn a decent living, but I will probably never take home anything approaching what I did as an architect. It wasn't a bad line of employment, financially speaking, but it wasn't really emotionally rewarding. "Contrasting that with what I do now, well, I will never tire of seeing happy pupils re-emerge from the test centre to give me the good news. It's an uplifting experience on each and every occasion."

Paul will have been together with his wife Veronica for twelve years next month, and she has always been a supporter of his plans. "Paul tends to be quite spontaneous. His goals are always changing. When he was made redundant from the housing business, he didn't hesitate in refocusing his ambition on another project. "I, however, lack commitment to the professional aspect of my own life. "I've always been a homebody, so I think that's how we maintain the equilibrium."

Can you fill in a word or expression in the text box (three words maximum) which means:

Q28: Lost his job (two-word-verb)

....

Q29: Serving the purpose of increasing wealth (adj.)

....

Q30: The act of making a choice or decision (n.)

....

Q31: A person's principal business activity (three word expression)

....

Q32: A person happier around the house or not at work (n.)

1.11   Listening: A different kind of match

The next activity is a listening one.

You will need access to the sound file *hg-cesl2-1-2listening.mp3* to continue.

Listening: A different kind of match (15 min)   Go online ✳

Listen to the passage then answer the questions that follow.

Q33: How old is Jennifer?

a) Thirty
b) Twenty-nine
c) Twenty-three

....

Q34: Jennifer started having parties:

a) Because she and her friends were single
b) Because her hockey career had finished
c) To start up her new business

....

Q35: She decided to set up her company:

a) Because of the encouragement of friends
b) Due to her friends getting married
c) Because she realised she could earn a lot of money

....

Q36: Jennifer is aspiring to:

a) Expand and diversify her business
b) Sell wedding dresses and offer wedding services through her internet company
c) Buy more premises for her business

....

Q37: She believes that:

a) Her new career was perhaps what she was always meant to do with her life
b) She would have been a successful hockey player
c) Her life always brings her surprises

1.12   Writing

The final activity is a writing exercise. Make sure that you revise the topic before trying it.

Writing: Ambitions (60 min)

Write an article entitled *'My career ambitions'* for your school or college magazine.
Include all of the following points:

- Brief personal information about yourself
- What your dream job was when you were younger
- What qualifications and experience you have achieved in your life so far
- Your work goals in the short-term and long-term

Before you begin, consider the following questions:

- What is the purpose of the communication?
- Who is the audience of the article?
- What level of formality and register would be appropriate?

Make some notes or a mind map to help plan your writing before you begin.

Try to write around 300 - 350 words.

When you have finished your essay ask your teacher or tutor to check your work, or check it against the model answer provided.

1.13   Listening comprehension: Promotion

The next activity is the listening comprehension. You will need access to the sound file *hg-cesl2-1-3listening.mp3* to complete this.

Listen to the following dialogue which contains examples of many of the language areas you have covered within the topic.

Listening comprehension: Promotion (15 min)   Go online

You need access to sound file *hg-cesl2-1-3listeninget1.mp3* then you may try the questions which follow.

Listen to the recording again and try to answer the following questions:

Complete the gaps with the appropriate word or words.

Q38: Early promotions make people more _____ to stress and illness. Complete the gap.

....

Q39: Limitations on free time were _____ factors to poor health. Complete the gap.

....

Q40: The drive to climb the career ladder is causing more workers to become _____ and disenchanted. **(two words)**

Decide from what you heard if the following statements are: *true, false* or *does not say.*

Q41: People in promoted posts struggle to visit the doctor's surgery

a) true
b) false

....

Q42: Promotion can offer a lot of benefits

a) true
b) false

Q43: The writer thinks that the statement "Hard work brings its own reward":

a) needs to be changed
b) is completely incorrect
c) is a useful old expression in English

....

Q44: What is the main idea the passage is conveying?

1. Promotion makes people sick
2. The hidden danger of promotion
3. Most promoted people are unhappy

1.14 Reading comprehension: Ambitions

The following activity is a reading comprehension covering the work of this topic.

Before you begin read the passage and check that you understand it.

What are your ambitions? For many young adults, becoming a millionaire, being a sporting sensation or jet-setting around the globe, top the list of things they would love to be able to do. None of that interests Gordon Wylie, however, a sixteen-year-old with a much more anchored yet inspiring wish. Gordon just wants to be able to do the things that other teenagers can do.

Gordon was diagnosed with a rare debilitating muscular condition when he was four months old. The prognosis was bleak, specialists told his parents that the chances of survival beyond a year would be minute, but even at that age, Gordon was confounding the so-called experts. He pulled through against all odds and in doing so, rejected the first of many limitations that his condition typically imposes upon people.

Most children start to crawl a few months post-birth. Due to muscle wastage, Gordon spent his infancy in regimented rehabilitation sessions and on a strict dietary programme, which finally saw him able to manoeuvre on his hands and knees at age seven. Walking has been an even greater uphill struggle. One of the hardest decisions the Wylie family had to take was to opt for lower limb amputation and osseointegration of a prosthetic leg when Gordon was eleven. It was bankrolled by the sale of both the Wylie household's cars and the partial remortgaging of their home, but there were no regrets on anyone's part the day that Gordon walked out of the taxi from the hospital unaided, to be greeted at the front door by his mother's surprised, almost unbelieving gaze...

Many people would have felt fulfilled with that achievement, but Gordon always has his next goal in mind. Gordon agreed to be a test case for a new form of physiotherapy coming out of the USA, involving muscle memory techniques, and based loosely on the Roehampton approach. He will have been undergoing this pioneering physiotherapy treatment for exactly three years on Tuesday. "I will have ridden a bike for the first time by your next visit", he tells me.

Were you unfamiliar with the teenager in front of you, you'd have a sense of sadness that he dwells on impossible dreams and is quite deluded. Having spent an hour in his company, however, that feeling is surpassed by the knowledge of what he has already achieved and the infectious positivity that he exudes. I really don't think Gordon will be on a bicycle the next time we meet, I expect he'll have already conquered that challenge and be halfway toward the mastery of something more demanding by then.

Reading comprehension: Ambitions (30 min) Go online

Read the passage once more and answer the questions which follow.

What are your ambitions? For many young adults, becoming a millionaire, being a sporting sensation or jet-setting around the globe top the list of things they would love to be able to do. None of that interests Gordon Wylie, however, a sixteen-year-old with a much more anchored yet inspiring wish. Gordon just wants to be able to do the things that other teenagers can do.

Gordon was diagnosed with a rare debilitating muscular condition when he was four months old. The prognosis was bleak, specialists told his parents that the chances of survival beyond a year would be minute, but even at that age, Gordon was confounding the so-called experts. He pulled through against all odds and in doing so, rejected the first of many limitations that

---

his condition typically imposes upon people.

Most children start to crawl a few months post-birth. Due to muscle wastage, Gordon spent his infancy in regimented rehabilitation sessions and on a strict dietary programme, which finally saw him able to manoeuvre on his hands and knees at age seven. Walking has been an even greater uphill struggle. One of the hardest decisions the Wylie family had to take was to opt for lower limb amputation and osseointegration of a prosthetic leg when Gordon was eleven. It was bankrolled by the sale of both the Wylie household's cars and the partial remortgaging of their home, but there were no regrets on anyone's part the day that Gordon walked out of the taxi from the hospital unaided, to be greeted at the front door by his mother's surprised, almost unbelieving gaze. . .

Many people would have felt fulfilled with that achievement, but Gordon always has his next goal in mind. Gordon agreed to be a test case for a new form of physiotherapy coming out of the USA, involving muscle memory techniques, and based loosely on the Roehampton approach. He will have been undergoing this pioneering physiotherapy treatment for exactly three years on Tuesday. "I will have ridden a bike for the first time by your next visit", he tells me.

Were you unfamiliar with the teenager in front of you, you'd have a sense of sadness that he dwells on impossible dreams and is quite deluded. Having spent an hour in his company, however, that feeling is surpassed by the knowledge of what he has already achieved and the infectious positivity that he exudes. I really don't think Gordon will be on a bicycle the next time we meet, I expect he'll have already conquered that challenge and be halfway toward the mastery of something more demanding by then.

Q45: The most appropriate title for the article is:

a) Smaller ambitions than most
b) Refusing to give up
c) The dreams of an unlucky child

....

Q46: Find a word with the same/similar meaning to *firmly secured* in the article

....

Q47: Find a word with the same/similar meaning to *strictly organised'* in the article

....

Q48: Find a word with the same/similar meaning to *new and untried'* in the article

....

Q49: Find a word with the same/similar meaning to *display or spread'* in the article

....

Q50: In the phrase, *It was bankrolled*, what does *it* refer to?

....

Q51: How do Gordon's family feel about his ambitions? (choose the best answer)

a) They are supportive
b) They have found it a struggle
c) They think he is trying to do too much

....

Q52: How many examples of future perfect forms (simple and continuous) are there in the text?

1.15 Vocabulary list

This is a list of useful vocabulary which is intended to supplement what you have learned. It may also be useful to refer to when attempting the speaking and writing activities within the topic.

altruistic (adjective)	placing others' needs before your own
aspiring (adjective)	determined to achieve or reach a specific goal or target
to devote (verb)	to give or set aside time and effort to one particular idea or action
entrepreneur (noun)	an ambitious person who takes risks to start up their own business
to expedite (verb)	to speed up the process of something
to extend (verb)	to stretch or spread
humble (adjective)	not arrogant or overconfident; modest and unassuming
humility (noun)	the state of being humble
impulsive (adjective)	acting at the moment without thinking or planning; spontaneity
persistent (adjective)	continuing to try despite problems or setbacks
pride (noun)	the state of being proud; having a lot of confidence and self-esteem
purpose (noun)	the reason or aim of something
rewarding (adjective)	satisfying or valuable in a monetary or other sense
single-minded (adjective)	determined; driven to succeed or achieve
zest (noun)	an enjoyment/love for something

Unit 2 Topic 2

Preparing for the world of work

Contents

Learning objective

By the end of this topic you should be able to:

- use a wider range of vocabulary in the topic area of work and preparation for work

- understand and use participles and negative prefixes

- demonstrate your knowledge of writing genre through writing a discursive essay

- demonstrate your knowledge of note-taking

This topic will provide opportunities to practise skills relevant to academic life such as referencing and note taking. You will have the opportunity to extend your range of vocabulary through activities which will include work on all four skills: speaking, reading, writing, and listening. There will also be an opportunity to focus on pronunciation. Assessment opportunities occur at the end of the topic.

Certain sections contain sound files. You may download these here and use them on your mp3 player or equivalent to practise your pronunciation. This may be very useful if there are times when you will not have access to the materials online.

2.1 Reading: Family economy

This section includes two activities: a pre-reading and a reading activity.

Pre-reading activity: Family economy (20 min)

Discuss the following questions with a partner, if possible, or make some notes about them by yourself.

a) How much money do you think an average family in the UK spends each year on:

1. toys
2. computer games
3. clothes

b) Do you think people in your country spend more or less than British people on these things?

c) Do you think that parents are under pressure to spend money on toys, games and brand name clothes for their children?

d) How can parents avoid spoiling their children by overspending on the above?

Try to discuss your ideas with a classmate.

Reading: Family economy (35 min)

Q1: While reading decide on the main focus of each paragraph (1 to 5) for the list:

paragraph 1	responses to research findings
paragraph 2	issues around attitudes to time spent with families
paragraph 3	introduction and outline of the main discussion points
paragraph 4	recommendations and conclusions
paragraph 5	issues around attitudes to material goods

Read the text.

Paragraph 1

As Christmas approaches once again, the question of materialism and its place in the lives of ordinary families rears its head. Does materialism dominate family life? A recent UNICEF report on child well-being explores the issue in detail. The report, based on independent research by IPSOS, MORI and Dr Agnes Nairn was commissioned by UNICEF UK and examines children's perceptions of the relationship between materialism, inequality and well-being in the UK, Spain and Sweden. Prompting the research was an earlier report which revealed that the UK compared unfavourably with other countries, often significantly poorer countries, in the areas of child well-being and inequality. An interesting comparison is made between material well-being and subjective well-being and indicates that while the UK ranked 18th and 20th respectively in these categories out of 21 countries, Sweden ranked 1st and 7th and Spain 12th and 2nd. The research was conducted through observation and filming of families and interviews with 250 children.

Paragraph 2

There were some areas of consistency across the countries. Researchers found that children from the UK, Sweden and Spain all expressed desire for time spent with friends and family, and for activities outside the home. However, while it was very clear that most children perceived time with family as more important than material goods, parents in the UK seemed to be struggling more than Spanish or Swedish parents to provide this. It was evident that, in Spain and Sweden, families had less difficulty in making choices which emphasised family life over work. In both these countries there was also greater participation in outdoor and creative pursuits which were identified as being strongly linked to perceived happiness. In the UK, the level of involvement in sporting and other outdoor pursuits declined dramatically as children became older, and was particularly poor by the time they had reached secondary school age. This was especially true among lower income families.

Paragraph 3

The relationship with material goods was not straightforward. While it became clear that children and parents across the three countries were similarly affected by pressures to earn and consume, in the UK parents felt less equipped to deal with these pressures and, as a result, were more likely to succumb to them. Children expressed the desire to have 'things', but rather than being acquisitive, this was often found to be associated with a desire to fulfil 'utilitarian, symbolic and social' functions. Parents in the UK also appeared to have a complicated relationship with spending on material goods. They often bought almost against their own better judgement. Branded goods were purchased with a sense of protectiveness that their children should not experience a feeling of inferiority or be bullied as a consequence of not having the most highly rated brands. At the same time, parents expressed a sense of despair over their powerlessness and the pointlessness of over-consumption. Reference was made to boxes of toys, broken presents and unused electronics in the home. This trend was far less evident in the other two countries involved in the study.

Paragraph 4

How do ordinary parents view the findings of the study? When we conducted a survey of our own in a main shopping district in London, we found that the ordinary mother and father expressed both harmony and discord with the research report. One father thought that many parents nowadays were guilty of status anxiety, the need to keep up with the Joneses, as well as a feeling of buying presents at overinflated prices in order to assuage guilt. Another person we interviewed, a mother of three, blamed rampant Western materialism and economic pressure to keep capitalist society afloat.

Paragraph 5

UNICEF has made several recommendations as a consequence of the report. UNICEF UK calls on the UK government to examine the impact of income inequality and to promote a living wage. This would help to preclude the need for parents to work in more than one job and to spend more time with children which was clearly indicated as desirable. A second recommendation is that of investment in free play and leisure facilities for children and families. Finally there is a need to tackle materialistic culture. UNICEF UK applauds Sweden's 1991 ban on advertising aimed at children under twelve and suggests that a similar approach in the UK could help parents become more resilient against materialistic pressures.

For each question find a word in the text which matches the definition.

Q2: Formally appointed, chosen or assigned a task (paragraph 1)

....

Q3: (of a view or opinion) based on personal belief and feelings rather than fact (paragraph 1)

....

Q4: The state of remaining the same (paragraph 2)

....

Q5: To give in, to accept defeat (paragraph 3)

....

Q6: Where there is lack of agreement or harmony (paragraph 4)

....

Q7: Spreading in an uncontrolled way (paragraph 4)

Decide whether the following statements are **true** or **false** according to the article.

Q8: Children in the UK are objectively worse off than they think they are

a) true
b) false

....

Q9: Being outside makes children feel good

a) true
b) false

....

Q10: Children in the UK associate material goods with status

a) true
b) false

....

Q11: Parents in the UK think supplying children with material goods equates with caring

a) true
b) false

....

Q12: Parents in Spain and Sweden have fewer pressures to consume

a) true
b) false

....

Q13: The father who was interviewed believes that parents can and should make decisions that reduce spending on expensive toys

a) true
b) false

....

Q14: The UNICEF report indicates that economic support could enable families to spend more time with children

a) true
b) false

....

Q15: The UNICEF report advocates a ban on advertising

a) true
b) false

2.2   Writing: Ethical advertising

Writing: Ethical advertising (45 min)

Write a discursive essay in answer to the following question.

Advertising aimed at children under 12 should be banned in the UK.

Write an essay discussing this statement and supporting your example with some or all of the following ideas:

- The pressure advertising puts on parents

- Censorship of advertising

- Parental supervision of children

Before you begin consider the following questions:

1. What is the purpose of the communication?

2. Who is the intended audience?

3. What level of formality and register would be appropriate?

You should make notes or a mind map with ideas for both sides of the argument (for and against the statement in the question).

You should write between 300 - 350 words.

When you have finished your essay ask your teacher or tutor to check your work, or check it against the model answer provided.

2.3   Grammar: Participles

Sometimes we make our sentences shorter by using participles instead of the full verb. In order to avoid **ambiguity** it is important to ensure that the participle and the main verb have the same subject.

In the following example it is not clear which person was encouraged to go shopping and which person went shopping.

Example Having advised her eldest daughter to study all day, she went out shopping with her sister.

Ambiguity (25 min)

The following examples show ambiguity and then also demonstrate ways in which to clarify meaning.

Examples

1. Having done nothing to prepare for his presentation this week, his manager told him to spend the weekend working.

Having failed to prepare for his presentation this week he was told by his manager to spend the weekend working.

....

2. Being late for the meeting, the secretary told them they would have to wait outside.

Being late for the meeting they were told by the secretary to wait outside.

Q16: Not being clear about the answer to the question, the assessor marked me incorrect.

....

Q17: Being very domineering, her boss made her work twelve hour days.

....

Q18: Being guilty of plagiarism, her lecturer said she would have to appear before the university board.

....

Q19: Handing in her report late, the CEO said she was in danger of losing her job.

....

Q20: Lolling around in the cafeteria, I saw the laziest worker in the company.

....

Q21: Trying to write up his sales figures for work, Martin's flatmate partied until the early hours of the morning.

....

Q22: Having already got a degree, most undergraduates were less confident than postgraduate students.

....

Q23: Returning to full time education, most of her friends thought Sarah was mad.

2.4   Listening: Career change

Speaking: Career change

Before listening to the lecture you might like to consider the following questions

1. How many years would you expect to remain employed in the same job/organisation?

2. Think about your family and friends. How long have they been employed in one profession or organisation?

3. What life changes may result in someone making a career change?

4. Do you believe that there is a cut-off point or age beyond which it is impossible to make a career change?

Listening: Career change
Go online

Listen to the lecture again and write answers to the following questions in your notebook or using a text document. You can then compare your answers with the Display Answers.

You need access to sound file *hg-cesl2-2-1listening.mp3*.

Q24: What does the speaker indicate as the main purpose of the discussion?

....

Q25: How does the speaker expect the course to develop?

....

Q26: What is the speaker's purpose in describing an annual social gathering?

....

Q27: What prompted restructuring of the company?

....

Q28: Give the names of seven types of new employment which the speaker's colleagues have found.

....

Q29: What are the benefits of the annual get together? (give at least two answers)

....

Q30: What two questions do members of the audience ask

....

Q31: How does the speaker respond to those questions?

Key points of the lecture (25 min)

Use your notes and answers to the questions to rewrite in your own words the key points of the lecture and the post lecture question and answer session.

You can use the headings below:

1. Purpose of the lecture

2. Background to the occasion

3. New directions taken by former customer service employees

4. Current trends in society

5. Questions asked and responses given

You should ask your teacher or tutor to check your work.

2.5 Vocabulary: Work and academic language

Vocabulary: Work and academic words (20 min)   Go online

The following sentences contain vocabulary from the previous listening text. Complete each sentence with a word made from the word in capitals.

Q32: The party was by _____ only so it was quite exclusive. INVITE

....

Q33: Although I am Scottish, I do not _____ with Scottish culture. IDENTITY

....

Q34: I found it difficult to make the _____ from being full time nurse to full time parent. TRANSIT

....

Q35: I often find that I am stressed at work so I go for a _____ massage. THERAPY

....

Q36: We currently have a global _____ crisis as banks and mortgage lenders have encouraged excessive borrowing. ECONOMY

....

Q37: The _____ of the crash in our economy was a feature many banks chose to ignore. INEVITABLE

....

Q38: I am not a very _____ person. I am quite happy in my tiny flat without a TV or the internet. MATERIALISM

. . . .

Q39: The revelation of his corrupt business strategies put his colleagues in a very _____ position. COMPROMISE

. . . .

Q40: His comments are _____ of his faulty reasoning. ILLUSTRATE

. . . .

Q41: They have made a _____ to fight the closure of their department, but I am not convinced they will succeed. RESOLVE

2.6   Pronunciation: Word Transformation

Pronunciation: Word Transformation (20 min)   Go online

You will need access to the sound files *hg-cesl2-2-2pronunc1.mp3* to *hg-cesl2-2-2pronunc20.mp3*.

Q42: Listen to each word and decide on the position of main stress in each of the words from the previous activity and mark these on the words.

invite	invitation
identity	identify
transit	transition
therapy	therapeutic
economy	economic
inevitable	inevitability
materialism	materialistic
compromise	compromising
illustrate	illustrative
resolve	resolution

Listen and repeat the words to practise your pronunciation.

2.7 Negative prefixes

The prefix *un* is normally used to negate a word. It is normally attached to a noun or verb.

Example damaged

undamaged

Negative prefix *un* (20 min)   Go online ✳

Use the prefix *un* and the word in brackets to complete the second sentence while retaining the meaning of the first.

Q43:

1. The evidence against him was never (substantiated).
2. The evidence was _ _ _ _ _ _ _ _ _ _ _ _ _ _

   . . . .

Q44:

1. Her ambition to travel the world has, as yet, not been (realised).
2. Her ambitions are _ _ _ _ _ _ _ _ _ _ _ _ _ _

   . . . .

Q45:

1. With respect to my career I do not feel very (fulfilled).
2. I feel largely _ _ _ _ _ _ _ _ _ _ _ _ _ _ at work.

   . . . .

Q46:

1. The fears she had about meeting opposition at work have not had (foundation).
2. Her fears have been _ _ _ _ _ _ _ _ _ _ _ _ _ _

   . . . .

Q47:

1. I cannot (bear) the narrow minded attitude of some people at work.
2. I find the attitude of some people at work _ _ _ _ _ _ _ _ _ _ _ _ _ _

   . . . .

Q48:

1. The offer she has from Caledonian University does not have (conditions).
2. The offer is _ _ _ _ _ _ _ _ _ _ _ _ _ _

. . . .

Q49:

1. The decision to make so many employees redundant is without (justification).
2. The decision is completely _____

. . . .

Q50:

1. This massive restructuring is entirely without (precedent).
2. The restructuring is _____

. . . .

Q51:

1. She was not (sympathetic) when I failed my exams.
2. She was _____ about my failure.

. . . .

Q52:

1. The decision was found to have been against the (constitution).
2. The decision was _____ about my failure.

2.8   Reading comprehension: Valuable skills to learn

The following activity is a reading comprehension covering the work of this topic.

Read the passage quickly to grasp the gist of it.

How to take notes

Having just completed my third year of full time study at this amazing university, and having, by some freak accident, I can only imagine, been elected to vice president of the student union, I am very keen to share some wisdom with all newbies. For all of you out there who are embarking on the first stage of your university career with, no doubt, great fear and trepidation as well as major excitement, I would like to take this opportunity in the first edition of Campus this year to offer you all the information and tips I have for your edification on note taking.

Effective note taking is one of the most important skills you can learn for university study. It provides you with a record of all the lectures and tutorials which you attend and can therefore be used for exam revision, seminars, presentations and essay preparation. You can use notes to help you to identify the origins of your thoughts and as a starting point for development of your own thoughts and ideas. Another important point to remember is that good notes are invaluable as a trading commodity, because one day you will sleep in and miss a lecture or tutorial! If you have been generous with your notes then you can expect others to be equally generous with you on the occasion that you miss an important lecture.

Effective note taking involves a few basic principles, so let me begin with the skill of taking notes while reading. In the first place it is really important that you have ascertained what your task is! I am not being facetious here. There is no point in spending hours and hours as I have done to my cost, reading scores of pages of some dull tome hoping to extract key information without first working out what the essay or seminar question is. Targeted reading is crucial and will save a lot of time. Skim reading and scanning for an overview will also save time. After all,one can't spend all one's university days in the library can one? It is also crucial to get into the habit of asking yourself, what are the main points of this discussion? Try very hard not to use the writer's words; it is a tad slower but if you read, digest and then rewrite in your own words, not only will you have a better understanding of what you have read but you will also have a substantial amount of a possible future essay already written! Remember to record sources, particularly of quotes so that you can reference sources properly. Use diagrams, colour pens, highlighters and anything else you can think of to make information clear.

Now let me move on to taking notes while listening. Some of the strategies are the same, but of course while listening you are not really able to stop the process because you dozed off! It is vital to remain alert throughout and I have a few tips here too. Number one, try to get some sleep before lectures! Hmm, well okay it's not always possible! Seriously though folks, try to go prepared by reading around the subject beforehand and working out meanings of new concepts and vocabulary. Again target your listening, try to establish the main points under discussion and take relevant notes. Do not write everything down, but do use abbreviations to minimise time spent writing down important points. Mind maps, diagrams and pictures can help the visual learners among us. Try to pick up on what the main points in a lecture are, by watching and listening carefully to the lecturer. Body language and tone of voice often indicate key points. Thumping the lectern is not always temper! Finally, do not go back to bed after a lecture and forget all about it! Try to review your notes as soon as possible after the lecture and write a summary in your own words of what the lecturer had to say.

I know that I am probably making it sound very straightforward and manageable, when of course this note taking business is not easy at all. In my experience, lecturers will often go off on some tangent, making points and references which only he or she and his or her coterie of fellow 'obscure facts about Ibsen' fans find fascinating, thereby alienating the entire room (sorry Dr Davies, please forgive me!) However, if you follow my tips I am sure you will find things a little less overwhelming in the first few weeks. Take them with my blessing, and good luck one and all!

Reading comprehension: Valuable skills to learn (30 min)   Go online

Read the passage once more and answer the questions which follow.

How to take notes

Having just completed my third year of full time study at this amazing university, and having by some freak accident, I can only imagine, been elected to vice president of the student union, I am very keen to share some wisdom with all newbies. For all of you out there who are embarking on the first stage of your university career with, no doubt, great fear and trepidation as well as major excitement, I would like to take this opportunity in the first edition of Campus this year to offer you all the information and tips I have for your edification on note taking.

Effective note taking is one of the most important skills you can learn for university study. It provides you with a record of all the lectures and tutorials which you attend and can therefore be used for exam revision, seminars, presentations and essay preparation. You can use notes to help you to identify the origins of your thoughts and as a starting point for development of your own thoughts and ideas. Another important point to remember is that good notes are invaluable as a trading commodity, because one day you will sleep in and miss a lecture or tutorial! If you have been generous with your notes then you can expect others to be equally generous with you on the occasion that you miss an important lecture.

Effective note taking involves a few basic principles, so let me begin with the skill of taking notes while reading. In the first place it is really important that you have ascertained what your task is! I am not being facetious here. There is no point in spending hours and hours as I have done to my cost, reading scores of pages of some dull tome hoping to extract key information without first working out what the essay or seminar question is. Targeted reading is crucial and will save a lot of time. Skim reading and scanning for an overview will also save time. After all, one can't spend all one's university days in the library can one? It is also crucial to get into the habit of asking yourself, what are the main points of this discussion? Try very hard not to use the writer's words; it is a tad slower but if you read, digest and then rewrite in your own words, not only will you have a better understanding of what you have read but you will also have a substantial amount of a possible future essay already written! Remember to record sources, particularly of quotes so that you can reference sources properly. Use diagrams, colour pens, highlighters and anything else you can think of to make information clear.

Now let me move on to taking notes while listening. Some of the strategies are the same, but of course while listening you are not really able to stop the process because you dozed off! It is vital to remain alert throughout and I have a few tips here too. Number one, try to get some sleep before lectures! Hmm, well okay it's not always possible! Seriously though folks, try to go prepared by reading around the subject beforehand and working out meanings of new concepts and vocabulary. Again target your listening, try to establish the main points under discussion and take relevant notes. Do not write everything down, but do use abbreviations to minimise time spent writing down important points. Mind maps, diagrams and pictures can help the visual learners among us. Try to pick up on what the main points in a lecture are, by watching and listening carefully to the lecturer. Body language and tone of voice often indicate key points. Thumping the lectern is not always temper! Finally, do not go back to bed after a lecture and forget all about it! Try to review your notes as soon as possible after the lecture and write a summary in your own words of what the lecturer had to say.

I know that I am probably making it sound very straightforward and manageable, when of course this note taking business is not easy at all. In my experience, lecturers will often go off on some tangent, making points and references which only he or she and his or her coterie of fellow 'obscure facts about Ibsen' fans find fascinating, thereby alienating the entire room (sorry Dr Davies, please forgive me!) However, if you follow my tips I am sure you will find things a little less overwhelming in the first few weeks. Take them with my blessing, and good luck one and all!

Q53: Which adjective best describes the writer's tone?

a) serious

b) conversational

c) casual

....

Q54: What is the main purpose of the piece of writing?

a) Providing Instruction

b) Giving Rules

c) Sharing General information

....

Q55: What serious idea does the writer think might be received as a joke? What word tells you this?

....

Q56: What time-saving measures does the writer recommend to support note taking while listening?

a) Do not write down everything / use abbreviations

b) Do not write down everything / record the lecture

c) Record the lecture / use abbreviations

2.9   Listening comprehension: Carole

You will need access to the sound file *hg-cesl2-2-3listening.mp3* to complete this listening comprehension.

Listen to the dialogue and then try the activity.

Listening comprehension: Carole (30 min)   Go online

You need access to the sound file *hg-cesl2-2-3listening.mp3*.

Q57: What is the purpose of the lecture/talk?

....

Q58: Does the speaker think that the non-bookable PCs are safe option? What word in the text tells you this?

....

Q59: What is the advantage of being a final year or postgraduate student? (three word phrase)

....

Q60: What word indicates that the speaker expected a particular question?

....

Q61: What three word phrase in the text is used to describe the failure to accomplish something?

2.10 Vocabulary list

This is a list of useful vocabulary which is intended to supplement what you have learned. It may also be useful to refer to when attempting the speaking and writing activities within the topic.

to alleviate (verb)	to make pain or problems less severe
to advocate (verb)	to publically support / suggest an idea
compromising (adjective)	causing damage to reputation
discrete (adjective)	having a clear independent / separate shape or form
to envisage (verb)	to imagine or expect something in the future
fundamental (adjective)	of central importance
generic (adjective)	characteristic of a whole group or class
militates (against) (phrasal verb)	makes something less likely to happen
niche (noun)	job or position which is perfect for someone
nostalgia (noun)	feeling of pleasure combined with sadness which accompanies thoughts of the past
to perceive (verb)	believe or understand something
precedent (noun)	an action or decision which has happened before and can be used as argument for future decision
to resurrect (verb)	to bring back to life someone or something which has been dead
scores (noun)	large numbers
to substantiate (verb)	demonstrate something to be true
tangent (noun)	new and unrelated topic
therapeutic (adjective)	making one feel happier and more relaxed
unconstitutional (adjective)	not allowed within the rules governing a country
unduly (adverb)	more than is necessary
unpremeditated (adjective)	done without thought or planning

Unit 2 Topic 3

Politics

Contents

Learning objective

By the end of this topic you should be able to:

- use a wider range of vocabulary in the topic area

- use modal verbs with greater accuracy

- demonstrate your knowledge of writing genre through writing a discursive essay

- demonstrate an ability to undertake research and give a presentation

- demonstrate your knowledge of writing genre through writing a report

This topic examines politics, specifically political systems in the UK and overseas, political parties, figures and political issues. It revises grammar points which should be familiar to learners at this level, covering modal verbs. Advanced vocabulary relevant to the topic of politics is introduced and practised through a variety of activities. The topic includes work on all four skills: speaking, reading, writing, and listening. There are also supplementary pronunciation exercises. Assessment opportunities occur at the end of the topic.

Certain sections contain sound files. You may download these here and use them on your mp3 player or equivalent to practise your pronunciation. This may be very useful if there are times when you will not have access to the materials online.

3.1   Grammar: Modal verbs

Rules and Regulations

Political language contains many examples of obligation, permission and prohibition.   The grammatical concepts used to express these are commonly the modal verbs **must** and **have to**.

3.1.1   The verb: Must

Must is used when the obligation for us to do something comes from within.

> **Example** I must remember to cast my vote today.

Must can also be used, in some instances, in the same way as *have to*

> **Example** You must address the speaker as 'the Right Honourable Gentleman'.

Form

The form of must is the same in all persons, and it is followed by the base form of the verb.

I	must
you	must
he/she/it	must
we	must
you	must
they	must

 There is no must to in English.

Negative

Must not is the negative form in all persons and it expresses an obligation not to do something. It is followed by the infinitive of the verb.

Example The Prime Minister mustn't go back on his promise of tax cuts for the people.

Past

Must changes to *had to* in the past.

Example I must remember to contact my MP,
becomes
I had to remember to contact my MP.

 There is no negative form of must in the past. DO NOT use didn't have to because this has an entirely different meaning.

A close alternative to *mustn't* in the past would be:

Example You mustn't spoil your ballot paper. (Present with *must*)

You shouldn't have spoiled your ballot paper. (Present perfect with *should*)

 was/were not allowed to is another option for making must negative in the past.

Future

Must does not have any future form.

To express this idea of obligation in the future, we use *have to.*

Example I must remember to vote. (Present with *must*)

I will have to remember to vote tomorrow. (Future with *have to*)

3.1.2   The verb: Have to

Have to is used when we are obliged to do something under the orders of someone or something else, particularly official lawmaking bodies such as the government or police.

Examples

1. You have to pay your council tax if you don't qualify for an exemption.

. . . .

2. We all have to work until our sixties before we reach retirement age.

Form

The form of *have to* is the same in all persons except for third person (where *has to* is used), and it is followed by the infinitive of the verb.

I	have to
you	have to
he/she/it	has to
we	have to
you	have to
they	have to

Negative

Don't have to is the negative form in all persons except third person (*Doesn't have to*) and it expresses a lack of obligation, i.e. a choice. It is followed by the infinitive of the verb.

Example You don't have to vote in the general election. It's up to you.

Past

Have to becomes *had to* in the past.

Example I have to register my new voting address,
becomes
I had to register my new voting address.

 The negative form of have to in the past also expresses a lack of obligation on a deed already completed:

Example You didn't have to vote so early in the morning. The ballot boxes were open all day.

Future

Will have to' or '*going to have to*' are used for the future.

Examples

1. I will have to think about voting differently next time.

. . . .

2. I'm going to have to consider who to vote for very carefully.

3.2   Political vocabulary

This section contains a series of activities exploring different aspects of vocabulary in the context of politics.

Political vocabulary: Definitions (15 min)   Go online

Q1:   Match the words in the first list with their corresponding definitions taken from the second list.

1. undemocratic
2. monarchy
3. regime
4. coalition
5. boycott
6. constituency
7. legislature
8. referendum
9. partisan
10. rhetoric

A) an organised group with the authority to create laws
B) a true and loyal supporter of a political party or cause
C) the practice of putting forward a proposal to popular vote
D) a group of residents in an electoral district, or the electoral district itself
E) the art of speaking as a means of political persuasion
F) to refuse to deal with, or engage in discussion over, the acceptance of an idea
G) an alliance of two or more political parties, for example, to form a collaborative government
H) not in agreement with democratic practice or ideals
I) a type of government with a hereditary head of state who may or may not have significant political influence
J) a government which is currently in power

Political vocabulary: Spelling (10 min)   Go online

You will need sound files *hg-cesl2-3-1spelling1.mp3* to *hg-cesl2-3-1spelling10.mp3*

Listen to the following political words being read aloud. After you have listened to all ten, compare your spellings with the correct ones.

Q2:   *hg-cesl2-3-1spelling1.mp3*

....

Q3:   hg-cesl2-3-1spelling2.mp3

....

Q4:   hg-cesl2-3-1spelling3.mp3

....

Q5:   hg-cesl2-3-1spelling4.mp3

....

Q6:   hg-cesl2-3-1spelling5.mp3

....

Q7:   hg-cesl2-3-1spelling6mp3

....

Q8:   hg-cesl2-3-1spelling7.mp3

....

Q9:   hg-cesl2-3-1spelling8.mp3

....

Q10:   hg-cesl2-3-1spelling9.mp3

....

Q11:   hg-cesl2-3-1spelling10.mp3

3.3   Political vocabulary: Pronunciation

Pronunciation (15 min)

Q12: How many syllables does each of the following words have and where is the stress in each word?

1. undemocratic
2. monarchy
3. regime
4. coalition
5. boycott
6. constituency
7. legislature
8. referendum
9. partisan
10. rhetoric

3.4 Writing: Voter apathy

Writing: Voter apathy (60 min)

The table below shows the turnout (percentage of registered voters) in UK general elections in recent history.

Year	Turnout (%)
1992	77.7
1997	71.4
2001	59.4
2005	61.4
2010	65.1
2015	66.1

Your local MP has asked you to produce a report about voter apathy to help her prepare for her election campaign. In your report, you should:

- Look at the statistics in the table and discuss any trends or changes in the figures.

- Use your own knowledge and consult at least two external sources to discuss reasons for voter apathy .

- Consider ways that politicians can attract more voters in elections

Before you begin, consider the following questions:

1. What is the purpose of the communication?

2. Who is the intended audience?

3. What level of formality and register would be appropriate?

Make some notes or a mind map to help plan your writing before you begin.

Write a report of between 300 - 350 words.

When you have finished ask your teacher or tutor to check your work.

A model answer is also provided.

3.5   Vocabulary: More political words

Vocabulary: More political words (15 min)   Go online

Select one of the words from the given list to complete each sentence.

List: soapbox: backbench: by-election: devolution: autocracy: electorate: incumbent: spin: whip: veto:

Q13: Government ministers proposed to introduce tax reforms but there was a _____ due to the response of many backbenchers, so it looks unlikely to happen.

....

Q14: The president is just using social networking media as a new kind of digital _____ to put his point across.

....

Q15: They called it a successful consolidation of their overall national vote, but that was just _____ . In reality, they lost twenty-five seats across the country.

....

Q16: I think there will have to be a _____ for his seat. After such a scandal coming out in the press, there is no way he can remain an MP, never mind a member of the cabinet.

....

Q17: The Welsh Assembly may push further for their own cause, depending on the outcome of the _____ process in Scotland.

Spelling: More political words (20 min)   Go online

In each case, rearrange the letters to spell out further words connected to politics. Use the definitions as a clue to help you.

Q18: xpsobao: a (metaphorical) platform for people to put forward a political opinion

....

Q19: hkbeanbcc: the place where the ordinary MPs sit in parliament (not cabinet members)

....

Q20: ee-tblyocin: a special election held between regular elections, in order to fill a vacancy due to resignation, retirement or death of an MP

....

Q21: nevlodtiou: transference of rights or powers to another body from central government

....

Q22: ccraaytou: a system of government in which one person has unlimited power

....

Q23: taretceleo: the collective name for all the people entitled to vote

....

Q24: cimnubten: the present government is referred to as being this

....

Q25: nisp: to present political information in a slanted way to make it appear positive or negative

....

Q26: pihw: to gather all members of a party together for an important vote or parliamentary session

....

Q27: tove: one part of government or opposition acting to prohibit the proposal of another part of government

3.6 Speaking: Political systems

Revise this topic before you try the next activity.

Speaking: Political Systems (60 min)

The UK system of election (First Past the Post) is an example of a democratic electoral system. Consider this electoral system in comparison to another system of voting in an election. You should research at least two external sources either online or by making use of your school or college library, and use these sources to help you make notes about the advantages and disadvantages of each political system.

Think about the following points:

- Provide an introduction and explanation of the two systems of voting

- Discuss the fairness of each system

- Talk about the advantages and disadvantages each system has

- Provide a conclusion with your own opinion

You should prepare a Powerpoint (or similar) presentation with approximately 10 slides lasting 8 - 10 minutes on the above points. When you feel ready, you should present this in front of your class or your teacher (or you could video record yourself presenting, if you are studying from home).

Your teacher or other students should prepare questions to ask you at the end of your presentation.

Before you present, you should ask your teacher or tutor to check your work and give you feedback on your presentation.

3.7   Reading comprehension: UK Elections

The following activity is a reading comprehension covering the work of this topic.

Before you begin read the passage. Read the passage quickly to grasp the gist of it.

Despite the best efforts of opponents recently, the First Past the Post system remains the electoral system which is used in British society. At times of general elections or by-elections, registered candidates compete directly against each other in a numbers game, where the person with the most votes in their designated constituency gains the seat in that election. Due to the large volume of voters in constituencies nowadays, the process tends to be a straightforward one and recounts are rarely necessary.

The history of the First Past the Post system dates back hundreds of years, although in its earlier incarnations it was just as controversial as it is today, for very different reasons. In the eighteenth century, some of the boroughs which where contested were miniscule in size and population; in one English village an MP was elected by the solitary voter in the borough!

Proponents of the First Past the Post system cite its main advantage as being its simplicity. It is cheap and easy to administer (voters have only one choice to make on the ballot paper) and the turnaround from when votes are cast until they are counted and totalled is a relatively speedy process. For example, in the last general election, 99% of constituencies had returned their results within twenty-four hours of the ballot boxes closing.

The main critics of the First Past the Post system within the UK had long been the Liberal Democrat party. Since the 1970s, the Conservative and Labour parties have repeatedly traded places in the power stakes, leaving other parties looking in from the outside and making up the numbers. It is somewhat ironic then, that it is through this system that the Lib Dems achieved their elevation to becoming part of a coalition government.

The Alternative Vote system is what those who are against First Past the Post would like to see in its place. The Alternative Vote refers to a system of Proportional Representation, but it was overwhelmingly rejected by the British public when a referendum was held to establish public opinion.

The counter-argument from the supporters of First Past the Post is to direct attention towards nations which do not use the system, and the resultant political instability and regular change of government which occurs there. In addition to this, the subdivision of constituencies among MPs (a result of Proportional Representation) could lead to confusion about who is actually the representative member to contact when a member of the public needs direct political assistance.

There have historically been occasions in which the percentage of public vote has not been representative of how the nation voted. Twice in the history of the UK parliamentary election has a government been elected through First Past the Post while having a lower number of nationwide votes, and this scenario is commonplace in by-elections. Champions of Proportional Representation point to this as further evidence of how the First Past the Post system does not accurately reflect public opinion.

Is First Past the Post democratic? Is Proportional Representation fairer? There will always be split opinion on the matter, and vociferous campaigning for change from the minority parties, but while the Conservatives and Labour remain the heavyweights in the UK political arena, in no small part due to First Past the Post, that system is unlikely to be replaced in the foreseeable future.

Reading comprehension: UK Elections (30 min)   Go online

Read the passage once more and answer the questions which follow.

Despite the best efforts of opponents recently, the First Past the Post system remains the electoral system which is used in British society. At times of general elections or by-elections, registered candidates compete directly against each other in a numbers game, where the person with the most votes in their designated constituency gains the seat in that election. Due to the large volume of voters in constituencies nowadays, the process tends to be a straightforward one and recounts are rarely necessary.

The history of the First Past the Post system dates back hundreds of years, although in its earlier incarnations it was just as controversial as it is today, for very different reasons. In the eighteenth century, some of the boroughs which where contested were miniscule in size and population; in one English village an MP was elected by the solitary voter in the borough!

Proponents of the First Past the Post system cite its main advantage as being its simplicity. It is cheap and easy to administer (voters have only one choice to make on the ballot paper) and the turnaround from when votes are cast until they are counted and totalled is a relatively speedy process. For example, in the last general election, 99% of constituencies had returned their results within twenty-four hours of the ballot boxes closing.

The main critics of the First Past the Post system within the UK had long been the Liberal Democrat party. Since the 1970s, the Conservative and Labour parties have repeatedly traded places in the power stakes, leaving other parties looking in from the outside and making up the numbers. It is somewhat ironic then, that it is through this system that the Lib Dems achieved their elevation to becoming part of a coalition government in 2010.

The Alternative Vote system is what those who are against First Past the Post would like to see in its place. The Alternative Vote refers to a system of Proportional Representation, but it was overwhelmingly rejected by the British public when a referendum was held to establish public opinion.

The counter-argument from the supporters of First Past the Post is to direct attention towards nations which do not use the system, and the resultant political instability and regular change of government which occurs there. In addition to this, the subdivision of constituencies among MPs (a result of Proportional Representation) could lead to confusion about who is actually the representative member to contact when a member of the public needs direct political assistance.

There have historically been occasions in which the percentage of public vote has not been representative of how the nation voted. Twice in the history of the UK parliamentary election has a government been elected through First Past the Post while having a lower number of nationwide votes, and this scenario is commonplace in by-elections. Champions of Proportional Representation point to this as further evidence of how the First Past the Post system does not accurately reflect public opinion.

Is First Past the Post democratic? Is Proportional Representation fairer? There will always be split opinion on the matter, and vociferous campaigning for change from the minority parties, but while the Conservatives and Labour remain the heavyweights in the UK political arena, in no small part due to First Past the Post, that system is unlikely to be replaced in the foreseeable future.

Q28: Decide, from the passage, if the following statements are

- true
- false

1. First Past the Post always results in a clear outcome without need for a recount.
2. The Liberal Democrats were helped by the First Past the Post System in recent history.
3. The UK's traditional left and right wing parties are the chief beneficiaries of the First Past the Post system.

....

Q29: Find a word which means *shapes*, or *forms* in the article

....

Q30: Find a word which means *extremely small* in the article

....

Q31: Find a word which means *typical* or *usual* in the article

....

Q32: In paragraph 5, in the phrase "... it was overwhelmingly rejected by the British public...", what does the word 'it' refer to? (two or three word answer)

....

Q33: In paragraph 6, in the phrase "In addition to this...", what does the word 'this' refer to? (two word answer)

3.8 Listening comprehension: The monarchy

Now you have completed the topic, listen to the following assessment dialogue. It contains examples of many of the language areas you have covered within the topic.

You will need access to the sound file *hg-cesl2-3-2listening.mp3* to complete this listening comprehension.

Before listening think about the following:

1. Do you have a royal family in your country?

2. What do you know about your royal family, or the royal family in the UK?

3. Do you think people today are in favour of, or against the idea of a monarchy?

Listen to the passage before you try the activity.

Listening comprehension: The monarchy (30 min)   Go online

You will need access to the sound file *hg-cesl2-3-2listening.mp3* to complete this listening comprehension.

Listen to two speakers, Eleanor and Mike, giving their opinions about the monarchy. You may wish to take some notes as you listen in order to answer the questions which follow.

Q34: Decide which speaker (Eleanor or Mike) said each statement.

1. The monarchy dominate the newspapers.

2. A lot of royals have the best jobs.

3. Most of the country actually love the royal family.

4. MPs are a sorry group of untrustworthy people.

5. There's a lot of over the top ceremony involved with the monarchy.

6. The publicity the royal family brings is crucial.

Listen again and answer the following questions.

Q35: Which adjective does Eleanor use to describe the unclear history of the Commonwealth?

....

Q36: Eleanor says that people abroad appreciate royal visits. Is this true or false?

....

Q37: Eleanor is sad about the attitude of sports stars towards the monarchy. Is this true or false?

....

Q38: Which noun does Eleanor use to describe people who would prefer to have no monarchy at all, which she believes would result in chaos?

....

Q39: Which noun does Mike use to describe the lack of power associated with the monarchy these days?

....

Q40: Mike thinks the monarchy should end immediately. Is this true or false?

....

Q41: Mike has nothing positive to say about the royal family. Is this true or false?

....

Q42: Which adjective does Mike use to describe the idea of the royal family being out of date?

3.9 Vocabulary list

This is a list of useful vocabulary which is intended to supplement what you have learned. It may also be useful to refer to when attempting the speaking and writing activities within the topic.

to abdicate (verb)	to give up power (in the case of a king or queen)
bill (noun)	a proposed law under consideration by a legislature
bureaucracy (noun)	a government marked by its fixed rules and hierarchical structure
chambers (noun)	the houses comprising parliament
Commons (noun)	the lower house of the UK parliament
coup (noun)	a sudden uprising against, or overthrowing of a government by an opposition group
doctrine (noun)	a government policy statement
to lobby (verb)	to attempt to influence or persuade towards a desired outcome or action
Lords (noun)	the upper house of the UK parliament
to nominate (verb)	to put oneself or be put forward by others as a candidate for election
opinion poll (noun)	a survey of public opinion from a sample group representative of the wider population
parliamentarian (noun)	a member of a parliament
to petition (verb)	to make a formal (usually written) request for change
polling station (noun)	a place where the electorate go to vote in local or general elections, often within a community building such as a school
reform (noun)	an amendment to correct defective, out-of-date or unpopular policy
solidarity (noun)	a political unity based on common beliefs, interests or aims
speaker (noun)	the presiding officer of an assembly, such as the House of Commons
spoiled/spoilt paper (noun)	an incorrectly marked ballot paper in a vote (either deliberately or accidentally) which therefore does not count towards any of the parties' final standing
summit (noun)	a meeting or conference of high-ranking officials / heads of state
turnout (noun)	the total number of people who vote in an election

Unit 2 Topic 4

Global issues

Contents

Learning objective

By the end of this topic you should be able to:

- use a wider range of vocabulary in the topic area of climate change

- use adjectives with greater accuracy

- demonstrate your knowledge of writing genre through writing an opinion essay

- demonstrate your knowledge of writing genre through writing a report

This topic examines climate change and natural disasters around the world. It revives the use of adjectives, examining and practising the order of adjectives in English. Advanced vocabulary relevant to the topic of climate change and natural disaster is introduced and practised through a variety of activities. The topic includes work on all four skills: speaking, reading, writing, and listening. There are also supplementary pronunciation exercises. Assessment opportunities occur at the end of the topic.

Certain sections contain sound files. You may download these here and use them on your mp3 player or equivalent to practise your pronunciation. This may be very useful if there are times when you will not have access to the materials online.

4.1   Vocabulary: Climate change

Vocabulary: Climate change (20 min)

Find a word or phrase that fits each description.

Choose from the list provided:

Wordlist: reforestation: fossil fuel: acidification: famine: desertification: greenhouse gas: precipitation: deforestation: drought: emission

Q1:   A situation in which there is not enough food for people to eat, and there is widespread starvation:

. . . .

Q2:   A situation in which there has been no rain for a long period of time and the land dries out, making it impossible to grow crops:

. . . .

Q3:   The collective name for coal, oil and other naturally occurring resources which we burn for energy:

. . . .

Q4:   This absorbs infrared radiation and acts as a heat shield, thereby increasing the earth's temperature. Carbon dioxide and Methane are two examples of it:

. . . .

Q5:   This is the production and discharge of a gas into the atmosphere:

. . . .

Q6:   This is the process of a liquid or substance falling to the ground, e.g. rain:

. . . .

Q7:   This is the process of replacing trees in an area where they were previously logged or destroyed by natural causes:

. . . .

Q8: This is the process of something becoming acidic through contamination, e.g. rain:

....

Q9: This is the process of formerly arable land becoming dry and arid, unsuitable for growing crops, due to drought or human activity:

....

Q10: This is the process of logging, or removing trees from an area for use in construction or as fuel, or to clear areas for building:

Vocabulary in context (20 min)   Go online

Q11: Use the words in the list to complete the sentences. Some sentences use two of the options.

List: famine: drought: fossil fuel: greenhouse gases: emissions: precipitation: reforestation: acidification: desertification: deforestation

1. Don't you care about the damage you're causing to the environment? All those aerosols in that bathroom cabinet are adding to the build-up of_____

2. The amount of pollution in our atmosphere is causing _____ in rainfall. Harmful _____ like that can't be good for anything living on our planet.

3. The Kyoto Protocol was supposed to force the world's superpowers to reduce their _____, but there has been little sign of that and we are still burning our _____ resources at an alarming rate.

4. _____ has been a problem in the Amazon for some time, although the _____ efforts of conservationists are beginning to redress the balance. There is a long way to go, however.

5. _____ in parts of Africa, when combined with the problems they have with _____, means that _____ is an all too frequent and tragic consequence.

4.2 Pronunciation: Climate change

Pronunciation: Climate change (15 min)   Go online

You will need access to the sound files *hg-cesl2-4-1pronoun1.mp3* to *hg-cesl2-4-1pronoun10.mp3* to be able to complete the question which follows.

Q12: Look at the following word list

Listen to the words being read aloud.

How many syllables does each word have, and where is the word stress in each word?

1. famine
2. drought
3. fossil fuel
4. greenhouse gas
5. emission
6. precipitation
7. reforestation
8. acidification
9. desertification
10. deforestation

4.3 Grammar: Adjectives

Adjectives are everywhere in English. As a more advanced learner you will be aware of the function of adjectives in English to describe characteristics and properties of various objects, people and places. We will now revise the order of adjectives and the rules governing their use.

Adjective order:

The most commonly occurring type of adjective in English is the attributive. *Scary* is an attributive adjective in scary event. In English, attributive adjectives usually come*It was an event scary enough to make the residents leave their homes.*

The order of adjectives in a sentence has particular rules. The following mnemonic may help you remember adjectival order in English:

OSSACOM

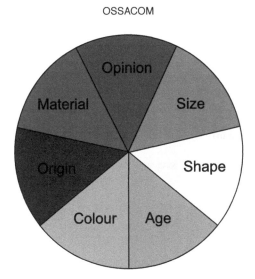

Opinion: what a person thinks or feels about something

    Example interesting, dangerous, terrible

Size: the dimensions or physicality of an object

    Example huge, small, gigantic

Shape: the physical form of an object

    Example round, oval, square

Age: how old an object/person is

    Example old, new, modern

Colour: the colour of an object

    Example red, green, black

Origin: where something/someone comes from

    Example Italian, American, alien

Material: what something is constructed from

Example wooden, metallic, plastic

 This is a guide which will help you remember the order of adjectives in most situations in English. However, there are exceptions to the rule above.

Adjective category (10 min)   Go online

Q13: Decide which category the following adjectives would fit into. Some may be suitable for more than one category:

1. synthetic
2. amber
3. destructive
4. ancient
5. cylindrical
6. conical
7. monstrous
8. historical
9. European
10. colossal

Adjective order (10 min)   Go online

Q14: Following the OSSACOM system, put the following adjectives into the correct order to describe the noun:

1. enormous - plume - suffocating - grey
2. molten - red hot - metal - hazardous
3. covering - deathly - white - fine

 It is uncommon to use more than three adjectives to describe one noun but not unheard of especially in reportage.

 Example *A terrifying huge red lava flow.*

4.4 Writing: Climate change

Writing: Climate change (60 min)

Climate change is a topic concerning many companies and individuals these days. There are differing opinions on its causes, its contributory factors and on government and individual responsibilities towards halting its effects.

Write an essay on this topic. You should include the following points and may add ideas of your own:

- What is climate change?

- What are the contributory factors?

- What can large companies and their staff do to prevent the problem escalating?

- What can the government do to help companies be more environmentally friendly?

Before you begin, consider the following questions:

1. What is the purpose of the communication?

2. Who is the intended audience?

3. What level of formality and register would be appropriate?

Make some notes or a mind map to help plan your writing before you begin.

Write an essay of between 300 - 350 words.

When you have finished ask your teacher or tutor to check your work or check it with the model answer.

4.5   Vocabulary: Natural disasters

Crossword: Natural disasters (20 min)   Go online

Q15: Complete the crossword with the clues provided.

Across

4   the act or process of spouting material or liquid forcibly from something, e.g. a volcano

5   molten rock which is sent forth from a volcano

6   the column of air which resembles a coiled spring, another word for tornado

7   molten rock material under the earth's crust

8   this affects a huge number of individuals within a population or country at once, and is often used to describe the spread of airborne viruses

9   snow, ice, earth or rock which travels quickly and suddenly down a mountain, covering everything in its path snow, ice, earth or rock which travels quickly and suddenly down a mountain, covering everything in its path

Down

1   a minor follow-up seismic event, which follows the main earthquake

2   this affects a huge number of individuals within several countries across borders and seas, and is often used to describe the spread of airborne viruses

3   rock or stone coming free from a hillside, cliff, or slope and travelling downward at a rapid speed

4   the act or process of escaping from a place in danger

Vocabulary: Natural disasters (15 min)   Go online

Q16: Complete each sentence with one of the words from the list.

List: avalanche: landslide: evacuation: aftershock: eruption: lava: twister: magma: epidemic: pandemic

1. The north run is closed today, so we'll have to ski over on the south run instead. Apparently there was an _____ yesterday.

2. The forces of nature are a sight to behold. Thankfully everyone got off the bus in time before the _____ flipped it into the air as if it were a toy. Amazing, and terrifying all at once!

3. Bird flu never quite became the _____ that everyone thought it might a few years ago.

4. Scientists are monitoring the stability of the _____ chambers to get an indication of the likelihood of the volcano's future activity.

5. The tsunami warning was observed by everyone in the village and the community leaders were pleased with their successful _____ rehearsal.

6. The parasitic infection caused by a new species of horse fly has now been discovered in twenty-one states in the USA. It could become an _____ .

7. The _____ flow engulfed the homes of all the townspeople who lived on the mountainside.

8. The _____ of Krakatoa is a legendary event in Indonesian history. That part of the world became enshrouded in darkness for weeks.

9. Mountain rescue teams were called in to help motorists who became stranded under rubble from the sudden _____ .

10. Residents were just starting to return to their homes when the first _____ hit. Fortunately, it seems that there were no casualties, but authorities are warning people to remain outside city limits for the time being.

4.6   Listening: Preserved in time

Listening: Preserved in time (25 min)   Go online

You will need access to the sound file *hg-cesl2-4-2listening.mp3* to be able to complete this question.

Listen to the dialogue twice.

Q17: Complete the passage by filling in the missing words.

The once proud Roman town of Pompeii is now 1._____ with only one event, the 2. _____ eruption of the sleeping giant, Mount Vesuvius, in AD 79. Indeed, for the best part of two 3. _____, Pompeii existed only in historical reference, the actual 4. _____ being buried by the age old remnants of an event which was as devastating to mankind at that time as the Hiroshima bomb was in the twentieth century. A lethal 5. _____ of ash and fumes rocketed more than twenty miles into the air, dispersing grey cloud across the region and turning day into night.

And so Pompeii lay, untouched and 6. _____ for around eighteen hundred years. Records show that 7. _____ started in the 1860s, and archaeological teams since that date have unearthed not only the ruins of foundations of Roman buildings within Pompeii, buried under the 8. _____ layers left by the 9. _____ flows, but some of the unsuspecting residents themselves, petrified in ash and forever preserved in an 10. _____, but intriguingly lasting testament to the carnage caused by the power of the volcano.

The pyroclastic flows, lava and lahars which ran down the mountainside at temperatures of 1300 degrees Fahrenheit, were the main killer. The vertical explosion and the resultant ash cloud added to the casualties, but the 11. _____ speed of the flows is what 12. _____ the town and more than 15,000 of its inhabitants.

Today, the once lost town of Pompeii is a popular tourist attraction, with millions of visitors worldwide travelling to see the ruins and experience the 13. _____ tale first hand. Vesuvius has not erupted since 1944, and never with the same 14. _____ as recorded in Roman times, but nevertheless, its silent threat looms large over the hordes of souvenir hunters, with experts theorising that the longer the volcano lies dormant, the greater the significance and 15. _____ any future eruption will have.

4.7   Writing: Coping with disasters

Writing: Coping with disasters (60 min)

Natural disasters usually strike quickly and unpredictably.   However, there are some precautions and emergency planning procedures that can be readied in advance.

The manager of the company you work for has asked you to write a report for all staff telling them how to prepare for an unexpected and sudden flood in the area.

You should include information on:

- What the company can do to physically prepare offices, e.g. equipment to buy

- What ideas and training can be put in place — escape plans, food / rations etc.

- General advice on how staff should react and behave in such a situation.

You should use your own knowledge and consult external sources to help you answer the question.

Before you begin, consider the following questions:

1. What is the purpose of the communication?

2. Who is the intended audience?

3. What level of formality and register would be appropriate?

Make some notes or a mind map to help plan your writing before you begin.

Write a report of between 300 - 350 words.

When you have finished ask your teacher or tutor to check your work.

A model answer has also been provided for you to compare with your work.

4.8   Reading comprehension: The most destructive volcano

The following activity is a reading comprehension covering the work of this topic.

Read the passage quickly to grasp the gist of it.

The most destructive volcano in the world is not situated in Italy or a remote mountain range in Asia, but in one of the USA's most frequented tourist destinations. . . and it is potentially thousands of times more devastating than Krakatoa. In recent years, buoyed by the wizardry of its CGI depiction in Hollywood movies, the Yellowstone 'Super-volcano' has become more than mere doomsday pseudoscience. Scientists predict that an eruption of the interconnected geothermal system bubbling under the park's hot sulphuric springs could bring an end to the world as we know it. Such an explosion from the 'Caldera', as it is known, would result in the blanketing of North America in thick ash. The knock-on effect could be cataclysmic, with the atmospheric shift caused by that event affecting global climate in a way that could lead to the extinction of the human race.

Geologists and historians have determined that the last eruption of the super-volcano most probably occurred over half a million years ago, and that, much like the regularity of the park's most famous geyser, Old Faithful, the approximate timescale can be predicted - although in this case the time frame is in hundreds of thousands of years - 500,000 to 700,000 years, meaning that we are potentially already within the danger zone. Volcanologists are constantly monitoring the tectonic activity of the super-volcano from the ranger outposts in the park. This ever-present early warning team are always on guard for clues toward anything unusual in the rumblings of the geothermal features, in case they give an indication of forthcoming catastrophe.

However, it is not quite as straightforward as listening out for signs of an impending eruption. Regular subterranean earthquakes, subsistence of the ground in and around the thermal features, and changes in the regularity of the eruptions of these features are all warnings of volcanic activity, but they are all commonly recorded phenomena within the region, and therefore it is more a question of the intensity of these features that concerns the experts, as opposed to the frequency of their occurrence.

The monitoring team in the park post regular volcano warning levels, not unlike the terror levels issued by western governments, but happily for all of humankind, since their watch began the monthly alert level has kept its default status of 'normal'. They are likely to change the status only in extreme circumstances, for example were there to be a huge hydrothermal explosion in the park.

Much of the science of the fragility and volatility of tectonic plates is outside the realms of scientific comprehension at present, and therefore the periodic past activity of volcanoes and earthquakes serves as the basis for much of the knowledge of probable future eruptions. The episodic nature of Yellowstone's volcanic history means that scientists are in agreement that it is a question of when, and not if, another eruption will happen. However, although they believe we are now at risk of the super-volcano detonating, scientists do console us by restating the theory that we may yet have a 200,000 year buffer before the big one. Perhaps, by that time, evolution and progress in science will have found a way to suppress or evade one of the biggest hazards that lurks just a few miles beneath our earth's surface.

Reading comprehension: The most destructive volcano (30 min) Go online

Read the passage once more and answer the questions which follow.

The most destructive volcano in the world is not situated in Italy or a remote mountain range in Asia, but in one of the USA's most frequented tourist destinations... and it is potentially thousands of times more devastating than Krakatoa. In recent years, buoyed by the wizardry of its CGI depiction in Hollywood movies, the Yellowstone 'Super-volcano' has become more than mere doomsday pseudoscience. Scientists predict that an eruption of the interconnected geothermal system bubbling under the park's hot sulphuric springs could bring an end to the world as we know it. Such an explosion from the 'Caldera', as it is known, would result in the blanketing of North America in thick ash. The knock-on effect could be cataclysmic, with the atmospheric shift caused by that event affecting global climate in a way that could lead to the extinction of the human race.

Geologists and historians have determined that the last eruption of the super-volcano most probably occurred over half a million years ago, and that, much like the regularity of the park's most famous geyser, Old Faithful, the approximate timescale can be predicted - although in this case the time frame is in hundreds of thousands of years - 500,000 to 700,000 years, meaning that we are potentially already within the danger zone. Volcanologists are constantly monitoring the tectonic activity of the super-volcano from the ranger outposts in the park. This ever-present early warning team are always on guard for clues toward anything unusual in the rumblings of the geothermal features, in case they give an indication of forthcoming catastrophe.

However, it is not quite as straightforward as listening out for signs of an impending eruption. Regular subterranean earthquakes, subsistence of the ground in and around the thermal features, and changes in the regularity of the eruptions of these features are all warnings of volcanic activity, but they are all commonly recorded phenomena within the region, and therefore it is more a question of the intensity of these features that concerns the experts, as opposed to the frequency of their occurrence.

The monitoring team in the park post regular volcano warning levels, not unlike the terror levels issued by western governments, but happily for all of humankind, since their watch began the monthly alert level has kept its default status of 'normal'. They are likely to change the status only in extreme circumstances, for example were there to be a huge hydrothermal explosion in the park.

Much of the science of the fragility and volatility of tectonic plates is outside the realms of scientific comprehension at present, and therefore the periodic past activity of volcanoes and earthquakes serves as the basis for much of the knowledge of probable future eruptions. The episodic nature of Yellowstone's volcanic history means that scientists are in agreement that it is a question of when, and not if, another eruption will happen. However, although they believe we are now at risk of the super-volcano detonating, scientists do console us by restating the theory that we may yet have a 200,000 year buffer before the big one. Perhaps, by that time, evolution and progress in science will have found a way to suppress or evade one of the biggest hazards that lurks just a few miles beneath our earth's surface.

Decide if the following statements, according to the passage, are **true** or **false** .

Q18: Underground activity gives the team their clues about when the volcano may erupt

....

Q19: The warning level of the volcanic eruption has only changed once.

Q20: Find a word or phrase with the same or similar meaning in the article for:

1. supported
2. disastrous
3. explosiveness or unpredictability

....

Q21: In paragraph 4, in the phrase *"They are likely to change the status..."*, what does the word *'they'* refer to?

....

Q22: Where would you find this article?

A) In a newspaper or magazine
B) In an academic journal
C) In a novel

4.9 Listening comprehension: Earthquakes

You will need access to the sound file: *hg-cesl2-4-3listening.mp3* to complete this listening comprehension.

Listen to the dialogue and then try the activity.

Listening comprehension: Earthquakes (25 min)	Go online

You will need sound files *hg-cesl2-4-3listening.mp3* to do this assessment.

Q23: Complete the passage which is a transcript of the sound file.

Perched upon a multitude of converging tectonic plates, or 'fault lines', Japan is perhaps the most _____ located country in the world when it comes to susceptibility from earthquakes. Over a thousand tremors are measured on mainland Japan and in the oceans nearby every year. The majority of these pass by unnoticed by the average Japanese commuter or tourist, as they are too far underground or too low on the Richter scale to be _____ at surface level. Nonetheless, the Japanese public are the most informed and prepared of any world nation for the possibility of a huge earthquake. Tokyo has been _____ anticipating an overdue major quake for the last ninety years.

The Great Kanto Earthquake of 1923 claimed the lives of one hundred thousand citizens of Tokyo. Since that time, Japan's government has placed earthquake damage limitation and _____ procedures high on its political agenda. Safety standards and building design are subject to rigorous _____ to ensure that they meet the required levels of earthquake proofing.

The focus on the capital city has itself been controversial and eye-opening for the people of Japan. The 2011 tsunami and the earthquake of 1995 in Kobe, in the west of Japan, served as a wake-up call to authorities whose efforts had arguably been too focussed on the most _____ and economically important areas of their country. Both of these events, although not the strongest earthquakes recorded in or around Japanese shores, _____ havoc and devastation on a _____ scale with tremendous loss of life. The lesson learned? An earthquake's magnitude is not the defining point in its ability to cause widespread destruction and despair. Indeed, regular earthquakes of 7 and 8 on the Richter scale are recorded in the seas surrounding Japan, but because the _____ is deep underwater and because of their geographic location, these quakes tend to cause minor, if any, damage to small fishing villages in rural Japan. Move the source of the earthquake one hundred miles nearer the mainland and pointing towards Tokyo, and such _____ activity would have an altogether different level of impact. The Kobe earthquake's epicentre was so near to the city that the _____ it caused was enormous.

The avoidance of a repeat of the Kobe earthquake in other major _____ is a conundrum for the Japanese government, as the number of variables when attempting to forecast earthquakes is enormous. Seismologists estimate a seventy-five per cent chance of a major earthquake occurring in the Tokyo vicinity within twenty-five years. Therefore, the authorities have an obligation to do all that they can to prevent it.

Fire safety has been improved in most homes and offices in Tokyo. State of the art sprinkler systems are installed as a matter of course nowadays, and _____ furniture is now illegal. Fires resulting from the aftermath of earthquakes are one of the biggest killers, and therefore reducing their likelihood is a controllable and measurable preventative action.

Computer aided design has enabled structural engineers to ensure that they are using the best resources when assembling new office blocks. New structures have to withstand the strongest of tremors, and not crumble or _____ under all but direct pressure. Of course, not all buildings in Tokyo are new - and many residents simply cannot afford the considerable expense needed to shore up their older homes structurally against the threat of earthquakes. It is these most vulnerable residents whom the Japanese authorities are racing against time to safeguard.

4.10   Vocabulary list

This is a list of useful vocabulary which is intended to supplement what you have learned. It may also be useful to refer to when attempting the speaking and writing activities within the topic.

to abate (verb)	to decrease in intensity or force
adaptation (noun)	the change or adjustment to particular environmental conditions
aftermath (noun)	the period immediately after a disastrous event
anthropogenic (adj)	the relationship between humans and their influence on the natural world
chlorofluorocarbons (noun)	gaseous compounds which commonly occur in household products, e.g. aerosols, cleaning agents. Linked to the damage of the ozone layer.
containment (noun)	the process of restricting or preventing the spread of something potentially harmful
contaminant (noun)	an agent which can poison or contaminate something, e.g. an airborne virus
cyclone (noun)	a storm system which acts in a rotational manner, bringing heavy rain, thunder, lightning and high winds
degradation (noun)	the impairment or dilapidation of a physical property
emergent (adj)	unexpectedly arising
glacier (noun)	a huge area of ice and snow moving slowly down a valley
to loot	to steal from shops / other people's homes, usually after a drastic event such as war or natural disaster
mitigation (verb)	An attempt to downplay the seriousness of a situation
ominous (adj)	foreboding
painstaking (adj)	diligent; very careful and attentive to detail
to perish (verb)	(of an event) to cause someone to die
subsistence (noun)	the minimum necessary to support life, in terms of food, drink and shelter
surge (noun)	a sweeping, fast movement, like that of a wave
toxicity (noun)	containing poisonous gas / liquid / material which can cause serious illness or death

Unit 3: ESOL in Context (Society)

Unit 3 Topic 1

Learning skills in context

Contents

Learning objective

By the end of this topic you should be able to:

- demonstrate greater knowledge and awareness of a variety of reading sub-skills including prediction and skimming

- demonstrate greater knowledge and understanding of effective dictionary use

- demonstrate a wider knowledge of American and British English language equivalents

- demonstrate a wider knowledge and understanding of prefixes, including negative prefixes

- demonstrate a wider knowledge and understanding of writing genre

- demonstrate a greater knowledge and understanding of writing purpose

- demonstrate wider knowledge of vocabulary in a range of study related contexts

- demonstrate a greater knowledge of writing genre and writing process through practice in a range of activities

This topic focuses on the development of reading skills and vocabulary extension. It includes work on developing good reading techniques, understanding the features of different genres, and textual analysis in a variety of formats. To support this, there are activities which focus on prediction, skim reading, British and American English, and dictionary skills. It includes work on all four skills: speaking, reading, writing, and listening, and additional activities on grammatical features. Assessment opportunities occur at the end of the topic.

Certain sections contain sound files. You may download these here and use them on your mp3 player or equivalent to practise your pronunciation. This may be very useful if there are times when you will not have access to the materials online.

1.1   Reading techniques

This section will explore two techniques:

1. Predicting

2. Skim reading

1.1.1   Predicting

'Predicting' refers to guessing what the theme of the text will be prior to reading any of it. It is a skill that you probably already have in your own language, but it can sometimes be harder to predict in a foreign language. The ability to predict before reading any of the content allows you to think about the genre of a text, its content and whether it is something you would benefit from reading for entertainment or education. In the following activities you will learn how to predict by looking at titles of texts in English and summaries of texts. In some contexts these are known as blurbs.

Book covers

Look at some book covers either on the web, in a book shop or in a library.

Try to find ones which indicate, from the cover, the kind of genre to which they belong.

Find one for each of the following, making notes of the content of the cover illustration and the book title.

1. Horror

2. Thriller

3. Romance

4. Classic

5. Biography

When you have finished, use your notes to discuss your findings with a classmate. Justify why you felt your choices were appropriate to a particular genre.

Book titles (15 min)   Go online

Try the following activity, paying close attention to the vocabulary in the book titles to help you identify what category (genre) they could be:

Q1:   Look at the following titles. What kind of book does each title suggest?

A) King and Country: One Man's Empire

B) Cyber Silhouette

C) Mikey the Marvellous Monster

D) Think you're successful? Look at your colleagues!

E) Dominique Van Roost - the Story of an Underdog

F) A Lone Pilgrimage

G) A Fight for Justice in the Developing World

H) Killer Zombie Cowboys

I) The Family Launderette - Making Millions from Other People's Misery

J) How are you? Fine, thank you . . . and you?

Choose from the following genres: Crime, Religion, Business, History, Children's, Science Fiction, Politics, Horror, Biography, Languages

---

The blurb (20 min)   Go online

Gore galore in the latest thrilling instalment of the teen vampire saga. Bettie and Paige have an unquenchable thirst for blood, and only Zander and his gang of slayers stand in their way as mayhem and carnage threaten the once quiet and sleepy town of Diresville. The self-proclaimed "Defenders of the Living" have their own identity problems though, as Zander risks succumbing to the charms of the enchanting vampish antiheroines, leaving Murphy and the rest of the gang with an unenviable decision to make over the fate of their fearless leader. . . all will be revealed in 'Moonstone: The Temptress'

Q2:   Who is the intended audience of this novel?

a) Adults
b) Adolescents
c) Children
d) Anyone

. . . .

Q3: What is the main genre?

a) Horror
b) Romance
c) Thriller
d) Drama
e) Comedy

....

Q4: What subgenre is present?

a) Horror
b) Romance
c) Thriller
d) Drama
e) Comedy

Andrei's job is to serve his passengers, no matter how obnoxious, belligerent or downright stupid they are. He was never meant to be serving cartons of unidentifiable slop to these cretins at thirty-seven thousand feet. He is a playwright after all, it's not his fault that the world just hasn't realised it yet. One day, the despair of this mundane, nameless existence gets too much for Andrei, and he decides to hold a captive audience on board flight BR413 to Palma. They will watch, listen, even perform in his latest epic... until the plane lands and Andrei realises he may well have written his last production...

Q5: Who is the intended audience of this novel?

a) Adults
b) Adolescents
c) Children
d) Anyone

....

Q6: What is the main genre?

a) Horror
b) Romance
c) Thriller
d) Drama
e) Comedy

....

Q7: What subgenre is present?

a) Horror
b) Romance
c) Thriller
d) Drama
e) Comedy

1.1.2 Skim reading

Skim reading, or skimming, is a technique used to identify the main theme, or gist, of a text. When skimming, you do not read every word of a text or focus on unknown vocabulary. Instead, you are looking for the overall idea of what the text is about, what it is telling you. This is a particularly common and useful technique for reading newspapers, magazines and websites. It can also be helpful when conducting academic research, reading journal articles to determine whether they are useful or not.

How to skim read:

- Read the first sentence of the article
- Look for key words
- Look for related words about a particular topic

Extracts (15 min)   Go online

Read the following newspaper extracts and match them with the following topics:

Q8: The orbiter Endeavour touched down at 6am local time to complete the historic final voyage of the 30 year NASA programme. It was a day of mixed emotions for the ground staff, with many of them facing the prospect of redundancy only 24 hours after their involvement in this momentous occasion for humankind.

a) Social Unrest
b) Education
c) Space Exploration
d) Market News
e) Unemployment Crisis

....

Q9: The rioters took to the streets without warning, catching the authorities unawares and wreaking havoc among what are typically regarded as some of the quietest districts in the city. MPs have been quick to condemn the behaviour and promise to bring the perpetrators to justice.

a) Social Unrest
b) Education
c) Space Exploration
d) Market News
e) Unemployment Crisis

....

Q10: Sales of the lastest iPad have helped Apple to a buoyant year in the stock exchange, with share prices going through the proverbial roof both when the product was first announced and on its launch date.

a) Social Unrest
b) Education
c) Space Exploration
d) Market News
e) Unemployment Crisis

....

Q11: The crisis deepens for the incumbent government, as the jobless figures only look like rising further in the short to medium term. Analysts warn that without heavy government investment in the public sector, the number of teachers, nurses and similar workers will drop to an all-time low imminently.

a) Social Unrest
b) Education
c) Space Exploration
d) Market News
e) Unemployment Crisis

....

Q12: The demand for places is still expected to be high, despite the unprecedented hike in fees. It is thought that some students from England may choose to enter Scottish universities, where the fees system has been less affected than that of south of the border.

a) Social Unrest
b) Education
c) Space Exploration
d) Market News
e) Unemployment Crisis

1.2   Vocabulary: Dictionary skills

In academic reading it is likely you will encounter texts which contain vocabulary specific to that subject area, and therefore not widely used in everyday life. Sometimes it is difficult to predict or guess the meanings of such words from the context. In these situations, it is helpful to consult a dictionary.

Dictionary practice (25 min) Go online

Read the following text. It contains several words specific to the subject area of Law.

The tenant is contractually bound to accept any changes associated with damage incurred as a result of improper use of the amenities and facilities associated with the property at 8 Cresswell Drive. Failure to pay said charges promptly may result in the exercising of clause 4.2, namely the imposition of further financial penalty or the immediate cessation of the above named tenant's lease without the previously agreed due notice. Infringements outside of the above stated will be investigated and pursued separately, and without proof of mitigating circumstances may also result in the same financial penalty or early termination of the rental agreement.

Use a dictionary to help you answer the following questions.

Q13: What does *bound* mean?

a) obliged
b) forced
c) expected

....

Q14: What does *incurred* mean?

a) taken
b) caused
c) subjected

....

Q15: What does *promptly* mean?

a) immediately
b) quickly
c) now

....

Q16: What does *imposition* mean?

a) levy
b) payment
c) bill

....

Q17: What does *cessation* mean?

a) interruption
b) break
c) end

....

Q18: What does *mitigating* mean?

a) unknown
b) exceptional
c) difficult

British and American English (40 min)   Go online

British English and American English are similar but there are some subtle differences. Look at the following passage of text and try to identify examples of American English vocabulary. You can check your answers and the British English equivalents in the subsequent exercise. You may use a dictionary or online resources to help you.

Q19: The following text contains 18 examples of American (U.S.) English. Can you highlight them and provide a British English equivalent?

Henry strode out of his apartment and onto the sidewalk. After that long shift he was overcome with hunger, so he made his way as quickly as he could to the diner. "Two hot dogs and a pitcher of beer", he barked at the waitress. "We're all outta dogs, all we got left are some cookies... you want one with your beer?" Henry had always liked the waitress, she had cute bangs and a tempting smile, even if she managed to make serving drinks look like brain surgery. "Sure", he replied, "...and you got an eraser? I just started this crossword and I think I got one wrong..." "An eraser, Yeah, I'll have a look for you honey, why not? You want me to get you a pacifier and change your diapers while I'm back there?" Henry was too focussed on the couple who'd just entered the diner to deliver one of his typically sharp ripostes. They'd parked their station wagon just by the other door, the one facing the busy intersection, before saddling in, arm in arm, the fresh faced girl chewing on a granola bar and carrying a soda. "Why am I not with this granola girl, or even the waitress?" Henry wondered to himself, as he took his diabetes shot. I need to get myself outta this job, this town, that apartment with that damn leaky faucet and that insufferable boarder... "Check, please!" he shouted through the back to the waitress, "But you've not even eaten yet!" came the puzzled reply. Henry had already left a ten dollar bill on the counter and made his way out, determined to kick start his day, maybe even his life...

. . . .

Q20:

Match the American English words and their British counterparts:

apartment	drink
sidewalk	fringe
pitcher	bill
cookies	estate car
bangs	jug
pacifier	pavement
diapers	note
station wagon	flat
intersection	nappies
soda	dummy
faucet	biscuits
check	crossroads
bill	tap

1.3   Reading: How best to read

The following activity is a reading comprehension covering the work of this topic.

Read the passage quickly to grasp the gist of it.

How not to read

Reading is a skill that most people develop in their own language at an early stage in their cognitive development. Whether reading in your mother tongue or in a second language, there are some fundamental principles which apply, in order to make reading a more successful and pleasurable experience.

The first thing you need to learn to do is to stop talking to yourself! Research has shown that people who talk to themselves while reading believe they are aiding their comprehension of the written word, and more so their retention of whatever literature they have just devoured. Apart from the funny looks that you will draw from strangers on the train, talking while reading is actually counterproductive to understanding. The vocalisation of words (pronouncing aloud to oneself) slows down the rate at which you read, due to the fact that speech is a more laboured activity than reading. Subvocalisation, pronouncing the words in your head in a silent way, is also counterproductive to efficient reading technique. Your eyes can move more quickly than your lips, so the key is to try and have them operate independently from your vocal cords, and not allow yourself to sound out words as you go.

This is a difficult skill to master. Perhaps the best analogy is to think of a written text in the same way you would look at a work of art, a painting or a sculpture, and run your eyes across it to take in the ideas and the deeper meaning as opposed to scrutinising every last detail and missing the artist's intention.

Another common mistake that people make when reading is to try to read every word individually. In the same way that vocalisation affects speed, fixing your gaze on every solitary word will also inhibit the rate at which you read. Reading chunks of language, rather than separate words, can enable you to derive meaning more easily from sentences, due to linguistic features such as collocation, which can be missed if reading singularly. The eye, including the peripheral vision, is able to focus on groups of four, five or even six words at a time, and naturally occurring phenomena like phrasal verbs, articles and prepositions are often embedded in our inner lexicon, making them flow directly from the page to the brain.

Regression is a further giveaway of poor processing skills. Re-reading the same words, phrases or sentences is often a sign of a lack of concentration, and not, as the reader may believe, an inability to grasp the intended meaning. Skipping back through sentences means that the flow is lost and therefore it may actually hinder your comprehension of the overall text rather than help it. Using a physical pointing device, such as a pen, or even your finger, can assist your eyes in following the direction of the writing or print. Your reading speed may increase, as you will find that the rate at which you move the pointer is in keeping with the rate at which your eyes cross the page. Consider the genre, tone and style of the text you are reading, and use predictive techniques - paragraph headings, captions and so on, to help you establish the meaning and context of the piece, then you may find you do not struggle as much with the overall comprehension.

Finally, in keeping with the previous point, consider how the author intended the text to be consumed. Poems, plays and songs were never meant to be read into oneself, they were designed to be either performed, read or sung aloud. As such, attempting to speed read those kind of texts would clearly be conflicting with their purpose. Such texts should be read with care, and the time they deserve. On the other hand, magazines, newspapers, and most internet sites are designed to be skimmed and scanned, disposable material ideal for speed readers.

Reading: How best to read (40 min)

Q21: What is the main purpose of this text?

a) To help people read more quickly
b) To eliminate bad reading habits
c) To teach people how to read different texts

....

Q22: Vocalisation is something that many readers inaccurately believe helps their reading

a) True
b) False

....

Q23: How we read should be determined by what we read

a) True
b) False

....

Q24: The writer believes that good writing is similar to good artwork in how it is appreciated

a) True
b) False

....

Q25: Find a word which means *consumed*, or *used quickly* in the text

....

Q26: Find a word which means *harmful*, or *impeding* in the text

....

Q27: Find a word which means *exceptional or remarkable circumstances or happenings* in the text

1.4 Listening: Talking literature

Pre-listening: Talking literature Go online

You will need access to the sound file: *hg-cesl2-5-1listening.mp3* to complete this listening comprehension.

Q28: Before listening look at the four titles below, if you have read the novels they entitle then answer the following questions from memory otherwise try to predict the answers.

a) What is the genre of the novel?
b) What is the subject matter of the novel?

1. The Time Traveler's Wife
2. The Baroque Cycle
3. Therese Raquin
4. Ordinary Thunderstorms

Check your answers to the above question by listening to Martin, Janine, Freya and Grace talking about books. (sound file: *hg-cesl2-5-1listening.mp3*)

Listening: Talking literature (40 min)   Go online

You will need access to the sound file: *hg-cesl2-5-1listening.mp3* to complete this listening comprehension.

Q29: Why do the characters begin a conversation about books?

a) Martin is an author
b) Janine has just finished a book
c) Freya is thinking about reading a new novel

....

Q30: What aspects of their chosen novel does every speaker character discuss? Pick three from the list:

a) timing

b) the characters

c) death

d) the author

e) the language

....

Q31: What word indicates that the Time Traveler has no control over his destiny?

....

Q32: In the Baroque Cycle, what word is used to indicate that the writer is able to change the imaginary people?

....

Q33: What three word phrase does Freya use to describe the degeneration of the characters in Therese Raquin?

....

Q34: What two word phrase describes the vanishing of Kindred in Ordinary Thunderstorms.

Attribute the themes to the novels / speakers. Some themes are explored in more than one novel.

Q35: murder

....

Q36: travel

....

Q37: science fiction

....

Q38: love

....

Q39: modern life

....

Q40: humour

1.5   Text analysis

Genre analysis   Go online

Read the following extracts and decide which genre or type of writing they are representative of

Q41: Sir, I refer to the article in Saturday's edition entitled 'The New alliances' in which the writer, purporting to have the best interests of Scotland at heart, nevertheless promotes moves which would undermine many years of relatively peaceful co-existence within the UK, in favour of entirely new allegiances. I object strongly to his remarks which I believe are deliberately incendiary...

a) magazine article
b) email to a friend
c) discursive essay
d) letter of complaint
e) theatre review
f) letter to a newspaper
g) report

....

Q42: As the curtain opened to reveal the solitary figure of Ms Redgrave, dressed in sand coloured suit in the foreground with a backdrop of the sepia coloured waves of a cool and cloudy day, the atmosphere could not have been more poignant. Her opening lines, delivered with rock like stoicism not quite masking an hysterical edginess, set the tone...

a) magazine article
b) email to a friend
c) discursive essay
d) letter of complaint
e) theatre review
f) letter to a newspaper
g) report

....

Q43: I recently ordered and paid for a year's subscription of the monthly magazine, 'Universal ' through your organisation, for a friend as Christmas gift. It is now July and my friend has not received a single edition of the magazine. Not only am I disappointed at this apparent inefficiency but am also extremely embarrassed. . .

a) magazine article
b) email to a friend
c) discursive essay
d) letter of complaint
e) theatre review
f) letter to a newspaper
g) report

....

Q44: Like many other British children, I was brought up on various maxims which punctuated our family lives, offering solace or advice, advising caution or courage. 'Many a true word spoken in jest' , 'marry in haste repent at leisure', 'look before you leap' 'strike while the iron is hot' One saying which I always found a little discouraging with its allusion to age and mortality was 'you can't teach an old dog new tricks' something which I am delighted to report here is completely untrue. . .

a) magazine article
b) email to a friend
c) discursive essay
d) letter of complaint
e) theatre review
f) letter to a newspaper
g) report

....

Q45: . . . The recent inspection has indicated that there are also weaknesses which should be addressed as a matter of urgency. In the first place there is a need for radical improvement in the areas of communication between management and staff. Communication among staff within various departments also needs to be addressed. The issue of Disciplinary procedure was highlighted as an area of weakness, as was use of Information and Communications Technology (ICT). . .

a) magazine article
b) email to a friend
c) discursive essay
d) letter of complaint
e) theatre review
f) letter to a newspaper
g) report

....

Q46: Hi Gill how're you doing? Haven't seen you for ages but guess what? I've got to come down south for work next month. If you're free, we could get together? There's a conference on the 24th and I'll be there all day but on the 25th it's just a half day and then I'm free! If you're not already booked up I thought we could head over to Covent Garden, do some shopping and grab a bite then maybe see a play or something?. . .

a) magazine article
b) email to a friend
c) discursive essay
d) letter of complaint
e) theatre review
f) letter to a newspaper
g) report

. . . .

Q47: Many parents and teachers are delighted by current trends in schools, with results in Standard Grades, Higher and Advanced Higher indicating a greater number of good passes at higher levels each academic year. Nevertheless there are many who question the process which enables this apparent success. Sceptics believe that exams are easier than in the past. At the same time universities are struggling to accommodate large numbers of school leavers.

a) magazine article
b) email to a friend
c) discursive essay
d) letter of complaint
e) theatre review
f) letter to a newspaper
g) report

Identifying purpose

Go online

After the extracts of text you will find a list of seven descriptions of the writer's purpose. Match each extract with the corresponding description of purpose. (Answer with a number from1 to 7).

Extracts

1. Sir, I refer to the article in Saturday's edition entitled 'The New alliances' in which the writer, purporting to have the best interests of Scotland at heart, nevertheless promotes moves which would undermine many years of relatively peaceful co-existence within the UK, in favour of entirely new allegiances. I object strongly to his remarks which I believe are deliberately incendiary?. . .

2. As the curtain opened to reveal the solitary figure of M/s Redgrave, dressed in sand coloured suit in the foreground with a backdrop of the sepia coloured waves of a cool and cloudy day, the atmosphere could not have been more poignant. Her opening lines, delivered with rock like stoicism not quite masking an hysterical edginess, set the tone. . .

3. I recently ordered and paid for a year's subscription of the monthly magazine, 'Universal ' through your organisation, for a friend as Christmas gift. It is now July and my friend has not received a single edition of the magazine. Not only am I disappointed at this apparent inefficiency but am also extremely embarrassed...

4. Like many other British children, I was brought up on various maxims which punctuated our family lives, offering solace or advice, advising caution or courage. 'Many a true word spoken in jest' , 'marry in haste repent at leisure', 'look before you leap' 'strike while the iron is hot' One saying which I always found a little discouraging with its allusion to age and mortality was 'you can't teach an old dog new tricks' something which I am delighted to report here is completely untrue...

5. ... The recent inspection has indicated that there are also weaknesses which should be addressed as a matter of urgency. In the first place there is a need for radical improvement in the areas of communication between management and staff. Communication among staff within various departments also needs to be addressed. The issue of Disciplinary procedure was highlighted as an area of weakness, as was use of Information and Communications Technology (ICT)...

6. Hi Gill how're you doing? Haven't seen you for ages but guess what? I've got to come down south for work next month. If you're free, we could get together? There's a conference on the 24th and I'll be there all day but on the 25th it's just a half day and then I'm free! If you're not already booked up I thought we could head over to Covent Garden, do some shopping and grab a bite then maybe see a play or something?...

7. Many parents and teachers are delighted by current trends in schools, with results in Standard Grades, Higher and Advanced Higher indicating a greater number of good passes at higher levels each academic year. Nevertheless there are many who question the process which enables this apparent success. Sceptics believe that exams are easier than in the past. At the same time universities are struggling to accommodate large numbers of school leavers.

Q48: Objective description of facts or findings

....

Q49: Subjective response to entertainment

....

Q50: Expression of dissatisfaction with goods or services

....

Q51: Making contact with a friend

....

Q52: Entertainment and/or information

....

Q53: Expressing personal opinion of media or current affairs / issues

....

Q54: Exploring a contentious issue and convincing the reader

Features of language: Genre (15 min) Go online

Q55: Match the following features of language to the genre in which they would be most appropriate.

Features of language

A) use of first person

B) idiomatic language

C) passive voice

D) ellipsis and substitution

E) contractions

F) formal language

G) informal language

H) inversion

I) colloquial language

J) metaphorical language

Genre

1. report

2. theatre review

3. letter of complaint

4. email to a friend

5. article

6. letter to a newspaper

7. discursive essay

Features of language: Writing conventions

Look at the texts again and answer the questions which follow. The first question refers to text 1, the second question to text 2 etc.

1. Sir, I refer to the article in Saturday's edition entitled 'The New alliances' in which the writer, purporting to have the best interests of Scotland at heart, nevertheless promotes moves which would undermine many years of relatively peaceful co-existence within the UK, in favour of entirely new allegiances. I object strongly to his remarks which I believe are deliberately incendiary?. . .

2. As the curtain opened to reveal the solitary figure of M/s Redgrave, dressed in sand coloured suit in the foreground with a backdrop of the sepia coloured waves of a cool and cloudy day, the atmosphere could not have been more poignant. Her opening lines, delivered with rock like stoicism not quite masking an hysterical edginess, set the tone. . .

3. I recently ordered and paid for a year's subscription of the monthly magazine, 'Universal ' through your organisation, for a friend as Christmas gift. It is now July and my friend has not received a single edition of the magazine. Not only am I disappointed at this apparent inefficiency but am also extremely embarrassed. . .

4. Like many other British children, I was brought up on various maxims which punctuated our family lives, offering solace or advice, advising caution or courage. 'Many a true word spoken in jest' , 'marry in haste repent at leisure', 'look before you leap' 'strike while the iron is hot' One saying which I always found a little discouraging with its allusion to age and mortality was 'you can't teach an old dog new tricks' something which I am delighted to report here is completely untrue. . .

5. . . .   The recent inspection has indicated that there are also weaknesses which should be addressed as a matter of urgency. In the first place there is a need for radical improvement in the areas of communication between management and staff. Communication among staff within various departments also needs to be addressed. The issue of Disciplinary procedure was highlighted as an area of weakness, as was use of Information and Communications Technology (ICT). . .

6. Hi Gill how're you doing? Haven't seen you for ages but guess what? I've got to come down south for work next month. If you're free, we could get together? There's a conference on the 24th and I'll be there all day but on the 25th it's just a half day and then I'm free! If you're not already booked up I thought we could head over to Covent Garden, do some shopping and grab a bite then maybe see a play or something?. . .

7. Many parents and teachers are delighted by current trends in schools, with results in Standard Grades, Higher and Advanced Higher indicating a greater number of good passes at higher levels each academic year. Nevertheless there are many who question the process which enables this apparent success. Sceptics believe that exams are easier than in the past. At the same time universities are struggling to accommodate large numbers of school leavers.

Q56: Why does the writer use 'Sir' as a means of address?

....

Q57: The phrase 'rock-like stoicism' is an example of what kind of language?

....

Q58: Give an example of the use of inversion.

....

Q59: Give an example of the kind of publication in which this extract might appear.

....

Q60: Give an example of use of the passive voice.

....

Q61: The second sentence includes an example of ellipsis, which word (s) has (have) been omitted?

....

Q62: Give one or more example of formal linkers.

Features of language: Finding meaning in context (15 min)   Go online

Read the following text about education and answer the questions on vocabulary that follow:

Carl Rogers ideas about education are associated with his belief in the importance of creativity. He believed that without the ability to be creative, the survival of the human race would be under threat. Creativity is defined by Rogers as an intrinsic motivation, man's desire to fulfil himself, to expand and develop as an individual.

A similar approach to understanding human motivation was presented by Abraham Maslow. In Motivation and Personality, Maslow describes human needs in terms of a hierarchy. At the higher end of the scale of needs would be the desire to be all that one is capable of becoming. These needs would only emerge however after other more basic needs such as food, shelter and comfort had been met. The pyramid diagram illustrates Maslow's hierarchy.

As a consequence of his beliefs, in the context of education, Rogers found traditional classroom teaching limited. He argued that the traditional classroom situation, where the teacher directs classroom activity on the basis of externally defined standards of curriculum design and achievement, is not conducive to meaningful learning. In order for an individual to learn in a way that is significant, meaningful and creative, learning had to engage mind and feelings in the learning process. Learning should have a relevance to the individual learner.

The role of the teacher in this process is as a facilitator. The teacher would be a member of a community of learners. To this extent the classroom would be negotiated rather than imposed.

Find words from the text with the following meanings:

Q63: characteristic of person or thing

....

Q64: to satisfy or make happy

....

Q65: system in which people or things are organised in terms of perceived value

....

Q66: providing conditions in which something may flourish

....

Q67: arouse and maintain interest in someone

....

Q68: degree to which something is deemed important to present discussion or event

....

Q69: person who helps others to do something

....

Q70: where something or someone is forced upon one

1.6   Writing: Letters

There are a number of situations in which you might feel compelled to write a letter of complaint particularly in the context of disappointing customer service.

Generating ideas (15 min)

Before embarking on a writing task it is useful to generate a list or mind map of relevant ideas.

1. Make a list of problems which can spoil your evening in a restaurant in the categories of food/customer service/atmosphere.

2. Think of the steps which restaurant staff might make to encourage you to continue to eat in a restaurant following a bad experience.

Writing a letter of complaint (75 min)

You booked a restaurant for a meal for you and a few classmates on a Friday evening in your favourite local restaurant to celebrate your exam results. You are extremely disappointed with your starter which you are unable to eat. There are various other problems as well but when you express your dissatisfaction with the quality of the food and service, far from being appeased you are asked to leave the restaurant.

You are going to write a letter to the proprietor, Mr McGinley, complaining about the food and the service.

Before you begin writing consider what type of language is appropriate.

Q71: Look at the sentences below and highlight those which would be appropriate in your letter of complaint to the restaurant. Think about why the other examples are inappropriate.

1. Hi John
2. I am writing to complain about the standard of service in your restaurant
3. I hate your restaurant
4. The evening was beautiful and sunny
5. I am highly extremely disappointed in the attitude of your staff
6. Best wishes
7. We are unlikely to visit your restaurant again
8. Yours sincerely
9. Dear Mr McGinley

10. Restaurants like yours should be closed down

Using the ideas and information above, write your letter in an appropriately formal style. You should write approximately between 300 - 350 words.

When you have finished you can compare your answer with the model answer provided.

1.7 Listening comprehension: Giving feedback

Listening comprehension: Giving feedback (30 min)   Go online

You will need access to the sound file: *hg-cesl2-5-2listening.mp3* to complete this listening comprehension.

You will hear a conversation in which three students at a further education college complete a feedback form.

Before listening to the text consider the following questions:

1. Have you ever been asked to complete a feedback form about your school or college?

2. What kind of things do you think schools and colleges might ask students in order to gauge their satisfaction?

3. What features, if any, of your school / college experience would you like to see improved?

Read the questions below in order to prepare.

1. What three subjects are the respondents studying?

2. Each student indicates what motivated their choice of study. Use up to five words to say why each student chose to go to college.

3. Which two phrases suggest that the college course is not Anne's real ambition.

4. Which word/phrase indicates a change in Marie's self-belief?

5. With which aspect of college life is Thomas disappointed?

6. In Marie's opinion, what is notable about her tutor?

Listen to the dialogue and then try the activity.

You will need access to the sound file: *hg-cesl2-5-2listening.mp3* to complete this listening comprehension.

Q72: What three subjects are the respondents studying?

. . . .

Q73: Each student indicates what motivated their choice of study. Use up to five words to say why each student chose to go to college.

. . . .

Q74: Which two phrases suggest that the college course is not Anne's real ambition?

. . . .

Q75: Which word/phrase indicates a change in Marie's self-belief?

. . . .

Q76: With which aspect of college life is Thomas disappointed?

. . . .

Q77: In Marie's opinion, what is notable about her tutor?

1.8   Writing: Reports

Writing: Reports

The next activity is based on the listening comprehension. You will need the sound file *hg-cesl2-5-2listening.mp3* then you should listen to the recording again taking more notes if necessary.

Now, write a report for your college tutor describing the information you have heard.

You should write in a formal style summarising the information in clearly titled paragraphs.

You should write between 300-350 words. You may use the following headings:

Reasons for study
Aspirations
Positive and Negative Comments

When you have finished you can compare your work to the model answer provided.

1.9   Reading comprehension: Curriculum for Excellence

The following activity is a reading comprehension covering the work of this topic.

Before reading the text you might wish to think about the following questions:

1. Do you prefer working alone or as part of a team?

2. Do you have a favourite subject, if so what is it and why do you enjoy it?

3. Do you think ideas should be explored within subject boundaries or across subject areas?

4. What, if anything do you know about Curriculum for Excellence?

Read the passage quickly to grasp the gist of it.

Curriculum for Excellence the Scottish Government's new standard for education in Scotland has caused some controversy among educationalists, teachers and parents. Detractors are concerned by difficulties in implementing the curriculum and by variation across centres. Critics are also concerned about a perceived lack of emphasis on knowledge. Those in favour of the new approach stress the potential for innovative teaching, unconstrained by traditional subject boundaries, and for more meaningful learning.

One argument against Curriculum for Excellence which has been raised by some teachers is the difficulty anticipated in implementation of the system. The notion of key concepts for learning has been criticised as vague. However there have already been many examples of good practice across Scottish schools. Learners have collaborated on projects which have involved not only a range of different disciplines within schools but also external links with the community and local business. Such projects have created invaluable learning experiences in an innovative way.

Another concern with the new curriculum is that there may be wide variation in its interpretation across schools. This could lead to a great disparity in what is taught. However the culture of openness and involvement which the curriculum promotes should enable teachers to share ideas and ensure that learners' experiences are comparable.

Finally it has also been suggested that the standard lacks sufficient detail to encourage breadth and depth of thinking. As a result learners will fail to develop an adequate knowledge base and will not develop critical thinking strategies. This argument has been rejected by proponents who argue that the curriculum offers great potential for challenge, meaningful learning and progress to in-depth study.

While there is some trepidation over the design, implementation and assessment of the new standard, there is also excitement about the opportunities which the new curriculum should bring. The focus on interdisciplinary learning should encourage openness and collaboration, enable initial problems to be resolved and enhance learning and teaching.

Reading comprehension: Curriculum for Excellence (30 min) Go online

Read the passage once more and answer the questions which follow.

Q78: To what genre does this piece of writing most closely conform?

A) Report

B) Formal letter

C) Discursive essay

. . . .

Q79: The writer's attitude to the new standard is

A) generally favourable
B) generally unfavourable
C) neutral

....

Q80: Paragraphs 2-4 develop from initial topic sentences. What key criticisms are dealt with in each paragraph?

....

Q81: What counter arguments are offered for each criticism?

....

Q82: What is the purpose of the introduction?

....

Q83: Select three words from the conclusion which emphasise the writer's stance.

1.10 Vocabulary list

This is a list of useful vocabulary which is intended to supplement what you have learned. It may also be useful to refer to when attempting the speaking and writing activities within the topic.

coherence (noun)	the quality of being coherent; having clarity and understandable order
colloquialism (noun)	a regional dialect expression
connotation (noun)	a positive or negative association carried by a particular word
contraction (noun)	the shortened form of a word, e.g. don't instead of 'do not'
denotation (noun)	the direct and specific meaning of a word
to emphasise (verb)	to place importance on something; to stress something
figurative (adjective)	expressing one idea using language which normally denotes another, i.e. metaphor
genre (noun)	the category of literature, art, film etc identifiable by particular features in style
hyperbole (noun)	overstatement or exaggeration
idiom (noun)	a saying or expression particular to a region, country or group of people
narrative (noun)	the representation of a story within literature or art
to proofread (verb)	to carefully check a document or text for errors
prose (noun)	the style of writing used in literature, resembling everyday language more than other styles (such as poetry) do
protagonist (noun)	the main character in a story or real life event
register (noun)	the levels of formality and varieties within language used in differing social circumstances
setting (noun)	the location(s) where a story or event takes place
slang (noun)	nonstandard and informal vocabulary which is often particular to a regional or social group
to summarise (verb)	to reduce a large amount of text to a smaller amount; to make a summary
syntax (noun)	how linguistic features, e.g. word order within grammar are assembled into comprehensible phrases or sentences
tone (noun)	the general feeling, mood, quality or character of a text
allegiances (noun)	loyalties to a particular belief system, group or individual.
appeased (verb)	to make concessions to the opposition in war or opponent in argument
conducive (adjective)	where the conditions enable something to flourish
contentious (adjective)	likely to cause disagreement
convivial (adjective)	friendly and welcoming
diminishes (verb)	reduces in size

edginess (noun)	state of agitation
feasible (adjective)	able to be done
field (noun)	subject area, discipline
imperious (adjective)	commanding
incendiary(adjective)	provocative
indispensable (adjective)	something or someone you cannot manage without
irrespective (adverb)	without consideration of factors
maxims (noun)	proverb or saying
prospective (adjective)	people who are about to do something e.g. buy a house prospective buyers
proponent(noun)	one who is in favour of an idea or plan of action
stoicism (noun)	the quality of suffering without complaint
unconstrained (adjective)	free, without constriction

Unit 3 Topic 2

Further education opportunities

Contents

Learning objective

By the end of this topic you should be able to:

- identify key information by reading and listening in the topic area

- display a greater awareness of commonly confused words

- display a greater awareness of educational vocabulary

- demonstrate your knowledge of writing genre by writing academic and discursive essays

- demonstrate greater understanding of word classification

This topic examines education, including current issues at school, further and higher education levels. It includes work on the development of vocabulary, through activities on commonly confused words and new lexical terms related to the topic. The topic includes work on all four skills: speaking, reading, writing, and listening. Assessment opportunities occur at the end of the topic.

Certain sections contain sound files. You may download these here and use them on your mp3 player or equivalent to practise your pronunciation. This may be very useful if there are times when you will not have access to the materials online.

2.1   Vocabulary: Commonly confused words

Vocabulary: Commonly confused words (20 min)   Go online ❄

There are several words in English that are commonly confused, even by native speakers. The confusion in use is often due to similar spelling or pronunciation.

For each of the examples, choose the correct option from the two possibilities to complete the sentence.

Q1:   The _____ is making sweeping changes to the school. (principal / principle)

....

Q2:   There is a danger that the college will _____ the contract for those classes next year. (lose / loose)

....

Q3:   Would lecturers please inform the administrative assistants of any _____ requirements for the forthcoming academic year. (stationary / stationery)

....

Q4:   These sections must be correctly completed before the university can _____ with your application. (precede / proceed)

....

Q5:   The full _____ of the increased budget will be felt by the next intake of engineering students. (affect / effect)

....

Q6:   Speak to the UCAS tutor. She'll give you helpful _____ about your application. (advice / advise)

....

Q7:   The teacher says that school sports class today is dependent on _____ or not it stays sunny outside. (weather / whether)

....

Q8: Staff _____ is at an all-time low due to the latest round of compulsory redundancies. (morale / moral)

....

Q9: You can treat your prelim exams as _____ for the final exam. (practise / practice)

Parts of speech: Definitions (25 min)   Go online

For each definition given:

1. choose the word from the given list to which it refers

2. decide what part of speech this word is. (noun, verb, adjective etc)

Wordlist:

weather: effect: advice: precede: expend: practice: morale: loose: principle: lose: stationary: proceed: affect: advise: whether: moral: practise: stationery: expand: principal:

Q10: the head of a school or college

....

Q11: to fail to win

....

Q12: a moral belief or opinion

....

Q13: not moving

....

Q14: a change as a result of something happening

....

Q15: writing and other office materials

....

Q16: to come before something

....

Q17: to move forward with something

....

Q18: to do something repeatedly; to rehearse

....

Q19: expressing doubt between choices

....

Q20: not tight; incorrectly fitting

....

Q21: a lesson which can be taken from a story / situation

....

Q22: to make a difference to something

....

Q23: to make larger

....

Q24: to tell someone what to do

....

Q25: atmospheric conditions; wind, sun, rain etc

....

Q26: information given to tell someone what to do

....

Q27: confidence or spirit in a person / people

....

Q28: the use or application of a method

....

Q29: to use up a resource

2.2   Reading: University challenge

Reading: University challenge (30 min)

Read the following article carefully.

The demand and competition for university places in the UK has been escalating for the past three decades. What was once the domain of the privileged few has gradually become more and more accessible to the masses, in no small part due to the political drive for widening participation. Still, for those in the very lowest socio-economic groups there remains an insurmountable financial hurdle and, at times, a further barrier in the form of academic snobbery. Young people from middle class backgrounds are currently three times more likely to go to university than their less comfortable peers.

The recent doubling, even trebling of tuition fees at some institutions has led to further concerns that the rich-poor divide has only broadened of late.

The Centre for Inclusion and Curriculum at the Open University, the world's pioneers in distance learning courses and inclusivity, concur that the type of student that widening participation schemes have targeted over the last twenty years (those on the lowest incomes, from poorer areas and often with lower self-confidence) have most likely been the biggest victims of the financial hikes imposed by most universities on their undergraduate programmes.

There is an underlying belief among some commentators that the UK higher education system is unfair. On the surface, anyone can go to university, whether that is via excelling academically at secondary school or via the mature student route, where consideration is given for life experience in lieu of qualifications. However, qualification and achievement are not the whole story.   The poorer societal groups are struggling to muster the necessary funds a university career entails.   In addition to the increasing fees, there are the general living expenses of rent, bills, food and so forth to consider.

There is a further obstacle facing the low-income entrants too, and this is one that no loan or grant will help alleviate. . . the sense of feeling unwelcome. The perceptual class barrier that confronts people from lower socio-economic groups is becoming a major factor. Quite simply, they often convince themselves that they do not belong at university. Proponents of the current financial system point out that sociological factors like that will be difficult to break down, but argue that high fees and loans should not be a deterrent to lower earners; theoretically they will leave university on an equal footing with their wealthier friends (in spite of entering at a disadvantage), and they would be protected by the loan repayment threshold, meaning they would not have to pay back their debts until they were earning over £21000 per year.   But for those already trying to keep the wolf from the door before they even consider applying, the overwhelming fear of years of debt-ridden struggle is more likely to sway their decision than the opportunity to earn the national average salary.

Q30: The main topic in this text is:

a) The unfairness of university fees
b) The struggles young people on low incomes face
c) Both of the above
d) Neither of the above

. . . .

Q31: Which of the following things are mentioned in the article? (Choose three answers)

a) Government defence of the university finance system

b) Additional support for the poorest students

c) The psychological concerns of potential students

d) The history of student loans

e) Methods of postponing repayment

f) Entrance routes to university

. . . .

Q32: Find a word in paragraph 1 which means *too big to deal with*

. . . .

Q33: Find a word in paragraph 3 which means *agree with*

. . . .

Q34: Find a word in paragraph 4 which means *gather together*

. . . .

Q35: The class barrier is stopping potential students from going to university.

a) true

b) false

. . . .

Q36: The Open University is concerned that the student inclusion policy is suffering.

a) true

b) false

2.3   Writing: Tuition fees

Writing: Tuition fees (60 min)

The table below illustrates the average cost of a four-year undergraduate degree course which a university student in the UK would have expected to pay when starting their Higher Education in the given year. The figures represent the total including tuition fees and the cost of future loan repayments.

Year	Approximate Cost
Pre 1998	0*
1998	£4000
2009	£12000 - 15000
2012	£20000 - £36000
2017	£20000 - £36000

* Student grants and loans were available at this point, but not all students applied for them unlike loans since 1998 which have been necessary to cover the actual tuition fees.

Consider the following question in relation to the table. Use the information above to help you answer the question.

1. *University education in the 21st century is no longer in reach of all young people. Being in reach of all young people is a long forgotten aim.*

   Discuss this statement by using the statistics to help you discuss any trends or changes in the figures.

Before you begin, consider the following questions:

- What is the purpose of the communication?

- Who is the intended audience?

- What level of formality and register would be appropriate?

Make some notes or a mind map to help plan your writing before you begin.

Write an essay between 300 - 350 words.

Ask your teacher to check your work when you have finished and / or compare your answer with the Model answer provided here.

2.4 Vocabulary: Academic context

Correct word choice (15 min) Go online

For each question use two words/phrases from the given list to complete the sentences.

Wordlist:

resit: continuous assessments: prelim: appeal, faculty: Honours: postgraduate: sandwich: vocational: lifelong learning:

Q37: Constance's grades were disappointing, probably due to her illness prior to the exams. We will initiate an _____ on her behalf, as it would be an unfortunate outcome had she to _____ this year.

....

Q38: I am sorry, but the conditions for attachment to the external Higher examination were made abundantly clear from the outset. The decision is based on both your _____ result and the successful completion of all _____.

....

Q39: Emily is investigating the possibility of a five-year course of study, with a _____ placement in Russia prior to the _____ year.

....

Q40: That's right, yes. Our evening provision is primarily geared towards those without an academic background, and those who have been outside of academia for some time. We pride ourselves on our commitment to _____ courses, widening participation and _____.

....

Q41: Professor Wood, from the Social Science and Linguistics _____, will be able to answer any questions you have about _____ study, and she will also be able to discuss the requirements of the dissertation.

Vocabulary: Academia (20 min)   Go online

For each question, rearrange the letters to spell out further words connected to education. Use the definitions as a clue to help you.

Q42: stier

a second opportunity to take an examination or assessment, granted on the grounds of prior academic achievement or medical or other extenuating circumstances

....

Q43: socuunonti tasnemssse

an alternative to exams when measuring student achievement over an academic year

....

Q44: lepirm

a practice examination which normally takes place a few months before the final examination

....

Q45: pleapa

a request by the student or educational establishment to the examination board for special consideration to change a student's grade when it has been poorer than expected

....

Q46: clutyaf

The teaching staff of a university or college, or of one of its departments or divisions

....

Q47: nrshuoo

a class of degree considered higher or more specialised than an ordinary degree

....

Q48: stapdrogtaue

typically a one year advanced level degree for students who have already completed a first degree, or the name for such students

....

Q49: wdincahs

a degree course which contains an extra placement year for students to gain real-life work experience

....

Q50: lvoancoait

a non-academic course, focussing more on practical aspects useful in the student's intended career

....

Q51: gnielolf ianrelgn

the notion of studying in all aspects and all stages of life, and the idea of widespread inclusion

2.5   Listening: Robot teachers

Listening comprehension: Robot teachers (30 min)

This section relies on the sound file *hg-cesl2-6-1listening.mp3*. You will need access to it to complete the section and the related activity.

Listen to the lecture.

Q52: The company has so far only built one model of the Maria robot.

a) true
b) false

....

Q53: Maria can walk around the classroom helping students.

a) true
b) false

....

Q54: The Gina robot will replace the Maria robot in schools in the future.

a) true
b) false

....

Q55: Maria's principle purpose in the short term will be:

a) To teach primary school classes when teachers are sick
b) To give out homework and respond to student questions
c) To act as a teaching assistant to a real teacher

....

Q56: Maria was not used as a traffic policewoman because:

a) The authorities decided it was too risky
b) She was not programmed to be used that way
c) There were financial implications

....

Q57: How does Professor Nakamura feel about opposition to his robot teachers?

a) He is confident he will change the minds of opponents
b) He does not care what the critics think
c) He is worried that critics will scare others into thinking negative thoughts

....

Q58: The author's opinion on the idea of robotic teachers is:

a) unclear
b) quite positive
c) very positive

2.6 Writing: Technology in the classroom

Writing: Technology in the classroom (60 min)

Interactive whiteboards, online virtual learning environments, podcasts, wikis, blogs. These are just some of the multitude of technological advancements within education over the last ten to fifteen years. Consider how these technological developments have benefited the students of today, while taking into account any detrimental effects they have had on the learning and teaching process. Write a discursive essay including the following points:

- the student learning experience and how it has changed

- the changing role of teachers and the skills they require

- the future of technology in education

Before you begin, consider the following questions:

- What is the purpose of the communication?

- Who is the intended audience?

- What level of formality and register would be appropriate?

Make some notes or a mind map to help plan your writing before you begin.

Write a discursive essay of between 300 - 350 words.

Ask your teacher to check your work when you are finished and / or compare your answer with the Model answer provided here.

2.7 Listening comprehension: Scotland Street School

The following assessment dialogue contains examples of many of the language areas you have covered within the topic.

You will need access to the sound file *hg-cesl2-6-2listening.mp3* to complete this listening comprehension.

Listen to the dialogue and then try the activity.

Listening comprehension: Scotland Street School (30 min)   Go online

You need access to the sound file 2-listening-hg-esl5-6et1.mp3 then you should listen to the recording again and try to answer the following questions:

Q59: Scotland Street school still has pupils enrolled today

a) True
b) False

....

Q60: The school was in excellent condition when it was converted to a museum

a) True
b) False

....

Q61: The school has three functioning classrooms from the 1960s which can be visited

a) True
b) False

....

Q62: Which word meaning *strongly associated with, or related to Mackintosh* was mentioned in the dialogue

....

Q63: Which word meaning *lifelike and realistic experience* was mentioned in the dialogue

....

Q64: Rival schools were a critical factor in the closure of Scotland Street

a) True
b) False

....

Q65: The overall aim of the listening dialogue is:

a) To advertise the museum
b) To inform the general public
c) To train staff about the museum's facilities

2.8 Reading comprehension: Mind your language

The following activity is a reading comprehension covering the work of this topic.

Read the passage quickly to grasp the gist of it.

What do you call someone who speaks three languages? 'Trilingual'. What do you call someone who speaks two languages? 'Bilingual'. What do you call someone who speaks one language? 'British'.

Jokes of that nature may not be around for much longer, should Education Secretary Darren Green have anything to do with it. He is aiming to eradicate the perception of the obstinate Brit who need not acquire any linguistic skills beyond that of his native tongue simply because "English is a global language". According to Green, that argument does not stand up in today's progressive society, particularly one in which China is quickly heading towards the position of the world's leading superpower.

Green is at the centre of a drive to address the shortage of language classes for children in primary and secondary schools across the country. It is his fundamental belief that every child aged five and over should have the opportunity to learn a foreign language. Given the reductions in provision by previous governments, this radical turnaround will not happen overnight. Whatever his motive, there is no denying that the existing investment in language teaching in the UK pales in comparison to every other country in Western Europe, a fact that the minister describes as shameful.

Critics argue that Mr Green is merely paying lip service to a problem highlighted by Modern Foreign Language teachers for over a decade now and that the government needs to back its statements about supporting languages by putting its money where its mouth is. The National Union of Teachers has been reticent about offering its full backing to Green's plans, apparently concerned at allusions to extensions of the school working day and the supplanting of existing subjects and staff to accommodate this move.

The task faced by the present government to reverse the decline in language teaching is an unenviable one. The number of pupils studying a foreign language at secondary school has halved between the late 1990s and today, and Green believes by the time students are thinking about taking GCSEs or National 5 qualifications, it is too late to persuade them to consider languages. The interest must be sparked at an earlier developmental stage.

Green cited examples of his linguistic revolution that are already up and running which he hopes to replicate on a national level, such as primary schools in deprived areas which have drafted in Spanish teachers to teach children's Primary One classes.

According to Green, not only does learning a language improve neural networks leading to improved brain power, it also leads to a more employable and tolerant workforce. It could, in his opinion, boost the country's economy in the future by improving networking around the globe due to a collective understanding built through an appreciation of other languages.

"It's time to stop believing in our colonial past, and the notion that the acquiescence of other nations to our language is sufficient", he said. "Speaking slowly and loudly just isn't acceptable as a way of working with our international colleagues any more - we should stop expecting others to compromise and start proactively changing our attitude to foreign languages. We have to do this at grass roots level and implement the changes now so they benefit future generations in this country."

Reading Comprehension: Mind your language (25 min)   Go online

What do you call someone who speaks three languages? 'Trilingual'. What do you call someone who speaks two languages? 'Bilingual'. What do you call someone who speaks one language? 'British'.

Jokes of that nature may not be around for much longer, should Education Secretary Darren Green have anything to do with it. He is aiming to eradicate the perception of the obstinate Brit who need not acquire any linguistic skills beyond that of his native tongue simply because "English is a global language". According to Green, that argument does not stand up in today's progressive society, particularly one in which China is quickly heading towards the position of the world's leading superpower.

Green is at the centre of a drive to address the shortage of language classes for children in primary and secondary schools across the country. It is his fundamental belief that every child aged five and over should have the opportunity to learn a foreign language. Given the reductions in provision by previous governments, this radical turnaround will not happen overnight. Whatever his motive, there is no denying that the existing investment in language teaching in the UK pales in comparison to every other country in Western Europe, a fact that the minister describes as shameful.

Critics argue that Mr Green is merely paying lip service to a problem highlighted by Modern Foreign Language teachers for over a decade now and that the government needs to back its statements about supporting languages by putting its money where its mouth is. The National Union of Teachers has been reticent about offering its full backing to Green's plans, apparently concerned at allusions to extensions of the school working day and the supplanting of existing subjects and staff to accommodate this move.

The task faced by the present government to reverse the decline in language teaching is an unenviable one. The number of pupils studying a foreign language at secondary school has halved between the late 1990s and today, and Green believes by the time students are thinking about taking GCSEs or National 5 qualifications, it is too late to persuade them to consider languages. The interest must be sparked at an earlier developmental stage.

Green cited examples of his linguistic revolution that are already up and running which he hopes to replicate on a national level, such as primary schools in deprived areas which have drafted in Spanish teachers to teach children's Primary One classes.

According to Green, not only does learning a language improve neural networks leading to improved brain power, it also leads to a more employable and tolerant workforce. It could, in his opinion, boost the country's economy in the future by improving networking around the globe due to a collective understanding built through an appreciation of other languages.

"It's time to stop believing in our colonial past, and the notion that the acquiescence of other nations to our language is sufficient", he said. "Speaking slowly and loudly just isn't acceptable as a way of working with our international colleagues any more - we should stop expecting others to compromise and start proactively changing our attitude to foreign languages. We have to do this at grass roots level and implement the changes now so they benefit future generations in this country."

Q66: Which adjective is used in the text to describe the inflexible nature of many British people towards speaking another language?

....

Q67: What is Mr Green's main motivation for change:

a) Political point scoring

b) A genuine concern for today's youth

c) Fear of the UK being left behind

....

Q68: What is the view of the National Union of Teachers?

1. Indifferent about the changes as they are unclear

2. Apprehensive about the impact of some changes

3. Completely opposed to the idea

....

Q69: Which word in the article means, *suggestion or indirect reference*?

....

Q70: Which word in the article means, *to put an end to; to delete or remove*?

....

Q71: Which word in the article means, *to replace, often by force*?

....

Q72: Mr Green is voicing an opinion long held by some teachers.

1. true

2. false

2.9   Vocabulary list

This is a list of useful vocabulary which is intended to supplement what you have learned. It may also be useful to refer to when attempting the speaking and writing activities within the topic.

alumni (noun)	Graduates of a college or university are known collectively by this term.
confer (verb)	The process by which the academic board of a college or university formally agrees to award a degree.
curriculum (noun)	The subjects which comprise a course of study in an academic programme.
diagnostic assessment (noun phrase)	A test, or series of tests, which is intended to discover specific areas of student strength or weakness, typically near the beginning of an academic programme.
formative assessment (noun phrase)	A type of assessment in which the participant is given feedback on their efforts, in order to aid their development and aptitude for their future (summative) assessment attempts. An example would be coursework handed out during the year.
invigilator (noun)	A person who supervises and oversees the administering of formal examinations and monitors and prevents cheating during said examinations.
learning style (noun phrase)	The preferred method of learning for a student. There are a variety of models discussing this idea, but in general it describes a preference for learning through different applications and combinations of senses, e.g. visual / kinaesthetic learning.
postgraduate (noun)	A student who has already completed a first degree and is embarking on a higher level of academic study.
summative assessment (noun phrase)	Assessed work which counts towards the overall outcome of a student's degree or course, for example: external examinations, essays or presentations.
undergraduate (noun)	A student who is currently on a programme to try and achieve a first degree.

Glossary

Acronym

This is an abbreviation which consists of the initial letters of more than one word pronounced together as a new word

Adjectival phrase

A group of words consisting of an adjective and either complement / modifier, which together function in the same way as a regular adjective

Affirmative

positive or standard form

ambiguity

having or expressing more than one meaning

Initialism

This is an abbreviation which consists of the initial letters of more than one word pronounced separately

Interpretation

A view, explanation or opinion.

Inverting

changing the order of

Metaphor

Makes a comparison between two things that are unlike each other in many respects but are implied to have something in common.

Perceived

clearly understood

Prepositional phrase

A phrase consisting of a preposition and an object with the value of an adjective or adverbial

Punctuation

Symbols used to help convey the meaning in a piece of text: Symbols include . , ( ) ' ""

Simile

Compares things by suggesting they are alike.

Answers to questions and activities for Unit 1

Topic 1: Personal profile

Reading: Mixed tenses (page 6)

Q1: Keira considers herself to be Scottish, although **her family is** from overseas. **She has lived** here for the best part of fifteen years and **she has developed** a strong Scottish accent in that time. "When I make new friends, **they never guess** that I was not born here", she says. Keira is currently a student at the Royal Dance Institute and in recent weeks **she has been practising** for her final practical exam. She is worried because **she has been experiencing** difficulties with some of the more complicated moves. **She is thinking** about specialising in ballet next year and therefore **she is keeping** her fingers and toes crossed that **she achieves** the required results in her exams.

Grammar practice: Mixed tenses (page 6)

Q2: I usually eat a sandwich for lunch at college.

Q3: Jonathan is working in a bank for his work experience placement.

Q4: We have visited the south coast many times on holiday.

Q5: She is sitting her dance exam later today.

Q6: Vishesh is waiting for you at the bus stop.

Q7: People have become very dependent on their mobile phones.

Q8: Jitka has never failed her English exams.

Q9: Wajdi has always been the hardest working student in the class.

Q10: Sara, on the other hand, has never tried to improve her grades.

Q11: I have been revising every day for a month because I am worried about my exam.

Reading: Gayle's story (page 7)

Q12: b) false

Q13: a) true

Q14: b) false

Q15: a) true

Q16: b) false

Vocabulary: Definitions (page 8)

Q17:

Gayle: The English Teacher

Gayle has been working as an English teacher for ten years, and she would not swap her job for anything else in the world! To Gayle, teaching is more than an occupation, it is a **passion** (1). She studied Accountancy at university, where she gained **distinctions** (2) in her studies and found the course an **absorbing** (3) experience, but she realised that dealing with figures on a day to day basis did not appeal to her. She considers herself a social animal and therefore decided to **pursue** (4) a career in a more people-oriented environment, so she enrolled on a teaching course. The most rewarding part of her job is seeing her students progress over time, from speaking very little English at the **outset** (5), to finding jobs or university places, and feeling that she had a part to play in that process. However, she does admit that it has been hard to keep in touch with former students when they leave her class.

Listening: Follow your dreams (page 9)

Listening transcript

Jeremy has been living in the UK for as long as he can remember. Both he and his brother were born overseas but when he was an infant and his brother only three years old, they came to Scotland with their parents. Jeremy's father has long since retired, but when he first moved his family abroad, it was in search of work in the printing trade. He had lost his job as a chef in his country and wanted to try something different. Jeremy attended school in Edinburgh, where he was a high-flier and gained five Highers at A and B grade. He had the world at his feet, and his family gave him their encouragement to study law at university. After considering degrees in Marketing and Fine Art, Jeremy went along with his family's suggested course. However, being a creative person, Jeremy felt stifled on the law course and was convinced that his talent lay elsewhere. He dropped out after just eighteen months. To the surprise of all his family and friends, he then chose to follow in his father's footsteps and now he is the happy owner of a franchise of a famous eatery in central London.

Q18: a) since his childhood

Q19: c) does not work

Q20: a) very successful at school

Q21: b) Law

Q22: c) owns a restaurant in London

Physical appearance (page 10)

Q23: d) slender

Q24: a) pale

Q25: d) yellow

Q26: e) neck length

Q27: e) undulating

Q28: b) black

Q29: e) orange

Q30: c) folded

Physical appearance adjectives (page 11)

Q31: 1D: 2B: 3A: 4C

Q32:

flattering	unflattering	polite/neutral
slim	fat	plump
slender	obese	stocky
muscular	thin	overweight
athletic	skinny	elderly
	ugly	old
	unattractive	underweight
	plain	
	ancient	

Describing appearance (page 12)

Q33: If someone has tanned or brown coloured skin, we can describe them as having a **dark complexion**

Q34: **Dimples** are the small dents or areas on your cheeks that show when you smile. They are considered attractive.

Q35: When people dye small strips of their hair a different colour, these are called **highlights**.

Q36: **Freckles** are several light brown coloured spots on your skin, often on the face and arms.

Q37: Short hair that hangs over a person's forehead is known as a **fringe**

Q38: Models are often chosen because they have **high cheekbones**

Q39: The strips of hair that grow down both sides of a man's face are called **sideburns**.

Q40: An early sign of baldness could be a **receding hairline** when young.

Q41: Most people have a few **wrinkles** around their eyes and mouth when they are older.

Q42: **Rosy cheeks** are an attractive and healthy redness around the centre of the face.

Writing: Appearance (page 13)

Model answer

David Beckham is quite tall and he has an athletic build. He has a fair and clear complexion - you couldn't say he has freckles. He is very popular all over the world because he is successful but also because of his appearance. At the moment he has short blonde hair with highlights and he sports a goatee beard and stubble, but he is always changing his style, so perhaps next year he will have dark spiky hair... who knows?!

Idioms using physical features (page 14)

Q43:

He is under the thumb.	To be controlled by another person, often a husband/wife.
Tracy's new car cost her an arm and a leg.	Something that is very expensive.
Tell me what you know. I am all ears!	To give your full attention to something.
Tim resigned after the argument. I think it was a knee jerk reaction.	To make a decision quickly without all the facts, or without thinking properly.
Sean's eyes are bigger than his stomach. He will never manage that!	He will never manage that! To think you are hungrier than you actually are.
I need to speak to my boss. There are a few things I have to get off my chest.	To tell someone how you feel about something, after a long time of staying quiet.
We used to be good friends, but we do not see eye to eye now.	To disagree about something; to have differing opinions.
Her dad had a lump in his throat the day she was married.	To be overcome with emotion and unable to speak.
The mayor had butterflies in his stomach as he prepared to break the bad news.	To feel nervous about something you are going to do.
John always invites himself to parties to try and rub shoulders with celebrities.	To meet someone socially.

Compound adjectives (page 15)

Q44:

1. Hard-working
2. Absent-minded
3. Well-mannered
4. Bad-tempered
5. Easy-going
6. Hot-headed
7. Quick-witted
8. Kind-hearted
9. Old-fashioned
10. Open-minded

Compound adjective meanings (page 16)

Q45:

Hot-headed	To do things without thinking about the consequences; to act rashly
Absent-minded	To forget things or be unaware of your surroundings
Hard-working	To put in a lot of effort into a job or a task
Old-fashioned	To believe and follow ideas which are no longer relevant, or from the past
Bad-tempered	To become easily angered
Kind-hearted	To be generous and caring towards others
Easy-going	To be friendly and kind towards people; to be of a relaxed nature
Quick-witted	To be able to think of good ideas and responses instantly
Well-mannered	To behave in a polite fashion
Open-minded	To be willing to accept new ideas and other people's opinions

Compound adjectives: Antonyms (page 16)

Q46:

Hot-headed	Cautious
Absent-minded	Attentive
Hard-working	Idle
Old-fashioned	Trendy
Bad-tempered	Even-tempered
Kind-hearted	Mean-spirited
Easy-going	Uptight
Quick-witted	Ponderous
Ill-mannered	Polite
Open-minded	Intolerant

Writing: Describing yourself (page 17)

Model answer

My name is Mike and I am 32 years old. I am originally from Warsaw in Poland but I have been living in Edinburgh for the last 7 years. I like living in Scotland because I think it suits my personality. People tell me I am a friendly and easy-going person, and that I am kind and helpful to my classmates and my work colleagues. Perhaps this is true but I know I can also be hot-tempered at times if things do not go exactly as I plan. I work in a factory here, although I am tall and quite well-built I am not actually that physical so I would prefer to do something more academic with my life. How would I describe my looks? Very handsome, of course! I'm joking... but I think I fit in well in Scotland because I have red hair and freckles, and quite a pale complexion! (152 words)

Vocabulary review (page 17)

Q47:

Sibling	A brother or sister.
Nuclear family	Family including only parents and children.
Single parent	Woman or man with children but no partner.
Maternal	Caring and protective feelings associated with mothers.
Adopted	Child whose legal parents who are not their original parents.
Extended family	Family including parents, children, grandparents, aunts, uncles.
Divorced	Describes a couple who have legally separated.
Upbringing	Process in which a child is trained and educated in life.
Childcare	Care and supervision of a child at home or outside.
Paternal	Attributes or characteristics associated with being a father.

Wedding terms (page 18)

Q48:

1. bride
2. bridegroom
3. best man
4. bridesmaid
5. flower girl
6. page boy

Reading: Wedding (page 19)

Q49:

Progressive	Enlightened
Traditional	Conventional
Dating	Going out with
Uncharacteristically	Atypically
Diplomatic	Tactful
Unsolicited	Uninvited
Nerve-racking	Worrying
Gravity	Seriousness
Unruffled	Relaxed
Reception	Party

Reading: Agony Aunt (page 21)

Q50: a) true

Q51: a) true

Q52: b) false

Q53: a) true

Q54: Close

Q55: Felt left out

Q56: On her plate

Vocabulary: Family problems (page 22)

Q57: Christopher is **insecure** because of his parents' divorce and the closeness of the relationship between his **siblings** and their mother. His father seems to lack any **paternal** emotions where Christopher and his sisters are concerned. His mother is trying to provide **security** and boundaries in her son's life which Christopher is desperate to escape. His aunt, a **single mother** seems to offer a compromise, offering the Christopher security which he needs in a less **rigid** environment.

Making collocations (page 23)

Q58: 1B: 2G: 3J: 4H: 5A: 6I: 7E: 8D: 9F: 10C

Understanding collocations (page 23)

Listening transcript

A sign of the times

I was brought up in quite a traditional way, by parents who had a strong sense of family values and expected their children to support each other. Although there was definitely an element of sibling rivalry among my brothers and sisters, and we squabbled a little, we were essentially loyal to each other. My father was very much a traditional father figure. He was the main breadwinner in the family, although my mother also had a part-time job. My mother has a very strong maternal instinct, she was very nurturing. She enjoyed cooking and knitting and taking care of her children. I cannot imagine either of my parents having an affair; they seemed to have made a very strong commitment to each other which they would not jeopardise. Most of my friends were brought up in the same way. However, perhaps it is a sign of the times, but when I think about the marital status of my contemporaries, they seem to be very different. Several of my friends and colleagues are separated or divorced and many are single parents.

Q59: c) Traditional

Q60: a) Similar to hers

Q61: b) Mostly no

Collocation meanings (page 24)

Q62:

Sibling rivalry	Competitiveness among sisters and brothers
Bring up	To care for and educate
Make a commitment	A promise of loyalty and steadfastness
Maternal instinct	A desire to protect, nurture and care for others
Single parent	A man or woman with children but no partner
Father figure	A person who takes on the role of father in a family or other situation
Breadwinner	One who earns money in a family
Marital status	Description of state of being married or otherwise
Family values	A belief in the moral value of a family
Have an affair	To have a relationship with someone to whom you are not married

Using collocations (page 24)

Q63: sibling rivalry

Q64: having an affair

Q65: family values

Q66: bring up

Q67: make a commitment

Q68: marital status

Q69: father figure

Q70: breadwinner

Q71: maternal instinct

Q72: single parents

Writing: A report (page 26)

Model answer

The table shows the number of divorces in England and Wales, by age at divorce, in thousands and by gender. It is clear from the table that the number of divorces instigated rose gradually with age, to reach a peak of just over twenty thousand at age forty to forty-four. Up to this age there were more women than men instigating divorce. At age forty-five the numbers of men and women divorcing experienced a decline, although in the fifty to fifty-nine year old age group, the numbers of men divorcing increased slightly to around nineteen thousand.

The chart indicates that in younger years, rates of divorce were higher among women. In the twenty to twenty-four year old age group, in general, numbers of divorces were low. Similarly in the sixty and over age group the number of divorces instigated was quite low, although at this life stage as indeed after the age of forty, men were significantly more likely to divorce.

163 words

Q73: Formal

Q74: No. It is not necessary to explain any reasons for divorce rates changing. You should only describe the trends in the graph.

Q75: No. It is not necessary to explain any reasons for divorce rates changing. You should only describe the trends in the graph.

Writing: Email to a friend (page 27)

Model answer:

Dear friend

I got your details from the exchange programme at my college and I decided to send you an email. In the old days people would've sent chain letters or handwritten notes to penfriends, so I suppose this is the modern day equivalent.

Anyway, as this is our first contact then I should introduce myself. My name is Joseph and I'm 23. I live in Aberdeen and I have a Scottish mother and South African father. I'd describe myself as being hard-working and easy-going, and in terms of appearance I'm tall and slim, I have curly hair and freckles... that's definitely from my mum's side of the family. Other than that I don't think I have many distinguishing features.

At the moment I am studying towards an engineering qualification at college. It is something that my siblings also study and we all take after our dad, it was his chosen profession first. We're a close family and there's no sibling rivalry however, everyone helps each other out with their studies.

I also work part-time at a restaurant here. To be honest I don't like it that much, the manager is hot-tempered and he's pretty lazy. But, it gives me a little extra money each month to spend on my hobbies which are skateboarding and video games. I'm also saving up to buy a car — I think I might need one for when I graduate and start my first job.

So, I hope that has given you an introduction to who I am. It would be great to hear back from you and maybe we can become online friends. Perhaps we could even visit each other's countries one day in the future?! Let me know all about you.

Best wishes

Joseph

(291 words)

Reading comprehension: Email to Marie (page 29)

Q76: informal. Examples are: contractions, exclamation marks, phrases like *how about that?*

Q77: a) They are friends

Q78: nuclear

Q79: extended

Q80: b) false

Q81: a) true

Q82: b) false

Q83: a) true

Listening comprehension: Claire and Edwin (page 31)

Listening transcript

Edwin and Claire have been planning their wedding for the last six months. Edwin, a twenty-seven year old doctor originally from the Netherlands, met Claire, twenty-three, while they were working together at the Northern General Hospital. Claire is a nurse in ward twenty-four and the care profession has been her occupation for over two years now. Claire's family are English but she moved to Scotland when she was nineteen to live with her previous boyfriend. That relationship did not last, Claire explains, "He was so hot-headed, he never listened to anyone's advice. We were always in trouble, but I guess I was young then, I probably found that attractive about him. Well, that and the fact that he was really quick-witted, he would always know the right thing to say in every situation. I'm a lot less attentive, a bit dreamy and absent-minded to be honest. They say opposites attract, and maybe they do, but they don't tell you that the attraction soon wears off!" Claire goes on to explain the differences between her ex-boyfriend and her fiancé, Edwin, "Edwin is so kind-hearted, with him being a doctor I suppose I expected that..." The present and past loves of Claire's life do not have a lot of similarities in terms of appearance either. "Barry, that's my ex, was tall and, well... a bit overweight. He had a dark complexion, a ridiculous goatee beard that I never liked, and to make matters worse he had blonde highlights. Actually he was quite unattractive now that I think about it!" "I'm no oil painting myself, of course, in fact I'm a bit of a plain Jane, but Edwin sees something in me that he likes". "The only criticism I would make of Edwin is his dress sense, he isn't exactly what you'd call a trendy guy, but if that's the only problem with him I think I can live with it!"

"People always say you should try and stay friends with your ex, but to be honest I just don't see eye to eye with Barry any more. He has changed so much from when I first knew him. I suppose I have been changing too, but I've never been happier than I am today. My wedding is just around the corner, I have butterflies in my stomach just thinking about it, my life has never been better. Thank goodness Edwin came into my life!"

Q84: b) while they were working in the hospital

Q85: a) impatient and smart

Q86: a) not having a good attention span

Q87: b) false

Q88: b) false

Q89: b) false

Q90: a) true

Q91: c) Claire's relationships past and present

Topic 2: Lifestyle

Vocabulary: Medical practitioners (page 34)

Q1: A8: B10: C5: D2: E3: F4: G7: H9: I1: J6

Pre-reading activity: A Winter's Tale (page 36)

Q2: 1F: 2H: 3B: 4I: 5N: 6G: 7L: 8D: 9A: 10M: 11C: 12K: 13E: 14J:

Reading: A Winter's Tale (page 38)

Q3: b) false

Q4: b) false

Q5: a) true

Q6: a) true

Q7: a) true

Q8: b) false

Q9: b) false

Q10: elation

Q11: distress

Q12: adequate

Q13: transformation

Q14: rewarding

How healthy are you? (page 40)

Q15: a) 7 - 8 hours

Q16: c) 1 - 3

Q17: c) three times a week

Q18: a) 2 litres

Q19: a) 28 / 21

Q20: b) at least five

Q21: a) I have at least one close friend or family member I can confide in

Q22: b) Eat, drink, and exercise in moderation

Alternative therapies (page 42)

Q23: b) reiki

Q24: g) chiropractic

Q25: f) shiatsu

Q26: c) reflexology

Q27: d) hypnotherapy

Q28: a) acupuncture

Q29: e) herbalism

Therapy synonyms (page 44)

Q30: healing

Q31: diagnosis

Q32: organisation

Q33: correspond

Q34: imbalance

Q35: flow

Q36: ailments

Recognising passive structures (page 46)

Q37:

1. is recognised
2. are affected
3. has revealed
4. has been established
5. is thought
6. is exposed
7. has been shown
8. be adopted
9. have been found
10. is believed

Stress

It **is recognised** that some stress is a positive thing since it can motivate us to act, increase productivity and improve our performance. However, too much stress can have a very negative impact on our lives in the short term, and can have long term consequences as well.

Sufferers of stress **are affected** by a range of unpleasant symptoms including insomnia, poor appetite, sweating, and difficulty concentrating. In the long term we are more likely to suffer further health problems such as high blood pressure, strokes, headaches and feelings of anxiety and depression.

A recent study **has revealed** that there is also a clear link between stress and heart disease. Although this connection **has been established**, the process by which it occurs is not altogether clear. It **is thought** that stress may have an indirect link to heart disease because it may lead to an increase in blood pressure and also cause people to overeat, indulge in alcohol or smoke more. High levels of stress mean the body **is exposed** to unhealthy levels of hormones such as adrenalin and cortisol.

It **has been shown** that the ability to deal with stress depends upon a range of factors including quality of relationships, emotional intelligence, approach to life and inherited factors. For example, if you have a strong group of friends and family you are likely to be more resilient when under stress.

There are a range of approaches which can **be adopted** to help tackle stress. Methods which **have been found** effective in dealing with stress include setting realistic goals, and prioritising tasks. It **is believed** that finding distractions, and in particular, exercise, can counteract the negative symptoms of stress, as can learning to express emotion and channelling positive thought.

Using passive structures (page 46)

Q38: You should take one to two tablets every four to six hours. One to two tablets **should be taken** every four to six hours.

Q39: Before you travel you should ensure that the doctor gives you all of the necessary injections. Prior to departure ensure that you **have been given** all of the necessary injections by your doctor.

Q40: Researchers have confirmed a link between stress and heart disease. A link **has been confirmed** between stress and heart disease.

Q41: Researchers have established that cutting down on overtime should reduce the risk of heart disease. It **has been established** by researchers that cutting down on overtime should reduce the risk of heart disease.

Q42: The British Medical Association recommend eating five portions of fruit and vegetables each day. Eating five portions of fruit and vegetables a day **is recommended** by the British Medical Council.

Idiomatic phrases part 1 (page 47)

Q43:

1. under the weather
2. off colour

3. clean bill of health

4. out of sorts

5. run down

6. on the mend

Idiomatic phrases part 2 (page 48)

Q44:

1. As fit as a fiddle

2. A cast iron stomach

3. Pins and needles

4. Recharge my batteries

Idiomatic phrases: Match phrases to definitions (page 48)

Expected answer

Q45:

1. cast iron stomach

2. under the weather

3. off colour

4. pins and needles

5. out of sorts

6. on the mend

7. clean bill of health

8. run down

9. to recharge your batteries

10. as fit as a fiddle

Answers from page 48.

Q46: 1, 4, 7, 10 and 11 are appropriate

Writing: A report (page 49)

Model answer

Introduction

This report is based on a survey conducted with 150 school pupils regarding our school canteen, snack shop and the van outside the gates. The report will present findings in each category and then provide recommendations regarding ways of improving the quality and availability of the food offered in school.

The canteen

Pupils were reasonably satisfied with the overall quality of the food served. The homemade soup was particularly popular. Pupils stated that they only had a choice of two main courses and this lack of variety in the canteen food also applied to desserts and fruit —only the most traditional kinds of fruit were available. Vegetables were thought to be overcooked and desserts "quite stodgy". The water fountain was broken throughout the survey period.

The snack shop

The food in the snack shop was limited to unhealthy snacks, and although pupils enjoy the range of cakes and sweets there were no healthy alternatives for their consideration such as fresh fruit or yoghurt.

The van parked outside the school

Food available from the van also tended to be quite unhealthy, consisting of burgers, pastries, sugary drinks and sweets rather than fresh fruit or juice. Many pupils indicated they used the van because it was cheaper than the snack shop or the canteen.

Recommendations

The results indicate a need to extend the range of food on offer and to focus on developing a healthier approach to the selection of foods at school and in our cooking methods.

249 words

Listening Comprehension: Eastern and Western medicines (page 50)

Listening transcript

The Practice of Acupuncture

What exactly is acupuncture and how did you become involved in it?

I have been practising acupuncture for around ten years now, however I feel that I am still learning and refining my practice. I believe that this is a process which I will be working on for the rest of my life. The therapy is based on the principles of ancient Chinese beliefs about healthcare, emphasising the need for balance in the flow of energy, or qi, within the body. Where there is pain and illness, the acupuncturist believes that there is imbalance and uses fine needles in points in the body to restore equilibrium and enable the body to heal itself.

What kind of training have you had?

The course which I completed lasted three years and encompassed two subtly different approaches to acupuncture. The first is Traditional Chinese Medicine (TCM) or yin yang theory and the other, Five Element Acupuncture. This blend enabled us to benefit from the two approaches. Traditional Chinese Medicine focuses on the symptoms which a patient is experiencing discovered by questions and observation. In Five Element Acupuncture, the accent is placed upon the nature of the person since everyone is likely to have a different response to a condition. In Five Element Acupuncture the therapist considers emotion, tone of voice, colour of the skin and smell in diagnosis and treatment.

Can you tell us about your course in bit more detail?

The course included study in five main areas which were Conventional Medical Science, Point Location, Professional Practice, Diagnosis and Treatment and Reflective Practice. The first of these enabled us to learn more about anatomy, physiology, pathology and pharmacology. It was necessary to learn about the body and conventional treatment of illnesses so as to be precise about use of needles, to compare Eastern and Western treatment, and to understand the impact of drugs and other traditional treatments when working with a patient.

What kind of techniques do you use in diagnosis?

Our course involved extensive practice in recognising signs and symptoms of ill health. To do this were trained in diagnostic techniques such as pulse taking and tongue examination. Point location requires extensive practise as there are nearly four hundred acupuncture points in the body and precision is essential. It was not until our third year that we were let loose on the public to practise our art! The practice of acupuncture is not confined to needles however so we were also taught cupping techniques and application of mugwort, a herb which is heated prior to use.

What place do you think acupuncture has in society?

I believe acupuncture is gaining popularity and I believe that it will continue to do so. I don't think that acupuncture will, could or should replace more conventional medicine but I believe that there is a place for both. What acupuncturists offer is a more holistic approach to ill health. Rather than looking for a quick fix, we are trying to determine the underlying causes of complaints in order to ensure more long term changes.

We live in an age which has a great deal to offer in terms of science and technology. In spite or perhaps because of this however, I think many people are searching for a different approach, one which really takes into account mind, body and spirit and this is where the acupuncture therapist can really help.

Q47:

1. imbalance
2. question and observation

Q48: emotion, tone of voice, colour of the skin and smell

Q49: conventional Medical Science

Q50: pulse taking and tongue examination

Q51: cupping and herbs

Q52: holistic

Reading comprehension: Women's health (page 52)

Q53: c) A newspaper article about health in the UK

Q54: stylishly thin

Q55: wives and girlfriends

Q56: psychological and emotional

Q57: True

Q58: False

Q59: defection

Q60: Osteoporosis

Q61: grounding

Q62: charitable organisation

Topic 3: Physical environment

Noun categories (page 58)

Q1:

1. proper
2. collective
3. collective
4. common
5. abstract
6. abstract
7. proper
8. concrete
9. concrete
10. common

Identifying types of noun (page 58)

Q2: A

Q3: B

Q4: B

Q5: A

Q6: A

Q7: A

Q8: B

Q9: B

Q10: B

Q11: B

Writing: City life (page 60)

Model answer

Living in a large urban metropolis can be a mixed experience. Coming from the city of Glasgow, a city of approximately one million inhabitants (including the surrounding suburbs), I have seen the best and worst that city life can offer.

In the first place, there is the issue of health. We benefit from a National Health Service, but there are a great number of unhealthy people in Glasgow. This in part is due to poverty, but it is also due to a lack of education about eating and other aspects of lifestyle. Scottish people are renowned for being among the unhealthiest in Europe - heart disease is high in the big cities where stresses of everyday life make people smoke and drink more than in other areas. Country life can make it easier to obtain fresh fruit and vegetables. Good quality produce can be hard to find in city supermarkets, and organic produce is often too expensive for many people.

Next, there is the issue of unemployment. In Glasgow, while there are jobs in business, banking and accounting, work is scarcer in other fields. Unemployment can lead to crime and in busy cities there is often a higher incidence of illegal activity. To that extent, the countryside may seem a safer option. However, you are more likely to find gainful employment in the city of Glasgow than in most other parts of Scotland. At the same time, if you know your way around a city you can generally avoid dangerous situations.

Finally, I would like to discuss the area of entertainment and leisure. In my city there are several cinemas showing a range of movies from mainstream to art house, hundreds of bars and restaurants and all the amenities you could want to enjoy a lively day out. Glasgow has a diverse and vibrant atmosphere and varied and interesting leisure options which are simply not available in other areas. In my view, the advantages of city life considerably outweigh the drawbacks.

Vocabulary: The city and the country (page 61)

Q12: 1I: 2H: 3B: 4G: 5C: 6E: 7J: 8A: 9F: 10D

Pronunciation: Syllable and word stress (page 62)

Q13:

1. outskirts (syllables = 2, stress = 1st)
2. picturesque (syllables = 3, stress = 3rd)
3. suburban (syllables = 3, stress = 2nd)
4. quaint (syllables = 1, stress = 1st)
5. bustling (syllables = 2, stress = 1st)
6. inhabitant (syllables = 4, stress = 2nd)
7. cultivate (syllables = 3, stress = 1st)
8. commuters (syllables = 3, stress = 2nd)
9. amenities (syllables = 4, stress = 2nd)
10. infrastructure (syllables = 4, stress = 1st)

Listening: City and country life (page 62)

Listening transcript

Living in the countryside is, to be honest, in equal parts a blessing and a curse. In many ways I feel fortunate to have grown up in a rural area. I wouldn't swap the memories I have of splashing around in rivers, climbing monkey puzzle trees and riding my uncle's horse around the hilltops, marvelling at the breath-taking views... I wouldn't swap that for anything. When we reminisce, I sometimes feel pity for those friends of mine who were raised among asphalt, high rise flats and exhaust fumes in the heart of the city.

Then again, when I was younger, some of my friends were dogs, cats and goats — we lived on a farm — and the highlight of the week was when the mobile library bus came to the nearest village. That was the only opportunity I had to see either a bus or city dwellers on a regular basis, until I went to university aged 18. Adapting to uni life was a real struggle. I feel like if I had lived in the melting pot of the city from a younger age I'd have integrated more adeptly. At times, I found it harder than the locals to interact. Ethnicity, culture, religion and tradition, even sexual orientation, are all much more diversely represented in the big city. It sounds like a cliché, but there are a good number of country folk whose belief sets have not progressed over the last fifty years. I put that down to their geographic isolation.

But, what I do know is that city life is much less healthy, what with all the waves radiating from wireless items like mobile phones and laptops, smog, dirty water — water in the countryside simply tastes purer and even looks cleaner... and as for the litter and the chewing gum everywhere in the streets, well, do I need to comment? The only people I remember getting sick from my childhood were the handful of adults who worked in the city and had to commute — they always looked more stressed and caught more germs and viruses than anyone else. The locals who grew their own crops and worked hard outdoors all day were always in the best of health.

Another plus point is the ability to work at your own pace as a countryside resident. There's not the same pressure of deadlines and schedules, nobody shouting at you to "have that done by lunchtime!" from their office in their pinstriped suit; you can more or less be self-reliant while living in the country. Life and work in the city can be hectic and that's something that I've never enjoyed about it, although you do miss the urban nightlife and leisure facilities when you're out in the sticks sometimes. Maybe the ideal set-up is to have a home in each place?!

Q14: b) false

Q15: b) false

Q16: a) true

Q17: b) Adults who went to work in the city had more illnesses

Q18: b) mobile phones, laptops and poor water quality

Q19: c) see positives and negatives in both

Q20: a) the leisure and nightlife

Q21: a) we don't know

Reading comprehension: Population control (page 65)

Q22: a) true

Q23: b) false

Q24: b) false

Q25: amercement

Q26: rigorous

Q27: macabre

Q28: dissuade

Q29: b) Holds a balanced view on the issue of population control

Listening comprehension: The New Atlantis (page 67)

Listening transcript

The New Atlantis?

News reports around the world recently broke the story that the world is going underwater, and fast. Before you rush out and buy your scuba-diving gear and put a down payment on a submarine, rest assured that it won't affect all but the most extravagant members of our civilisation. For the world under discussion is the archipelagic replica off the shores of Dubai. The rich and famous have, it would appear, quite literally been sinking their money into this ambitious property development which is now in peril from the sea, according to evidence brought forth at a recent tribunal.

Perhaps it is fortunate then, that this world is still largely unpopulated. In stark contrast to reality, only Greenland has a year-round population here, with the remainder of the country-shaped islands either incomplete, or the villas and hotels on them lying empty. Sports and movie stars were rumoured to have been among the investors, but there has been little in the way of stargazing to be had, and the tabloids have yet to capture any of the rich and famous in the area, so the rumours appear to have been unfounded. The company who won the contract to act as the "global ferry" to take people between regions of "the world", and back to the mainland, launched proceedings against the parent company of the project. They state that the islands are suffering erosion and the resultant clogging of the sea channels between them means they are no longer navigable.

The problems started with the financial crisis in Dubai, which saw many construction projects either scrapped, or at least indefinitely postponed. "The World" was undoubtedly the most ambitious and high-profile of all of these projects, and it quickly and unsurprisingly became the biggest casualty. The state owned conglomerate heading up the development of "The World" fell into debt of some thirty billion dollars in 2009. Since that time, various companies involved in the property development of the islands and the tourism promotion industry have filed actions against the chief developer.

Still, the obstinate corporate façade remains. The head developer claims that over seventy-five per cent of the luxury islands have been sold, and that the project has merely experienced a minor setback which has delayed the completion date. A spokesman for the parent company also refuted claims that the islands were sinking, stating that the sand did not require any further nourishment and that the project and the islands themselves were both still very much afloat.

Q30: A

Q31: False: it is the only island which is occupied

Q32: False: these were only rumours

Q33: False: many construction projects either scrapped, or at least indefinitely postponed

Q34: B

Q35: True: "minor setback"

Q36: True

Q37: A

Topic 4: Press and media

Analysing register in the press (page 71)

Q1: a) Tabloid

Q2: b) Broadsheet

Q3: b) Broadsheet

Q4: a) Tabloid

Q5: a) Tabloid

Q6: b) Broadsheet

Q7: a) Tabloid

Q8: a) Tabloid

Q9: a) Tabloid

Q10: a) Tabloid

Informal synonyms (page 73)

Q11:

Formal	Informal
recent	up to date
ascertain	find out
response	answer
acknowledge	admit
address	deal with
monitor	watch
vital	necessary
indicate	show
however	but
ensure	make sure

Newspapers: Vocabulary review (page 74)

Q12:

							¹J							
			²E	D	I	T	O	R	I	A	L			
							U			³C				
		⁴T		⁵P	R	E	S	S		I		⁶G		
		A		N			⁷C	A	R	T	O	O	N	S
		B		A			O		C	S				
		L		L			L		U	S				
		O		I			U		L	I				
	⁸A		I				S		M	A	P			
⁹B	R	O	A	D	S	¹⁰H	E	E	T		N	T	C	
T			E				I		I	O				
I		¹¹P	A	P	A	R	A	Z	Z	I		N	O	L
C			D						C		N	U		
L			L						H		M			
E			¹²I	N	T	E	R	V	I	E	W		N	
S			N						S					
	¹³L	E	T	T	E	R	S	P	A	G	E			

Reported speech (page 75)

Q13: a) Reported Speech

Q14: b) Direct Speech

Q15: a) Reported Speech

Q16: a) Reported Speech

Q17: b) Direct Speech

Q18: a) Reported Speech

Q19: b) Direct Speech

Q20: a) Reported Speech

Direct to reported speech (page 77)

Q21:

1. She said that she had taken a mobile phone out of her pocket and that Marzo had gone berserk and started hitting her.
2. She added that it was not the kind of thing she would do.
3. Bateman said that she had become used to that kind of thing and that it was part of the job.
4. The actress claimed that she had been stung in the past.
5. She said that she was sorry about the misunderstanding.
6. Marzo admitted that she had taken tranquillisers and alcohol before leaving home.
7. Marzo invited Lewis to her hotel room for an interview on the following day.
8. John Bishop told reporters that it was a PR stunt.
9. Bishop said that Marzo loved the attention.
10. Lewis pointed out that she had nothing to lose.

Speech equivalents (page 78)

Q22: 1B: 2E: 3C: 4A: 5D

Television (page 80)

Q23: f) soap opera

Q24: d) film

Q25: h) travel

Q26: e) reality TV

Q27: b) documentary

Q28: g) sport

Q29: a) comedy series

Q30: c) drama

Language of discussion (page 82)

Q31:

Agreeing	Disagreeing	Inviting opinion	Interrupting politely	Stating strong opinions
That's a good point	You have a point but...	What are your feelings on this?	If I could just make my point	I reject that view entirely
Exactly!	I agree with you up to a point	What do you think?	Could I just say	I really can't agree with you
Precisely!	I take your point but...	What are your views on the matter?	If I could just interject	I totally disagree
I couldn't agree more.	That's not quite how I see it	Do you have any thoughts on this?		I am firmly of the belief
Yes I agree with you	I see it a different way			I am convinced

Reading: Letters to the press (page 84)

Q32: b) To complain about a TV programme

Q33: c) angry

Q34: a) formal

Synonyms: Letters to the press (page 85)

Q35:

tedium	dullness
agonising	excruciating
endless	interminable
incoherent	inarticulate
shallow	superficial
greedy	avaricious
thoughts	reflections
acquisitive	materialistic
goals	aspirations
rebuked	berated
treating	indulging
chubby	podgy
familiar	common
rubbish	dross

Writing: Letters page (page 85)

Model answer

Dear Madam

I am writing to express my absolute delight with the recent 'Pets are Us' documentary on 'The Wild Channel' which explored the relationship between British people and their pets in a variety of different contexts.

The programme's researchers had unearthed some fascinating stories about unique bonds between animals and owners. My particular favourite was the bird which only sang on special occasions. However the programme did not confine its remit to heart-warming stories of favourite pets, it also delved into various psychological studies and recent research which has demonstrated the powerful impact which animals can have on our health and sense of wellbeing.

I was also fascinated to discover more about the various employment opportunities which exist involving working with animals both in paid and voluntary sectors. It was particularly uplifting to watch the positive responses of children with autism to equine therapy and elderly patients in hospitals to volunteer dog owners.

The strength of the show, in my opinion, lay in the quality of journalism. The programme makers managed to capture some special moments in the lives of ordinary people with pets without proceedings becoming overly sentimental.

This is one of the most interesting, entertaining and touching programmes I have seen in recent years. I only hope that there are more documentaries of a similar quality scheduled for the coming winter evenings. There is so much poor quality programming on television these days that I felt strongly compelled to write a letter supporting excellent documentary making by a channel which is always pushing the boundaries.

I would like to extend my gratitude to 'The Wild Channel' and I would encourage any of your newspaper readers who missed the programme to try to find it online on their catch-up service. They will not be disappointed.

Yours faithfully
Alexandra Jackson

(301 words)

Listening comprehension: Media (page 86)

Listening transcript

Jocelyn: Hi Gary how are you? Did you have a good weekend?

Gary: It was good but I didn't do an awful lot I'm afraid. What about that rain? Our street was flooded. The weather was so bad that even the football was cancelled. Anyway I stayed at home and watched a few matches on satellite TV. What about you?

Jocelyn: Do you know what? I quite like weekends like that, torrential downpours preclude going out, you have to be more resourceful. Anyway I spent the weekend reading newspapers and magazines. I cut articles out and I keep them in a scrapbook. Sometimes I use them here at work.

Gary: Why on earth would you bother to do that when there are computers? Hellooo it's the 21st century now! You have to "harness technology" as our head of department keeps saying!

Jocelyn: Very funny. Seriously though, are you telling me you don't read newspapers?

Gary: Never —I get all the information I need online and what's more I am sure I get far more than a newspaper can give. By the time the paper has gone to press it's already dated. I, on the other hand, get a blend of information and images from news agencies, and more importantly from real people. Citizen journalism is what it's all about. Look at all the major events that have taken place worldwide recently. Without people on mobiles taking pictures and sending messages we would really have struggled to get a clear idea of what was going on.

Jocelyn: Well Gary, I do agree with you that technology and the man in the street have a big part to play in dissemination of news. You do have a point there, but I just don't think you get the depth of analysis that you do in a good quality newspaper. Many journalists are really skilled at researching, analysing and writing. They can be more objective because they are not affected in the same way, they explore the issues and ask more interesting questions.

Gary: I think it's time that journalists realised they no longer have a monopoly on news. We can all publish now and lots of experts at home can challenge information that in the past we would have been forced to accept. We are no longer the passive recipients of what they choose to tell us.

Jocelyn: I can't agree with you on that one. That's just not how I see it. I can accept your point about the immediacy of news we get from citizens on the street at the time. That kind of information is invaluable but I think we have to look at various sources including newspapers, otherwise we just get a snapshot of events and no analysis. Oops, look at the time, interesting though this is I'll have to go .

Gary: It's just as well we are not planning to tie the knot Jocelyn can you imagine the daily battle over traditional versus modern? I can see it all now, computers flying out of windows and the like. . .

Jocelyn: I know, I'm surprised something like that hasn't happened here but there's still time! Do you know I am not sure people here believe we are actually friends.

Gary: I know. Hey, I'm going to see what my students think about this debate, newspapers or online news - bet I know what they'll say. The answer has been revealed

Q36: c) Comparing paper and online information sources

Q37: b) The speakers are colleagues

Q38: c) She was inhibited from going out

Q39: c) Ordinary people

Q40: b) More in-depth

Q41: A, D and E

Q42: a) Sceptical

Q43: b) Friendly chat

Reading comprehension: Media (page 88)

Q44: 1C: 2D: 3E: 4F: 5B: 6A

Q45: Autocratic regimes

Q46: Freedom of Information

Q47: b) false

Q48: a) true

Q49: b) false

Q50: b) An essay about freedom of information for students

Q51: c) Rights of the individual to privacy

Topic 5: Technology

Acronyms and initialisms (page 95)

Q1:

Computer Hardware	File Extensions	Internet	Television / Video	Other
RAM, USB, CPU	JPEG, PDF	ISP	HDTV, LCD, DVD	GPS, SMS

Q2:

1. ISP
2. GPS
3. JPEG
4. PDF

Reading: Cyberspace (page 95)

Q3: a) sarcastic and patronising.

Q4: b) a lifestyle column in a magazine.

Q5: a) True

Q6: b) False

Q7: b) False

Q8: obsolescence

Q9: supersede

Q10: blankly

Q11: freelance

Q12: consigned

Q13: advent

Relative clauses (page 100)

Q14: 1-b, 2-a

Q15: Steve Jobs, who co-founded Apple technology with Steve Wozniak, was credited with democratising the computer.

Q16: Social networking sites, which have arguably transformed the way we access news, give us more detail than journalists.

Q17: External hard drives, which prevent computers from losing processing time, are now essential in most organisations.

Q18: A local bus driver, who was using a mobile phone at the wheel, has been suspended.

Q19: Mark Zuckerberg, who is the founder of Facebook, still uses his networking site.

Q20: Bill Gates, who is the creator of Microsoft, is still the richest man in America.

Forming relative clauses (page 100)

Q21: Computer programmer: This is a person who specialises in writing computer software.

Q22: Blu-Ray player: This is a device which allows you to play movies in a high definition format.

Q23: Interactive whiteboard: This is a device which teachers use to display information to their classes.

Q24: Web designer: This is a person who builds websites for individuals and companies.

Q25: Digital camera: This is a device which allows you to take large numbers of photographs electronically.

Writing: Discursive essay on technology (page 103)

Model answer

There is no question that technology has brought a number of benefits to society, but at the same time, it could be argued that there are also negative factors associated with the advancement of technology. This essay will examine three of the more recent technological inventions, namely video games, social networking sites and digital cameras, and will explore both the advantages and disadvantages that they have had on society. Video games became hugely popular with children and teenagers in arcades in the 1980s. Today, they have grown beyond the youth market and are an integrated part of the entertainment industry.

Video games are often criticised by parents, schools and the government for having detrimental effects on those who play them. It is argued that they encourage sedentary lifestyles, prohibit the development of social skills and that they are bad for our eyes. This may be true, but video games also have many benefits. For example, people can link up with their friends online all around the world and chat while playing, therefore increasing opportunities for socialisation and countering claims that playing video games is a lonely, isolating experience. They also develop hand-eye co-ordination, a skill that is transferable to many real-life careers.

Social networking sites are often discredited in the same fashion as video games. Critics dismiss them as a waste of time and anti-social, but on the other hand many young people today organise their social lives and interests, and even their love life, very effectively through these websites.

Digital cameras perhaps have the most benefits, and fewest drawbacks of the three technologies. They allow us to take and store thousands of photographs instantly. They are inexpensive and highly convenient — many people now even use the inbuilt digital cameras on their mobile phones. Fifteen to twenty years ago, we had to buy film for our cameras, pay for expensive development and wait weeks to see photographs which may not even have turned out well. The only real drawback of the invention of digital cameras is that many photography stores have closed due to people being able to use computers and print pictures at home.

All new technology comes with its advantages and disadvantages, but generally the advantages tend to outweigh the disadvantages, and that is certainly true in the case of video games, the digital camera and social networking.

Pronunciation: Technology (page 103)

Q26:

Technological - Number of syllables: 5 Stress: 3rd

Capacity - Number of syllables: 4 Stress: 2nd

Prototype - Number of syllables: 3 Stress: 1st

Expansion - Number of syllables: 3 Stress: 2nd

Laboratory - Number of syllables: 5 Stress: 2nd

Integration - Number of syllables: 4 Stress: 3rd

Supersede - Number of syllables: 3 Stress: 3rd

Interconnectivity - Number of syllables: 7 Stress: 5th

Obsolescence - Number of syllables: 4 Stress: 3rd

Telephony - Number of syllables: 4 Stress: 2nd

Writing: Future technology (page 104)

Model answer

My city in the future will be a marvellous place to live. Nobody can say for certain what changes will take place, but based on evidence from the past few years and the changes that have already happened here, it appears likely that any change will have a positive effect on the wellbeing of the people and the economy.

Glasgow today is a progressive city. Only ten or twenty years ago it still resembled the shipbuilding hub that it was during wartime, but the redevelopment of the riverfront area and the razing of unappealing high-rise flats has really changed the face of the city and brought it into the 21st century. It is now a much brighter and more vibrant place to live.

I expect this trend to continue over the next two decades. Technology will clearly play a key role in the future of the city, and I expect that the road and rail infrastructure will be completely overhauled in this period. I am not convinced we will have flying cars or spaceships in twenty years, but I do believe the transport system will be much more efficient. Technological advancements will lead to people almost exclusively driving environmentally friendly vehicles, with cars running on solar power or electric charge. I also think we will see a change in people's work patterns, as more efficient computer technology and possibly robotics take away the strain from people in a lot of the labour-intensive tasks we face today. The result of this will be more free time, which can only be a positive thing for the health of the city's residents, as it should lead to reduced levels of stress and illness.

The move towards everything being more efficient will also affect our personal lives. People will have even more technology at home, but it will all be interconnected and easy to operate, perhaps even by voice. It is an exciting time to look forward to, and I think Glasgow will benefit from technological advances in the same way as the world's other major cities.

© HERIOT-WATT UNIVERSITY

Reading comprehension: The internet (page 105)

Q27: b: There must be more to the internet than this

Q28: a: Generally positive and optimistic

Q29: b: false

Q30: a: true

Q31: b: false

Q32: omnipresent

Q33: procrastination

Q34: infidelity

Listening comprehension: Technology (page 107)

Listening transcript

*Katy:*Well, if you resisted mobile phones like I did, and computers and digital cameras for a long time too, I wonder if you were finally won over and are now completely addicted to technology? Do you sleep with the mobile at the side of the bed? Skype your children when they are away from home? And are you committed to the daily ritual of checking your inbox? Many of us at one time, not so long ago, wondered if we would ever find a use for the technologies which we find indispensable today, but what about those of us with disabilities? Is the world of assistive technology developing at the same pace and producing indispensable gadgets to support disabilities?

*Katy:*Today my guest is Martin Kline, technology writer at the Tribune. Martin has just returned from this year's Techware conference which features presentations and speakers from around the world, and showcases recent innovations. Martin, welcome to the show.

*Martin:*Hello, Katy. Thank you for inviting me here. Yes, well, Techware have set up assistive technology events as you have said, focussing primarily on professionals and highlighting the role of technology in learning, work and society, for people with disabilities.

Katy: So, tell me, what caught your eye at this year's event?

*Martin:*Well, something which attracted quite a bit of attention from the Google stable is a mobile phone with a touch sensitive screen which enables blind and partially sighted users to make calls without the need to see the screen. The user touches the screen and this point represents the number 5. Other numbers are then found around the screen in terms of their relationship to that number. For example the number 8 would be just below where the number 5 was mapped on the screen and so on. An enhanced feature of the phone, which I particularly liked, was that if you make a mistake you simply shake it and start again! You can also get spoken feedback on what you have done.

*Martin:*A tip to remember is that if you pinch the phone this can increase accuracy of use. I really think this could be useful for people with physical disabilities too, as perfect aim is not a crucial factor in it use.

*Katy:*So, this is a technology that could target a wider market?

*Martin:*Yes, this could be beneficial in many ways - for those with physical disabilities, for the partially sighted and for sighted people too. It is really just an easier way to use the phone. This is important I think because many of those involved in assistive technologies believe the industry would benefit from making mainstream products more accessible and from making products which reach a wider market. There is an argument that assistive technologies focus on the most acute problems and don't really cater for the growing number of people who are partially blind or partially deaf, for example.

*Katy:*You say these numbers are growing?

*Martin:*Yes and with the aging population that we have, numbers will continue to grow.

*Katy:*So what other gadgetry did you encounter Martin?

*Martin:*Well I saw an amazing device called a PenFriend by the RNIB. Now this device is about the same size as a microphone. What you can do with this is record speech, in order to label anything from medicine to food packages. You simply attach a label to an object, register it with an optical scanner and then record your voice. When you point the scanner at the object you can then play back the recording of your voice, so if you wanted to remember dosages of medicine or contents and sell-by dates of foodstuffs, then that's the kind of information you could save.

*Katy:*Do you think that the IT industry has demonstrated sufficient interest in assistive technologies?

Martin: In the past, no, I think that this has been a missed opportunity. It is extremely disappointing that the revolutionary technology available at the research and design stage struggles to reach the market.

*Katy:*What lies ahead do you think?

*Martin:*Well I think that in the future, as a corollary of the aging population, there are likely to be far greater numbers of people who while not totally blind or deaf are partially so, and similarly we are likely to see greater numbers of people with memory disorders, so the market has to grow to accommodate that. At the same time there is also greater awareness of equal rights, so once again that will impact upon the industry and hopefully generate more enthusiasm around the whole subject.

*Katy:*Well let's hope so Martin. Thank you so much for coming in today.

*Martin:*Thank you Katy it's been a pleasure.

Q35: c) Assistive technology

Q36: A, D and F

Q37: relationship

Q38: feedback

Q39:

1. Attach a label to an object
2. Register it with an optical scanner
3. Record your voice
4. Point the scanner at the object
5. Play back your message

Q40: b) false

Q41: a) true

Q42: a) true

Topic 6: Planning a trip

Types of vehicle (page 112)

Q1: Road/overland: HGV, quad bike, moped
Rail/on track: freight train, tram, underground
Air: blimp, glider
Sea: hovercraft, yacht, cruise liner, trawler

Methods of transport (page 113)

Q2:

1. I didn't think there were many **hovercraft** around these days, but there are still several in use on the south coast of England. It's an exciting alternative to travelling by boat, and the kids love the idea that they are floating on a bed of air!

2. So, let me get this straight... in a **glider** it's just you up in the air in a plane with no engine? Sounds dangerous to me.

3. I'm just back from Rome. You should see the streets there - crazy traffic! Everyone is riding around on **mopeds**.

4. Scotland used to be famous for its **trams** but they were replaced with buses many years ago, and the rails have long since been removed.

5. Personally, I think that **quad bikes** should only be used off-road for sporting activities. They are too slow and the driver is too exposed to be on the road.

Parts of a vehicle (page 113)

Q3:

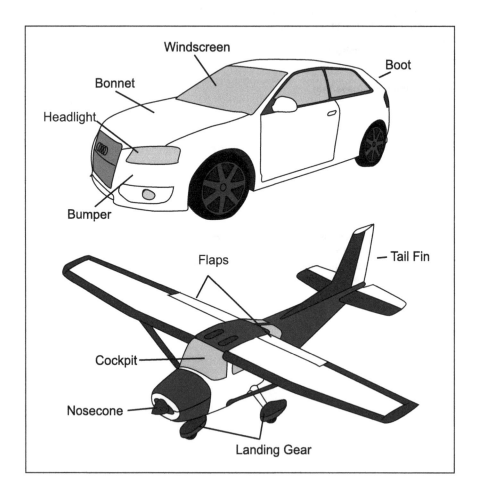

Punctuation (page 115)

Q4:

full stops	.
commas	,
capital letters	A
inverted commas	" "
parentheses	()
apostrophes	;

Reading: punctuation (page 115)

Q5:

Almost a million Anyplace Airways passengers face Christmas travel chaos, after the airline's cabin crew voted yesterday to back a twelve-day strike that will ground its planes beyond the New Year. The unprecedented walkout over staffing and salary cuts, which will last from the 22nd December (next Tuesday) to 2nd January, has left many customers scrambling to book on other airlines or trying to make alternative arrangements via crowded express trains. Anyplace Airways' sheer size as a long-haul carrier would make it difficult for other carriers to accommodate its passengers, according to observers within our industry. "If these strikes go ahead, a huge number of people will be stranded", said Tom Westland, aviation author and former pilot. "I cannot think of any route where flights would not have been fully booked, so there are going to be a lot of angry Anyplace Airways customers and possibly a lot of legal battles in the coming months."

Reading: Airline strike (page 116)

Q6: a) An aviation industry magazine

Q7: a) true

Q8: b) false

Q9: a) true

Q10: b) false

Synonyms (page 117)

Q11: 1H: 2F: 3J: 4A: 5I: 6C: 7D: 8E: 9B: 10G

Word stress (page 118)

Q12: d) five

Q13: b) second

Q14: c) four

Q15: c) third

Q16: b) three

Q17: b) second

Q18: c) four

Q19: b) second

Q20: a) two

Q21: b) second

Q22: c) four

Q23: b) second

Q24: c) four

Q25: b) second

Q26: b) three

Q27: b) second

Q28: a) two

Q29: a) first

Q30: d) five

Q31: b) second

Vocabulary: Holiday accommodation (page 122)

Q32:

1. 1G: 2I: 3D: 4B: 5E: 6F: 7J: 8C: 9H: 10A

Choice of accommodation (page 123)

Q33:

1. A hotel
2. A youth hostel
3. A chalet
4. A self-catering apartment
5. A campsite

Listening: Tourist haven? (page 123)

Q34:

Mallorca is the biggest of the Balearic Islands. It used to be one of the most **impoverished** parts of Europe and farming was the main source of employment. Forty years ago however things started to change and now Mallorca is one of Europe's **foremost** package holiday destinations, specialising in family holidays. Millions of visitors **flock** to the island, swelling the off-season **indigenous** population of seven hundred thousand. These visitors bring with them jobs and money, but at what cost?

One of the biggest problems caused by such a high level of tourism is the impact on the environment. A **massive** amount of building has taken place to accommodate tourists without much consideration for the environment. In many areas the coastline has been destroyed. Mass tourism has also brought traffic **circulation** issues and pollution. Mallorca has the highest level of car **ownership** per capita in Europe. Another major problem facing Mallorca is that of waste, which is increasing by 10 - 15% per year. Something **dramatic** would have to be done to solve this problem. There is also the issue of water shortage. At times, fresh drinking water has had to be shipped in from the mainland.

Many tourists are not interested in the environment or the culture of the country they are visiting. Indeed, even those who buy property and become resident in the country often form ghettos of their own nationalities, failing to **integrate** or show an interest in local culture and traditions. The purchase of property by foreign visitors causes property prices to **escalate**, making it more difficult for young locals to buy homes. This **exacerbates** the division between local people and the thirty thousand Europeans who have chosen to migrate to Mallorca. While the attitude of some tourists is **questionable**, since they seem to **disregard** the sensitivities of local people, they do bring employment and much needed cash to the community.

The economic impact of tourism in Mallorca has been **irreversible**, because tourism has all but put an end to farming. People have abandoned farming for easier jobs in the tourist industry. This has led to a critical loss of independence and has had a damaging effect on the culture of the island, as generic forms of entertainment replace more **traditional** ones, once again to meet tourist needs. The people of Mallorca find themselves in an unenviable position - where once they craved the **influx** of tourists and their spending power, now they are a necessary evil for the economic stability of the island.

Q35: Example answer

Phrasal verbs in context (page 127)

Q36: 1B: 2D: 3F: 4G: 5I: 6C: 7E: 8H: 9J: 10A

Phrasal verb synonyms (page 128)

Q37: 1D: 2A: 3C: 4I: 5B: 6F: 7J: 8G: 9E

A) Get around: travel

B) Account for: make/form a total

C) See off: say goodbye (to someone)

D) Check out: vacate (the premises)

E) Set off: start

F) Clamber in: climb across or into (somewhere with difficulty)

G) Fill up: replenish

H) Double back: retrace

I) Touch down: land

J) Check in: arrive (at a hotel or airport desk)

Writing: Informal email (page 129)

Model answer

Hi Georges,

How are you doing? It was great to hear from you. Susan and I can't wait to visit you - good thing we've been saving up too - flights are pretty pricey right now.

We had a few worries when we saw the news last week - it looks like there is a lot of tension and anger about the immigration changes. We're a little concerned that foreigners won't be too welcome right now, so can you reassure us or should we be thinking of putting off our visit for a while?

What's the easiest way to get there? We were thinking about a direct flight to the capital, and then taking the train, but perhaps you know a better route? Oh, and do we need any kind of jabs before we set off?

Shall we bother buying a phrasebook or can we get by in English? I doubt my Russian will help much, but we both know a little French, if that's any use?

Hoping it's still sunny when we arrive as we're planning on bringing shorts and t-shirts. The embassy staff told us not to carry cash but I thought I'd check with you to see how widely accepted credit cards are. Susan hates travellers' cheques, so I doubt we'll bother getting those.

One more thing, and I know it's right up your street... I'd love to take in a game when I'm there, see the local teams. Susan won't go for that, but she's keen to pay a visit to the Summer Palace - perhaps Aria could show her around while we hit the pubs and the big match? You'll know what else is worth going to see, so we'll leave that in your capable hands.

Get back to me when you can and we'll get this show on the road!

Cheers for now,

Mark

Reading comprehension: Holidays (page 131)

Q38: b) Potential holiday makers

Q39: a) In a tabloid newspaper supplement

Q40:

1. true
2. true
3. false

Q41: connotations

Q42: diligently

Q43: locales

Q44: (the length of) the journey

Q45: travellers' cheques

Listening comprehension: Holidays (page 133)

Listening transcript

Ross

I tend to find holidays, in the traditional sense, a bit problematic. I guess I am what you would call a workaholic. I find it really difficult to switch off. In fact I generally operate on the principle that a change is as good as a rest, and find that working on something other than my main job offers me a kind of relaxation. Having said that, I did start climbing several years ago - it seemed a logical progression from hill-walking, which I loved, and it has now become nothing short of an addiction. I think that climbing forces the mind to focus very deeply on a particular problem, the safest and most efficient way of getting to the top. At the same time, you also exercise almost every muscle in the body. After climbing I tend to feel both physically and mentally exhausted, and for me, that's the best place to be. The trip to South America came from nowhere. The guys who run the climbing centre, where I sometimes practise, were talking about a working holiday they had coming up. They were taking a group from London to Argentina on an adventure holiday and one of the climbing instructors had let them down. I jumped at the chance to stand in for him. Yes, I had to work when I was there, but I can honestly say that is how I enjoy myself. It was undoubtedly the best holiday I've ever had.

Alison

I had been going to painting classes quite regularly on Saturday mornings and had been thoroughly enjoying the process of developing my own style in a relaxed atmosphere. The teacher, Lisa, had a laid-back approach. She kind of enabled us to find our own way and offered advice and instruction when we were faltering. I thought a painting holiday in the south of Spain would be blissful, and even if I do say so myself I felt very hip as I set off with my borrowed portable easel and paint box. I met up at the airport with a couple of other people from the course and we set off in a taxi to find our accommodation, it was a castle and really was out in the back of beyond...! Anyway, that was where we would be based the following week. I think that the holiday could have been absolutely wonderful. The weather was good, the setting was breathtaking and most of the group were quite charming. But what transpired was unexpected. Monica, the teacher over there, was a very intense character. She had strong opinions and wasn't shy about sharing them with us. Far from feeling liberated and creative, I think we all began to feel a bit trapped in splendid isolation and under tremendous pressure to produce something wondrous to display at the end of the holiday. Happily for us, because the teacher was so bossy and controlling, us students bonded really well and kind of rebelled a little. One night we chose to eat in a local village rather than stay within the grounds and be forced to listen to Monica again! I wouldn't say I had a dreadful time, but it certainly wasn't the holiday I had anticipated and it didn't do much for my painting.

Sue

I had broken up with my boyfriend of several years and had been going through a particularly bad patch at work as well. I was dying for a break - it was either that or I'd probably have had a breakdown, so I started trying to visualise a context which would be therapeutic. Some friends invited me to join them on a package holiday to Greece, but I knew that I needed something which would be more nurturing and spiritually uplifting. When I saw an advertisement for a yoga retreat in India, I knew this was exactly what the doctor ordered! I had been practising yoga periodically in my local gym, but I was by no means an accomplished yogi! It turned out that this was irrelevant since the instructor at the Haven, as it was called, explained I would simply work to develop my own potential regardless of my prior experience. I'll tell you a secret - on holiday I tend to be a bit of a party animal, burning the midnight oil and then hiding my hangover under the duvet the next morning. But there was none of that wild behaviour on this holiday. I was up at the crack of dawn and in bed surprisingly early. There were yoga sessions available throughout the day from half six in the morning right through till dinner time, about five or so. I became totally focussed on the practice. There were also opportunities for meditation classes which I really got into as well. The food was all vegetarian, I knew that before I went, and as a meat eater I thought I'd find this a bit on the bland side, but each night a stunning array of delicious food was presented in an open air restaurant. As the holiday progressed, I began to unwind and relax in a way I had never managed before. It really was the most tranquil and uplifting experience I've had. When I came home, I felt rejuvenated and armed with inner resources to deal with my problems.

Q46:

1. Ross
2. Alison
3. Sue
4. Alison
5. Sue
6. Ross
7. Ross

Q47:

1. false
2. true
3. false
4. true
5. false
6. true
7. false
8. true
9. false

Topic 7: Current affairs

Vocabulary Review: Entertainment and leisure (page 138)

Q1:

1. theatre: play, musical, comedy, drama
2. music: classical, jazz, hip-hop, rap, blues, choral
3. art: still life, watercolour, installation, sculpture, expressionist
4. dance: tango, ballroom, ballet, flamenco
5. film: feature, romantic, drama, war, animation, comedy
6. literature: autobiography, non-fiction, poetry, romantic, crime
7. sport: racquet, water, spectator, team, winter

Entertainment Vocabulary in context (page 139)

Q2:

1. ovation
2. footlights
3. reviews
4. subtitles
5. aisle
6. romantic
7. conductor
8. installation
9. performances
10. backstage

Cleft and pseudo-cleft sentences (page 140)

Q3: What we decided in the end was to go to the cinema rather than stay at home.

Q4: It was the reviews that must have put people off going to see the play.

Q5: It was when we lived in London that we tended to go to the theatre more often.

Q6: What I have never understood is why people rave about opera.

Q7: What I wish is that people would refrain from consuming chips and crisps in the cinema.

Q8: What attracts me to travel writing is finding out about far-flung and exotic locations.

Q9: It wasn't until I was in my thirties that I started painting!

Q10: It is the joy of reading a good book that is one of my favourite forms of entertainment.

Word emphasis (page 141)

Q11: It is John who likes eating in restaurants, not Sally.

Q12: It wasn't until they were produced with sound that films became really popular.

Q13: It was ballet that she wanted to focus on, not tap.

Q14: It is talent that makes one a perfect musician, not practice.

Q15: It is not self fulfilment she is aspiring to, it's celebrity status.

Q16: It is the novel he wrote last year that he is famous for, not the other novels he has written about crime.

Reading: Film recommendations (page 142)

Q17: b) A film review

Q18: c) A magazine or online entertainment site

Q19:

1. What makes it even more compelling is the fact that it is based on a true story.
2. It is Ed Masry, played by Albert Finney, who is the legal 'expert'
3. but it is Erin who wins the confidence of the people of Hinkley, browbeating the opposition with her razor-sharp wit and ultimately emerging triumphant.
4. However, it is the future of her relationship with her new boyfriend about which we are left uncertain.
5. What happens between them is a kind of reversal of traditional gender roles.
6. It is a sense of feeling neglected and taken for granted, more often attributed to female roles, which prompts George to ask her to give up her job.
7. It is perhaps in the role of Brockovich that we see Roberts fully engaged with a character for the first time.

Q20: Erin and George

Q21: intoxicating

Q22: compelling

Q23: eponymous

Q24: brash

Q25: lowly

Q26: metamorphosises

Q27: razor

Q28: impacts

Q29: witty

Q30: understated

Listening: Music and emotions (page 145)

Listening transcript

Peter

I listen to classical music all the time, in my car, at work, when I am out running or walking or even in the bath. I was brought up with classical music, my mother plays piano and my father is a cellist. I can always find a piece of music which reflects my mood. When I go running I listen to something like Vivaldi's Four Seasons (perfect for the UK where we often experience all four seasons in one day). It makes me feel lively and optimistic even after a hard day at work when my energy seems depleted.

My favourite classical composer however is Beethoven I find his music completely awe-inspiring. It is so moving that I often lose myself completely, sometimes to my cost. More than once I've been sitting in a car, completely absorbed by my music, unaware that the traffic lights have changed from red to green, till some irate driver wakes me from my reverie!

Justine

I am absolutely addicted to Salsa. I first started listening to it a few years ago on a visit to South America and became totally hooked. For me it is the most upbeat music you can listen to. I defy anyone to feel low when there is Salsa playing. It is actually a name given to various Cuban derived genres such as Son and Mambo and has become astoundingly popular in the UK over the past decade. I dance to this music at home and at a local Salsa club. When I listen to Salsa it makes me feel invigorated and revitalised even on my most lethargic days.

Rachael

My favourite kind of music is Jazz. My father was a jazz musician and when I hear the sound of a saxophone, I experience a range of emotions. I find it really exciting and stimulating and yet also kind of mellow. A particular favourite is Billie Holiday. A friend introduced me to her music and I have spent a lot of time listening to her and reading about her life, which was one of terrible hardship. Perhaps that is why her voice seems to have such depth and richness. I feel I have an affinity with Jazz, probably inherited from my father, he is no longer with us sadly but the music stirs up a lot of memories of him. It makes me feel quite melancholy sometimes. Yes for me jazz rouses an intoxicating blend of feelings which no other music awakens.

Gerard

I am a big fan of rock music and I have always loved Bob Dylan. I have been listening to this music since I was a student about twenty years ago and even then it was apparently out of date! The lyrics are amazing and that's really important to me, Dylan is a true craftsman. When I listen to his music I find that it evokes the past and I enjoy reminiscing but it also relates to my life today. I find it therapeutic, uplifting, inspiring, relaxing ... you name it!

Q31: Peter and Justine

Q32: Peter

Q33: Rachael and Gerard

Q34: Peter

Q35: Justine

Q36: Rachael

Q37: Rachael

Q38: Peter

Q39: Depleted

Q40: Affinity

Q41: Irate

Q42: Blend

Q43: Evoke

Q44: Lethargic

Q45: Daydream

Q46: Reflect

Grammar: Prepositions (page 146)

Q47:

The novelist Jane Austen is known worldwide **for** her popular novels describing the society of pre-industrial England. She was born **in** Hampshire, England in 1775 and was one of eight children. Apart **from** three years at a school in Oxford, Jane received most **of** her education at home. She began writing seriously **in** the late eighteenth century and is credited **with** giving the novel its modern character through her treatment of everyday life. She focussed particularly **on** the rituals of courtship which she observed in her own family and **among** the professional and upper classes. Since writing was not considered an appropriate preoccupation **for** a woman Jane disguised her identity at the start **of** her literary career. Although the preoccupation of most of her heroines is courtship and marriage, she herself never married. She is thought **to** have had **at** least one proposal which she rejected because she would not marry someone she did not love. She spent the last eight years **of** her life **at** Chawton in a 17th century house which is now owned by the National Trust and preserved in her memory. She wrote some **of** her best and most popular works **in** this house.

Listening comprehension: Leisure (page 147)

Listening transcript

John

Do you have a taste for challenge and adventure? Do you dream of horse riding across the Andes or backpacking around the Far East? Well, perhaps you don't need to travel to the other side of the world to realise your ambition for excitement. Our reporter Miranda Bell has been finding out about what is becoming an increasingly more popular activity taking place on our own doorstep. Discover your own adventure, while mountain biking in the Borders of Scotland. Miranda what did you find out?

Miranda

Well John I have just returned from a fantastic week at Glentress, Scotland's biggest and most popular centre for mountain biking. It's just a mile and a half from Peebles, 24 from Edinburgh and 66 from Glasgow which makes it reasonably accessible for a weekend trip, but what I found amazing about Glentress is that you actually feel as though you have travelled to an entirely different country. The atmosphere is amazing - there is an incredible buzz around the place and the beauty of this kind of trip is that you can be outdoors pretty much all day if you want (and of course if the weather permits).

John

So why do you think so many people are drawn to mountain biking?

Miranda

Well I spoke to a group of guys from Edinburgh on a weekend break and the theme from all of them was very much the same. Biking is perhaps comparable with sports like climbing and skiing because it offers a physical and mental challenge. The mind is focussed on staying on the bike and on the track and of course doing this at speed is exhilarating. One cyclist told me it was the perfect antidote to a hard week at work, another said it was a sense of living in the moment that was so appealing. It can be a high energy, high adrenalin activity and that is part of the draw.

John

Why do you think that Glentress is so popular? After all, you could go almost anywhere to cycle on mountain bikes.

Miranda

Up to a point yes but there are some very good reasons to go to Glentress. The location is perfect. You don't need mountains for biking, but hills are good and this area offers a varied landscape with hills, forests and woodland. There has been a great deal of investment in Glentress by Visit Scotland, the National Tourist organisation, and it has paid off. There are a range of different trails which are colour coded according to difficulty. The red trail, for example, involves zigzagging through miles of single-track forest paths, while the black trail, the most demanding, involves twenty nine kilometres and a long gruelling climb.

John

Well we can see why this would attract the young and fit but what about families? Is this something you could do with children?

Miranda

Absolutely! This is something that the whole family can enjoy. As I said there are a range of different trails including some specifically aimed at the beginner. Instruction is available and there is a kids' club on Saturdays. There are lots of places to stay in the area including hotels and bed and breakfast accommodation and some good places to eat too. To really soak up the atmosphere though go to the hub cafe, the excitement there is contagious! What you experience in the hub is akin to the après ski experience. There's an element of bravado and competition among the thirty-something year olds, as they compare frame weight and kit and trade stories of their exploits, which I found hysterical. There are also loads of kids just yawning and stuffing food down in wide-eyed admiration at the tales they're hearing.

John

Finally Miranda do you have any tips for prospective visitors?

Miranda

Yes. The trails are rarely congested but there are a lot of visitors so if you plan to hire a bike book in advance to avoid disappointment. Apart from that remember it is Scotland so take some waterproof clothes and have a fabulous time!

John

Thanks for telling us all about it Miranda.

Q48: c) Describing a mountain biking centre

Q49:

1. The men interviewed by Miranda at Glentress said that mountain biking was the perfect antidote to work.
2. Another interviewee said that he enjoyed living in the moment.

Q50: a) Investment and varied landscape at Glentress.

Q51: b) It is long and it is a gruelling, difficult climb.

Q52: a) True

Q53: a) True

Q54: b) False

Q55: b) False

Reading Comprehension: Jane Austen Critique (page 149)

Q56: b) A critical essay of a novel

Q57: d) Human nature

Q58: b) False

Q59: a) True

Q60: b) False

Q61: a) True

Q62: short clauses and dashes

Q63: Town voice

Q64: Elegant language

Q65: Contrast and narration

Topic 8: Cultural awareness

Christina, Paul and Gosia (page 154)

Q1: Why did you decide to live in a different country?

Q2: Did you have any difficulty adapting to your new environment?

Q3: What differences did you find between your new country and your home?

Q4: Did you suffer from homesickness?

Q5: What were the advantages and disadvantages of living in a different country?

What they said (page 155)

Q6: b) The UK

Q7: a) Italy

Q8: b) false

Q9: a) true

Q10: b) false

Q11: a) true

Q12: c) The UK

Q13: a) Japan

Q14: b) false

Q15: a) true

Q16: a) true

Q17: a) true

Q18: c) Poland

Q19: a) The UK

Q20: a) true

Q21: b) false

Q22: a) true

Q23: a) true

Adjectives: Synonyms (page 158)

Q24: 1E: 2B: 3I: 4C: 5F: 6G: 7A: 8H: 9D: 10J

Answers from page 159.

Q25: past perfect simple

Q26: past simple

Q27: past perfect continuous

Narrative tenses (page 160)

Q28: When I **arrived** in Chile for a visit a few years ago, I **was** really excited and also a bit nervous. I **had not visited** South America before but **had done** some research on the country and I **had been practising** Spanish for a few months prior to leaving the UK. I **had packed** lots of summer clothes but **has also crammed** in some waterproof layers and some thermals, for visiting the south of the country. I **felt** quite well prepared and **had convinced** myself that there would be few surprises! We **had been encouraged** to visit one of Chile's beautiful national parks close to the famous Torres del Paine mountains and we **decided** to follow this recommendation. We **travelled** for three hours through the most magnificent scenery I **had ever seen** to reach our accommodation, a hostel in a log cabin. Unfortunately, as a vegetarian, I **did not find** much to eat at dinner time. We **slept** in bunks in small rooms with other hikers. I **had never been** so cold in my life and went to bed wearing all of my clothes including my hat and gloves! The distances we **covered** were immense and I simply **had not been prepared** for the incredible cold. However, despite this, we **had** had a fantastic trip, the scenery **proved** spectacular and the people very friendly.

Word class (page 161)

Q29:

Noun	Verb	Adjective
socialisation	socialise	sociable
offence	offend	offensive
expression	express	expressive
perception	perceive	perceptive
adaptation	adapt	adaptable
identity	identify	identification
culture	**no verb**	cultural

Polite behaviour (page 162)

Q30: a) a newspaper or magazine

Q31: d) irritated

Q32: disgruntled

Q33: incensed

Q34: universality

Q35: outmoded

Discourse markers (page 164)

Q36:

Additive (Giving more information)	and, what is more, similarly
Contrastive (introducing a point of contrast)	but, on the other hand
Concessive (concedes an unexpected point)	however, nevertheless
Resultative (introducing an outcome)	as a result, consequently

Analysing writing (page 164)

Q37: Talking about plans for the evening /shared expenses

Q38: A couple

Q39: Written — a note or text message

Understanding style (page 165)

Q40: Informal language, colloquial expressions, abbreviations, informal linkers, contractions.

Answers from page 166.

Q41:

1. To describe a visit
2. Colleagues at school/college, relationship of equals
3. Written

Q42:

- neither formal or informal,
- colloquial expressions
- formal and informal linkers
- title
- introduction
- conclusion
- abbreviations.

Features of writing: A visit to a foreign city (page 166)

Model answer

When my friend emailed an invitation to Perugia, she told me to give it some thought, sixty seconds later, I emailed her back to accept. I couldn't resist! Anna had said the architecture in Perugia was amazing, and that it was full of incredibly famous paintings. Perfect for art lovers! For foodies, it's full of wonderful Italian delicacies. What's not to like? I flew to Florence in July, and caught a train to Perugia. The trains seemed old-fashioned, the people lively and exuberant. Due to the sizzling heat, passengers were leaning out of open windows chatting to others. I found the singsong of the Italian accents and the strong smell of ground coffee in the air intoxicating. Perugia is the capital of Umbria and a centre of medieval art. It's full of amazing structures, like the San Lorenzo Cathedral in the city centre and a Roman aqueduct which connects two of the city's hills. In the surrounding area, Assissi is worth a visit. The countryside is a pleasant contrast to the hustle and bustle of the city. Umbria hosts a jazz festival every year in July. The city was buzzing with visitors and we were spoiled for choice in terms of musical entertainment. I can't recommend Perugia enough for a visit. For me, the scenery, architecture, food and entertainment all deserve ten out of ten!

Q43: 1F; 2A; 3G; 4E; 5B; 6D; 7C:

Appropriate language (page 167)

Q44: couldn't, you're, I'd, can't

Writing: School magazine article (page 168)

Model answer

So near and yet so far!

Last month our English teacher, Miss Lucas, decided we should visit London for a couple of days. She decided to visit Shakespeare's Globe Theatre to see Hamlet (which we are studying) and take in some museums. We left Glasgow for the "the big smoke" on a rainy Thursday in March.

Compared to Glasgow Airport, Heathrow is enormous and sprawling. Without Miss Lucas we would still be in Terminal Five. Londoners clearly had no idea what we were saying when we asked directions!

Everyone seemed incredibly busy! People of all sorts were running down escalators to catch the tube. I couldn't believe how many people were crammed into the carriages.

We were delighted to discover the weather in London was ten degrees warmer than in Glasgow. We were particularly pleased about the good weather as the Globe theatre has no roof!

On the first day some of us went to the British Museum. We all met at a traditional restaurant on the Thames for dinner. The menu included roast beef and Yorkshire pudding; not popular in Glasgow! On the second day we went to the Tate Modern and finally to the Globe. The performance was fantastic.

It was great to spend time in London. In many ways it's like home. However the city is much bigger and more densely populated than Glasgow and strangers don't chat to you like they do in Glasgow!

Intonation (page 169)

Q45: a) Rising

Q46: b) Falling

Q47: b) Falling

Q48: a) Rising

Q49: b) Falling

Q50: a) Rising

Intonation in a dialogue (page 170)

Listening transcript

Julie: Hello Carol! How are you?

Carol: I'm fine thanks ...you?

Julie: Oh I'm all right

Carol: You don't sound it! Is there something wrong?

Julie: Not really it's just that I was supposed to be going to the cinema tonight and I was so looking forward to it but John just cancelled!

Carol: Oh that's a shame

Julie: Yes I know I haven't been out for two weeks - I've been studying really hard.

Carol: Look I don't have any plans for tonight I'll come with you!

Julie: Really!

Carol: Yes I'd love to come

Julie: Great! Let's do that!

Q51:

The stressed words are in capitals and the patterns of intonation are in italic and described in the brackets.

Julie - **HELL**o **CAR**ol! How are *YOU*? (rising interested)

Carol - I'm **FINE** thanks ...*you*? (rising interested)

Julie - Oh **I'M** all *right* (falling - sounds a bit flat)

Carol - You don't **SOUND** it! Is there something *WRONG*? (rising then falling - sympathetically)

Julie - Not **REALLY** it's just that I was supposed to be going to the **CIN**ema tonight and I was **SO** looking forward to it but John just *CANcelled*! (falling on cancelled - fed up)

Carol - Oh *THAT'S* a *SHAME* (falling sympathising)

Julie - Yes I know I haven't been out for **TWO WEEKS** - I've been **STUD**ying **REALL**y *hard.* (falling on hard- fed up)

Carol - Look **I** don't have any plans for tonight **I'LL** come *with you*! (rising very enthusiastic)

Julie - *REALLY!* (rising very interested)

Carol - Yes I'd **LOVE** to *come* (rising)

Julie - **GREAT!** Let's *DO* that! (Rising)

Listening comprehension: Paula and Jamie (page 171)

Listening transcript

Paula

Interviewer: Why did you decide to live in a different country?

Paula I really wanted to expand my awareness of different cultures but I felt that to do this really effectively, I had to immerse myself completely in another culture.

Interviewer: Did you have any difficulty adapting to your new environment?

Paula No, I adapted straight away, I loved it! There were a few things I had to get used to though, like the pace of life. That seemed to be a lot slower than I was used to. I had been working in Scotland and was used to making plans. I crammed a lot of events into my days. When I went to Spain I had to accept that plans could be changed at the drop of a hat.

Interviewer: What differences did you find between your new country and home?

Paula The weather was very different so I enjoyed living in a hot and sunny climate. The lifestyle, as I said before, was very different as well especially with respect to socialising. It was commonplace to eat and stay out very late at night. I was doing evening work and finishing at about ten, but there was still a lot of time to hang out with friends. The weather in Scotland, as much as anything else, makes that kind of thing difficult.

Interviewer: Did you suffer from homesickness?

Paula I didn't really suffer much from homesickness, but ultimately you do perhaps do a bit of soul searching sometimes and wonder about how family and friends back home are doing and what you are missing out on.

Interviewer: What were the advantages and disadvantages of living in a different country?

Paula The advantages of living in Spain, for me, were the climate, the lifestyle, the opportunity to learn a new language and make new friends. Disadvantages hmm well, there were some differences which I found more difficult to acclimatise to. To give you an example, if I asked people round they didn't really let me know if they weren't coming or if they had to cancel. That seems to be normal in Spain but it would be perceived as a bit rude in the UK. Also, smoking still seems to be very popular and acceptable in Europe, while in the UK it's much more frowned upon.

Jamie

Interviewer: Why did you decide to live in a different country?

Jamie Well, I went to Zimbabwe, to go to university there. It was like a kind of an exchange thing, I spent six months at the University of Zimbabwe in the capital, Harare.

Interviewer: Did you have any difficulty adapting to your new environment?

Jamie It was tricky actually . . . a bit difficult at first, you see it was my first trip abroad ever, well pretty much, and it was completely different to the UK. I was a bit uncomfortable because I am British and because of Britain's colonial history there. I wasn't sure how I'd be received. I wasn't sure if people would be friendly or not but in fact people were really welcoming, I made a lot of friends quite quickly. The food was different as well, I'm vegetarian and eating out was much more difficult back then than perhaps it is now, so I had to adapt to that.

Interviewer: What differences did you find between your new country and home?

Jamie Well, food, as I said. Transport was different as well and of course the weather, which was much better than home, so I really enjoyed that aspect of the change. I was there in the winter so it was a nice warm temperature in the day time but surprisingly chilly in the evening.

Interviewer: Did you suffer from homesickness?

Jamie Yes I did and I found myself missing unexpected things, like the rain. I wished sometimes it would just rain. The sense of humour over there is good, but to be honest, I still think nothing beats the kind of humour which is based on shared experience. I think it's easier to identify with and be empathetic to the humour in your own country. Also, I didn't have a TV and though that's good in some ways, sometimes you just want to chill out in front of the TV.

Interviewer: What were the advantages and disadvantages of living in a different country?

Jamie What I loved about it most was my lifestyle, it wouldn't have been the same for everyone but I enjoyed being a student there. There were only two universities over there which was very different from the UK so anyone at university had got there through sheer hard work. Having got there students would work their socks off to make the most of it. That was a real eye opener for me. It influenced me a lot and encouraged me to capitalise on the opportunity really.

Q52: The UK, Scotland

Q53: Spain

Q54: b) false

Q55: b) false

Q56: a) true

Q57: People in Scotland are more **punctual** than people in Spain.

Q58: People in Spain **socialise** differently because the weather is better.

Q59: In the UK people are expected to accept or decline invitations. It would be **perceived** as rude not to respond.

Q60: The UK

Q61: Zimbabwe

Q62: a) true

Q63: a) true

Q64: b) false

Q65: b) false

Q66: Sense of humour is often best where people have shared **experience**.

Q67: At universities in the UK not all students **capitalise** on the opportunities they have.

Reading comprehension: Natalie (page 173)

Q68: b) she is on an exchange visit

Q69: a) Gabriella is easily pleased where food is concerned

Q70: c) are louder but just as friendly

Q71: b) false

Q72: a) true

Q73: a) true

Q74: b) false

Q75: b) false

Answers to questions and activities for Unit 2

Topic 1: Personal ambition

Uses of the be going to future tense (page 180)

Q1: Planned future events: A, D and E

Prediction based on evidence: B and C

Uses of the will future tense (page 182)

Q2: b) Prediction based on opinion or belief

Q3: b) Prediction based on opinion or belief

Q4: a) Unplanned action or event

Q5: a) Unplanned action or event

Q6: b) Prediction based on opinion or belief

Going to and will forms (page 184)

Q7: My daughter Morgan is only six years old, but she has more ideas, opinions and plans than most of my adult friends. She knows what secondary school and university she's going to attend, which boy from her class will be her future husband and how much money she will earn when she's thirty! Yes, it seems I as a parent will have little input because Morgan has already got it all figured out. "I'm going to wear my red dress today because I want to look pretty for singing class", she says, and in restaurants she assumes control, "I think I will have the fillet of sole, but not too much sauce". Times have changed since I was young, and it's hard to stop your kids behaving this way when all their friends are doing likewise. Compared to some of her playmates, Morgan isn't that bad, in fact. I've heard stories of credit cards being used, "I'm going to buy Barbie a new car" and holidays plans being ruined, "I'm not going to stay at gran's house because it's boring, so you will have to cancel your holiday to France", all because of spoiled and petulant children. Will our kids, or our children's children, ever enjoy the naïve innocence of childhood that we once had? I'm not going to put money on society reverting back to how it was, put it that way. Morgan will be an adult before she knows it and only then will she realise how much she has missed out on. Having said that, she tells me she's going to be a princess with six palaces by the time she's twelve, and I've been promised one of them, so perhaps it's not all bad news!

How ambitious are you? (page 184)

Q8:

Ambitious: A, D, H, I, J, L

Unambitious: B, C, E, F, G, K

Word class (page 185)

Q9:

Noun	Adjective	Adverb
determination	determined	determinedly
dedication	dedicated	dedicatedly
drive	driven	
listlessness	listless	listlessly
shiftlessness	shiftless	
indifference	indifferent	indifferently
apathy	apathetic	apathetically
passiveness	passive	passively
eagerness	eager	eagerly
aimlessness	aimless	aimlessly
discipline	disciplined	
resolve	resolute	resolutely

Pronunciation: Syllables and stress (page 185)

Q10:

oOo	determined				
ooOoo	dedicatedly				
ooOo	dedicated				
ooOooo	apathetically				
oooOo	determination				
Ooo	apathy	passiveness	shiftlessness	eagerness	resolutely
oOoo	indifferent				
oOooo	indifferently				

Reading: Ambition in the workplace (page 186)

Q11:

Did you hear about Brian, the new flight attendant? He's only been here a few months but I've heard gossip that the directors have an eye on him because they want to **fast track** him to a management post.

Not another person to get promoted ahead of me! I'm starting to tire of being **overlooked**. I'll have been here nine years next month and I'm standing still.

You'll get that promotion one day. I think it is just the luck of the draw, I really don't think there is a **glass ceiling** for female employees at this company.

Try telling that to Suzy. I've heard that she's being **demoted** from her position, probably so that Brian can be moved up.

That's not what I heard. Suzy will have been flying for twenty years soon, so she's going part-time because she wants to spend more time with her family. They're letting her cash in part of her pension now as well, it's one of the **perks** of having our job.

Oh, I didn't realise. That's not so bad. Well, good luck to Brian then - he's a nice guy and I suppose he deserves to move up the **career ladder**. I just hope I'll be next!

Definitions (page 187)

Q12: A4: B3: C5: D2: E6: F1

Understanding the future continuous tense (page 188)

Q13: 1C: 2A: 3B

1. They are going to be performing a new theatrical production at the Citizen's next month.
2. Will you be using your car a week tomorrow?
3. Linda shall be staying at John's house anyway, so I'm sure it's okay with her.

Use of the future perfect simple tense (page 189)

Q14: will have spent

Q15: will have taken

Q16: will have finished

Q17: will have graduated

Q18: will have left

Use of the future perfect continuous tense (page 191)

Q19: Shannon will have been riding horses for twenty five years (by next year).

Q20: James will have been learning/studying German for two years (by) next month.

Q21: We will have been living together for five years by January when my sister comes to see us.

Q22: Jill will have been writing that song for six months by Christmas.

Reading: A driving ambition (page 191)

Q23: b) false

Q24: b) false

Q25: a) true

Q26: b) false

Q27: a) true

Q28: laid off

Q29: gainful

Q30: volition

Q31: line of employment

Q32: homebody

Listening: A different kind of match (page 194)

Listening transcript

A different kind of match

As we catch up with Jennifer Owen, she's beaming with delight as she concludes a call with another satisfied customer.

"That's very pleasing to hear. I'll be delighted to come along to the reception".

She explains she is going to be attending another wedding, her ninth this year. A high number, but not anything too surprising for a girl on the brink of turning thirty, you may think. What is unusual though, is that Jennifer has in fact been responsible for all of these weddings taking place.

A talented hockey player with her fledgling professional career just beginning to blossom, Jennifer never had the chance to shine on the international stage as her career was cut short by a debilitating knee injury aged just 23.

"It was a tough time for me. Hockey was all I'd ever known since I was able to walk, to be honest. My life revolved around that sport, and my hopes and dreams were to be a successful professional and maybe captain my country one day."

Jennifer went through two years of demanding and intensive physiotherapy courses in an effort to restart her career, but ultimately it was in vain, as her doctor's prognosis was that resuming a hockey career could cause further health problems in later life. It was a hard period of Jennifer's life, but every cloud, as they say...

"I was so down at that stage. The only thing that kept me going was the parties I'd organise. I've always been a social animal, and my friends and I from the hockey scene were mostly single, so I used to throw parties, even prior to the injury, and try to set people up with each other, purely for fun on the off chance that something might happen." "It turned out I was quite good at playing Cupid, two couples I introduced at one of my first parties ended up getting married, and I had this light bulb moment where I thought... maybe I could do this as a career, I might even be able to earn some money from it!"

From that moment, Jennifer's new vocation has taken off in ways she never could have imagined. She's going to buy the premises she's been renting to run her internet and party dating business, "My Goal is Your Match", and is thinking about branching out into supplying bridal wear and wedding services in a traditional shop format.

"I will have been doing this for four years by March and in that time I will have brought together nearly one hundred couples through my dating service. "Like I said, I always thought my career path was going to be a sporting one, but life is full of surprises and perhaps matchmaking is my calling. After all, although I fell into it, I seem to have a talent for it, and who knows whether I would have done as well on the hockey field!"

Q33: b) Twenty-nine

Q34: a) Because she and her friends were single

Q35: b) Due to her friends getting married

Q36: a) Expand and diversify her business

Q37: a) Her new career was perhaps what she was always meant to do with her life

Writing: Ambitions (page 195)

Model answer:

As a twenty year old computing student, I have always wanted to be a successful IT professional. Well, before that I wanted to be a footballer, a cricketer or a famous actor, but I think all young children have slightly unrealistic and over the top dreams like that to begin with. My interest in computers started in my home country of India at a young age, I think I was about seven or eight years old when I got my first laptop. To begin with, I loved games and my dream job was to be a professional video game tester, but then I started to become interested in coding. I dreamed of programming my own games rather than just playing other people's. At school in Scotland I had the chance to learn the basics of programming and I passed my Higher Computing Science with a grade A. I also did well in Physics and Mathematics, which I think are helpful subjects for students who want to work with computers. Now I am in third year of my degree course at university, I am studying game design, and it is a placement year. I was lucky enough to get a placement in KITT, a multinational software company. I see it as a really good opportunity in the short-term to make contacts and network with like-minded professionals while learning on the job. In the future, I think that the experience and skills I am gaining at the moment will prove useful when I graduate and start applying for full-time positions in other organisations. If I really impress my manager on my placement year, I might be lucky enough to get a job with KITT when I graduate. My advice to anyone is to follow your dreams and above all else, work hard to achieve them!

Listening comprehension: Promotion (page 196)

Listening transcript

Striving for promotion is something that many young professionals find themselves doing in today's competitive workplace environment. But what happens when they achieve success and are awarded these elevated positions of responsibility? According to an independently commissioned research report by the University of West Lancaster, promotions are often nothing more than a poisoned chalice.

On the face of it, promotion brings opportunity for increased earnings, social status and all the trappings that life can offer, such as better cars, nice homes, expensive holidays and so on. But, the research shows that ambitious young professionals who receive early promotions are considerably more susceptible to increased stress levels, greater risk of heart attacks and generally poorer health all round. Is a more lucrative retirement fund worth such risk?

It is not just a person's physical wellbeing that is likely to suffer either. The eight-year study examined the mental health of participants in that time, and found that those who had received some form of promotion were 17% more likely to suffer from some form of mental illness, from anxiety attacks to complete mental breakdowns in the most severe cases. The increased limitations on free time or possibility of flexible shifts that are imposed upon a promoted employee were also contributory factors, as they made it more difficult for such people to make GP appointments or take part in any kind of physical exercise to release pent up stress.

'Hard work brings its own rewards' has long been an idiomatic expression in our language, but it would now seem to be in need of revision, because the perpetuation of the perceived rewards that climbing the career ladder brings are making more and more of our workforce into burned out, disenchanted wrecks, some of whom are now wishing that they had never applied for that step up in the first place.

Q38: Early promotions make people more **susceptible** to stress and illness.

Q39: Limitations on free time were **contributory** factors to poor health.

Q40: The drive to climb the career ladder is causing more workers to become **burned out** and disenchanted.

Q41: a) true

Q42: a) true

Q43: a) needs to be changed

Q44: 2. The hidden danger of promotion

Reading comprehension: Ambitions (page 197)

Q45: b) Refusing to give up

Q46: anchored

Q47: regimented

Q48: pioneering

Q49: exude (s)

Q50: lower limb amputation (and osseointegration of a prosthetic leg)

Q51: a) They are supportive

Q52: Three - will have been undergoing, will have ridden, will have already conquered

Topic 2: Preparing for the world of work

Reading: Family economy (page 202)

Q1:

paragraph 1	introduction and outline of the main discussion points
paragraph 2	issues around attitudes to time spent with families
paragraph 3	issues around attitudes to material goods
paragraph 4	responses to research findings
paragraph 5	recommendations and conclusions

Q2: commissioned

Q3: subjective

Q4: consistency

Q5: succumb

Q6: discord

Q7: rampant

Q8: b) false

Q9: a) true

Q10: a) true

Q11: a) true

Q12: b) false

Q13: a) true

Q14: a) true

Q15: b) false

Writing: Ethical advertising (page 206)

Model answer

A recent report published by UNICEF found that British parents felt under pressure to provide children with material goods. This report prompted discussion on the value of banning advertising aimed at children under twelve. While banning such advertising might reduce pressure on parents to buy products, such moves would not tackle the fundamental issue of parental responsibility.

The presentation on television of products which are attractive to children is perceived by some as immoral. These advertisements encourage materialistic attitudes in the young and breed an acquisitive culture among children, who often harass parents into spending beyond their means. At the same time, the desire for more 'things' alienates children whose parents simply cannot afford to keep up with the increasing demands of trends promoted by advertisers. These children can end up feeling isolated or even bullied at school due to them wearing the wrong brand of trainers or not having the latest video game console.

A total ban on advertising would alleviate some of the pressure on parents. However, it could be argued that such a ban would destroy a valuable opportunity through which children, with the assistance of parents, could learn about the ways in which advertising can be misleading and harmful. Furthermore, there is an argument that this move would set a dangerous precedent and that various other types of censorship would inevitably follow. It could open the floodgates for bans on various types of entertainment products and many people would question the authority of the government to make these decisions for them.

It is important to remember that children under twelve should generally be under the supervision of parents. As such, it is surely the responsibility of parents to educate children about advertising processes and to resist advertising pressure within the family, rather than rely on decisions made at a governmental level.

(305 words)

Ambiguity (page 207)

Q16: Being unclear about the answer to the question, I was marked incorrect by the assessor

Q17: Her boss being very domineering, she was made to work twelve hour days.

Q18: Finding her guilty of plagiarism, her lecturer said she would have to appear before the university board .

Q19: Handing in her report late, she was told by the CEO that she was in danger of losing her job.

Q20: I saw the laziest worker in the company lolling around in the canteen.

Q21: His flatmate partying until the early hours of the morning, Martin tried to write up his sales figures for work.

Q22: Having already got a degree, most postgraduates were more confident than undergraduates.

Q23: Returning to full time education, Sarah was thought mad by most of her friends.

Listening: Career change (page 208)

Listening transcript:

Stephen

Good morning everyone I hope that you are comfortable. My name is Stephen. I am here today to talk to you about changing career. The purpose of this initial talk is primarily to generate ideas for discussion and to indicate a clear path for future sessions. I envisage that over the next few weeks we will undoubtedly focus on the more practical aspects of career change, but I also hope that our future workshops and seminars will meet some of the needs identified today.

Let me tell you a story. Last week I attended a fantastic party in the city centre, an event at which there were over a hundred guests. It promised to be a really great occasion, but I have to say that I am not much of a party animal, so I arrived at eight, fully expecting to be back home in front of the fire by ten. Do you know that the first time I even glanced at my watch it was 1am? I was so busy talking and catching up with people that I lost track of time. Now the reason that I have brought this up is not because I intend to lecture you on party planning, but because I want to illustrate what has become a very important model of individual response to economic downturn.

What brought us together last week, is that we all worked in customer service for a highly successful travel company. For a while this company had several flourishing regional departments but, as the recession of the last few years began to bite, management decided to restructure. As a result, one hundred and fifty people were given a choice of taking a redundancy package or relocating to London. Not an easy choice. This was a group of people, largely female, many mothers, and some single mothers with networks of support in Scotland rather than London. Most had worked in travel for over fifteen years, many had no other qualifications and didn't think they had any other skills. In spite of this apparent lack of employability, for many continuing with the company was simply not an option.

So what did people do? Well it transpires they did a fascinating number and range of different things. Let me give you some examples. One lady was in the middle of a part-time Art History degree when redundancy struck. She has now completed that degree and a couple of post graduate diplomas as well and is working very successfully as a full-time curator. Several of the group have completed teacher training courses and have found work as teachers in schools and colleges. For others, redundancy provided an opportunity to reassess life and to explore hitherto unfulfilled dreams and ambitions. One lady realised her dream to work more creatively and independently. She completed a course in running a business supplying flowers for occasions. I talked to colleagues with new careers as diverse and far removed from travel as dog walking, massage therapy, systems analysis, and writing. No one claimed a completely smooth transition from the apparent security of their former existence but no one wished for their old life back. It was viewed with nostalgia rather than regret.

This gathering which takes place every year provides us with an opportunity to get together in a social context, but perhaps more importantly, and without having to try particularly hard, we have an opportunity to network. To put it another way, we have a chance to connect with friends and former colleagues. We inadvertently bounce ideas off each other in a way which has proved inspiring, influential and supportive. We make new contacts often in an entirely unpremeditated way.

Changes in the fabric of society today are well documented. Compared to the working lives of our parents and grandparents, we are all aware that nowadays jobs for life are far less common. Flexibility and change management are skills we need to master. Changes in the education system in Scotland today, involving movement away from learning discrete bodies of knowledge and towards learning to learn, reflect the demands of these new economic developments. Changes in the way we educate are underpinned by a need to furnish society with citizens who can demonstrate flexibility and generic skills and mirror changes we have witnessed in the economic climate in the UK over the last few decades.

In conclusion, and before inviting questions, I would like to say that far from being the blight anticipated, redundancy has opened the door to a new more rewarding future for many of my colleagues who discovered greater strength, determination and talent than they would have ever thought possible.

Thank you. Can I open the floor to questions now - yes, the gentleman in the third row first, and then you madam, just behind the gentleman.

Paul: Paul Tierney, housing manager. I listened to your talk with interest, Stephen, but I wonder how you would respond to the idea that the increasing centralisation of industry and business, rather than being a desperate response to a global economic crisis, is actually a cynical move on the part of a government keen to invest in areas south of the border, with a blatant disregard for the north.

Stephen: Thank you for your question. I would respond by saying that many of my former colleagues would completely agree with your comments, and that the majority fought this decision at great personal cost, both emotional and material. For a long period of time, the battle proceeded without resolution. I emphasise here that change is often excruciating, but in this case it was inevitable, and what I like to focus on are the positive outcomes.

Jane: Jane Walker, Travel Scotland. Stephen, I note your comment that you like to focus on the positive outcomes but can I ask you please at least to acknowledge the negatives. How many people didn't succeed in finding a new career?

Stephen: Well, Jane, of course a few people did not find a new niche. My colleagues were very lucky in that they were offered a decent redundancy package but, for some, that noted the end of their working lives. However, that group represents only a tiny minority; the least prepared, those who hid their heads in the sand and ignored what was happening and also those who had failed throughout their working lives to challenge themselves in any way. Some of these people have paid a high price for their previous lassitude. This is what these seminars are about, about arming people like you with strategies and skills which will protect you in difficult times and enable you to stay afloat when others around you are sinking.

Q24: The main purpose of the talk is to generate ideas for discussion and to direct future sessions

Q25: The speaker expects there to be practical sessions and seminars and workshops based on the current discussion

Q26: To use as a model for responses to economic downturn

Q27: Economic recession

Q28: Curator, teacher(s), florist (running a flower business), dog walker, massage therapist, systems analyst, writer

Q29: Networking, inspiration, influence and support

Q30: A. Government cynicism and B. lack of success in changing career

Q31: A. Agrees in principal but explains how people moved on from this B. Suggests people did not succeed because of a lack of preparation

Vocabulary: Work and academic words (page 209)

Q32: invitation

Q33: indetify

Q34: transition

Q35: therapeutic

Q36: economic

Q37: inevitability

Q38: materialistic

Q39: compromising

Q40: illustrative

Q41: resolution

Pronunciation: Word Transformation (page 210)

Q42:

invite (oO)	invitation (ooOo)
identity (oOoo)	identify (oOoo)
transit (Oo)	transition (oOo)
therapy (Ooo)	therapeutic (ooOo)
economy (oOoo)	economic (ooOo)
inevitable (ooooo)	inevitability (ooooOoo)
materialism (oOooo)	materialistic (ooooOo)
compromise (Ooo)	compromising (Oooo)
illustrate (Ooo)	illustrative (Oooo)
resolve (oO)	resolution (ooOo)

Negative prefix *un* (page 211)

Q43: unsubstantiated

Q44: unrealised

Q45: unfulfilled

Q46: unfounded

Q47: unbearable

Q48: unconditional

Q49: unjustified

Q50: unprecedented

Q51: unsympathetic

Q52: unconstitutional

Reading comprehension: Valuable skills to learn (page 214)

Q53: b. conversational

Q54: a. Providing Instruction

Q55: facetious

Q56: a. Do not write down everything / use abbreviations

Listening comprehension: Carole (page 216)

Listening transcript

Q57: Library induction

Q58: gamble

Q59: Document delivery service

Q60: pre-empt

Q61: drawing a blank

Topic 3: Politics

Political vocabulary: Definitions (page 223)

Q1:
1H: 2I: 3J: 4G: 5F: 6D: 7A: 8C: 9B: 10E

Political vocabulary: Spelling (page 223)

Q2: undemocratic

Q3: monarchy

Q4: regime

Q5: coalition

Q6: boycott

Q7: constituency

Q8: legislature

Q9: referendum

Q10: partisan

Q11: rhetoric

Pronunciation (page 224)

Q12:

1. undemocratic (syllables = 5, stress = 4th)
2. monarchy (syllables = 3, stress = 1st)
3. regime (syllables = 2, stress = 2nd)
4. coalition (syllables = 4, stress = 3rd)
5. boycott (syllables = 2, stress = 1st)
6. constituency (syllables = 5, stress = 2nd)
7. legislature (syllables = 4, stress = 1st)
8. referendum (syllables = 4, stress = 3rd)
9. partisan (syllables = 3, stress = 3rd)
10. rhetoric (syllables = 3, stress = 1st)

Writing: Voter apathy (page 225)

Model answer

Report for MP on Voter Apathy

For the Attention of: Jane Little MP

Please find below my report on voter trends and possible reasons for voter apathy in the UK as you recently requested. Should you have any further questions do not hesitate to contact me.

Summary of previous elections

The figures provided in the attached table illustrate the voting pattern of the UK electorate over an approximate twenty-year period, in terms of voter turnout. There was an extremely good turnout in 1992, with more than three-quarters of registered voters casting their votes at the ballot box. However, there was a severe downturn in the voting percentage over the course of the next two general elections, with turnout reaching crisis point and dropping beneath the sixty per cent mark in 2001. Since then, the numbers have been gradually rising again, up to a healthier 65% in 2010 and 66% in 2015.

Possible reasons for voter apathy

There are a number of reasons for the poorer voter turnout, and one of these is undoubtedly apathy on the part of the younger generations. This remains one of the hardest challenges for politicians to overcome —to win the hearts and minds of the future workforce. The youth vote has been targeted by both Labour and the Conservatives as being crucial to success. Tony Blair was perhaps the first Prime Minister to successfully appeal to younger voters (Source X), and the Liberal Democrat party made student rights and the tuition fee issue a centrepiece of their campaigning over several elections (Source Y), although lessons should be learned from their failure to deliver on their promises —this may only worsen voter apathy in future.

Suggestions

Campaigning on issues which matter to young people may help attract some of them to the polling stations. Engaging with the young vote and listening to and talking to potential young voters may also be a good strategy during your campaign.

(Word count: 322 words)

Vocabulary: More political words (page 226)

Q13: veto

Q14: soapbox

Q15: spin

Q16: by-election

Q17: devolution

Spelling: More political words (page 226)

Q18: soapbox

Q19: backbench

Q20: by-election

Q21: devolution

Q22: autocracy

Q23: electorate

Q24: incumbent

Q25: spin

Q26: whip

Q27: veto

Reading comprehension: UK Elections (page 229)

Q28:

1. false
2. true
3. true

Q29: incarnations

Q30: miniscule

Q31: commonplace

Q32: The alternative vote

Q33: political instability

Listening comprehension: The monarchy (page 231)

Listening transcript

Speaker 1: Eleanor

I feel really privileged to live in a country where we have the rich tradition and culture which the monarchy affords us. People know about the good deeds of our Queen and royal family all over the world, and the amount of positive publicity they generate for the nation just can't be overstated. Our Queen is above all of the political squabbling that parliament has degenerated into; we can always count on her to be impartial, and, well, just there for us. Prime Ministers and MPs come and go, some are more trustworthy than others, but the Queen, well, she's there in the times of prosperity and of recession, year in, year out. The historical significance of the Commonwealth is also huge. Perhaps our part in the history in some of these countries is slightly questionable, but nobody can deny that the Queen is the key link and the bind between us and the good work we have done in all these countries around the world. I think there are fifty-four countries in the Commonwealth, and they all still celebrate the Queen's role as the head of such an important institution. Look at some of the other countries in the world, and how the huge crowds go crazy for the royals when they go for official visits. In fact, there's just as much love for them here. The royal weddings are testament to that... and if any more evidence were needed, how about the collective outpouring of grief at the loss of Princess Diana? That truly showed the support for our monarchy, even from the people who claim not to be interested! The Royal Family acts as a focus for national unity and pride; there are national award schemes, like the Duke of Edinburgh scheme which supports enterprising young people, and look at our national sports people proudly singing the anthem when they represent their country. It brings a tear to my eye. There is no better symbol of 'Britishness' than Buckingham Palace and our Royal Family, and it will be a dark day if we ever let those anarchists and republicans have their way.

Speaker 2: Mike

The Royal Family? Waste of time if you ask me. Tax payers' money supporting something which belongs in a museum, not in castles and palaces and in our parliamentary system. Thankfully, they are more of a figurehead these days and don't really have any political influence any more, otherwise we'd all be living in a dictatorship. Saying that, I don't remember ever voting for the Queen, do you? I think we have a basic human right to elect our Head of State, rather than it just being the prerogative of one particular family. We are supposed to be a democratic country, after all, so I propose that we vote on the abolition of the monarchy. Anyone under 60 in the UK would probably be quite happy to see the back of them, and however the people speak, we should go along with it. There's always the argument that they generate income from tourism and that they act as great ambassadors with other countries, but let's be honest, the amount of good work that they do, and you have to give them some credit for their charity work and whatnot, but... it is detracted from by the amount of tabloid sensationalism that accompanies their every move. Does anyone really care about who the 9th person in line to the throne is going to a fancy dress party with? Should I have to read six pages about it in the papers and see it on the 10 o'clock news? As for our MPs, I feel sorry for them, and that's not something I'd ever expect to say. They have to swear an oath of allegiance to the Queen when they become a member of parliament - well, what if they don't believe in the Queen? You wouldn't make someone swear a religious oath these days, so why are they being forced to do this? It's all archaic pomp and ceremony. The monarchy represents all that is wrong about the class system in this country - they have no idea about what the everyday man and his family have to struggle with. Frankly, it's a discriminatory idea. Look at them giving themselves positions at the top of the military ranks, the heads of the charities and so on, without putting in the time and effort it takes everyone else to get there. It's all from a bygone era, when imperialism was the norm. Nowadays we don't need them. I'll be glad when this country finally becomes a republic.

Q34:

1. Mike
2. Eleanor
3. Eleanor
4. Eleanor
5. Mike
6. Eleanor

Q35: Questionable

Q36: True

Q37: False

Q38: Anarchists

Q39: Figurehead

Q40: False

Q41: False

Q42: Bygone

Topic 4: Global issues

Vocabulary: Climate change (page 236)

Q1: famine

Q2: drought

Q3: fossil fuel

Q4: greenhouse gas

Q5: emission

Q6: precipitation

Q7: reforestation

Q8: acidification

Q9: desertification

Q10: deforestation

Vocabulary in context (page 237)

Q11:

1. greenhouse gases
2. acidification, precipitation
3. emissions, fossil fuel
4. deforestation, reforestation
5. desertification, drought, famine

Pronunciation: Climate change (page 237)

Q12:

1. famine (syllables= 2, stress=1st)
2. drought (syllables=1, stress=1st)
3. fossil fuel (syllables=2, stress=1st) (syllables=1, stress=1st)
4. greenhouse gas (syllables=2, stress=1st) (syllables=1, stress=1st)
5. emission (syllables=3, stress=2nd)
6. precipitation (syllables=5, stress=4th)
7. reforestation (syllables=5, stress=4th)
8. acidification (syllables= 6, stress=5th)
9. desertification (syllables=6, stress=5th)
10. deforestation (syllables=5, stress=4th)

Adjective category (page 240)

Q13:

1. material
2. colour
3. opinion
4. opinion or age
5. shape
6. shape
7. opinion or size
8. opinion
9. origin
10. size

Adjective order (page 240)

Q14:

1. (A) suffocating enormous grey plume (of smoke)
2. (A) hazardous red-hot molten metal
3. (A) deathly fine white covering (of ash)

Writing: Climate change (page 241)

Model answer

Climate change has become a contentious but universal issue in modern times. Although there are some people and companies who deny its existence, the majority of people think it is real and that it is an escalating problem for the planet. Climate change is caused by greenhouse gases heating up the planet and affecting the global temperature and weather patterns. There are now droughts where there used to be plentiful supplies of water and vice versa.

Companies have as much, if not more of a responsibility to combat climate change as individuals do. Companies, particularly heavy industries which rely on large factories for their output, but also small businesses who use a lot of fossil fuels to power their offices should be thinking about ways to make themselves greener. One of the arguments opponents of green energy cite is that it is expensive or difficult to implement, but in fact some of the ways that this can happen are very simple and cheap to introduce. Reducing the wattage of electrical bulbs, replacing them with energy saving bulbs, can be a start no matter what size the company is. This, in the long term, will save the company money and it will also reduce electricity use. Similarly, using solar panels instead of gas or electricity to generate power is a very environmentally friendly step to take.

Governments should be taking the lead on this but unfortunately some are more interested in the economy than the future of the planet. If governments were to introduce grants for businesses to encourage them to go green, or schemes which help them to change over from gas and electricity to renewable energy sources then perhaps there would be a greater uptake and less resistance.

Companies, like individuals, have the choice to do as much or as little as they wish when it comes to preventing climate change but governments ultimately have the biggest responsibility for promoting greener energy.

(Word count: 323 words)

Crossword: Natural disasters (page 242)

Q15:

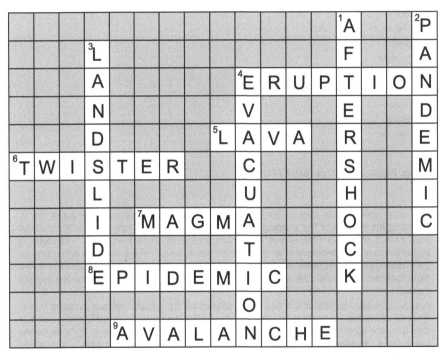

Avalanche: snow, ice, earth or rock which travels quickly and suddenly down a mountain, covering everything in its path

Landslide: rock or stone coming free from a hillside, cliff, or slope and travelling downward at a rapid speed

Evacuation: the act or process of escaping from a place in danger

Aftershock: a minor follow-up seismic event, which follows the main earthquake

Eruption: the act or process of spouting material or liquid forcibly from something, e.g. a volcano

Lava: molten rock which is sent forth from a volcano

Twister: the column of air which resembles a coiled spring, another word for tornado

Magma: molten rock material under the earth's crust

Epidemic: this affects a huge number of individuals within a population or country at once, and is often used to describe the spread of airborne viruses

Pandemic: this affects a huge number of individuals within several countries across borders and seas, and is often used to describe the spread of airborne viruses

Vocabulary: Natural disasters (page 243)

Q16:

1. avalanche
2. twister
3. pandemic
4. magma
5. evacuation
6. epidemic
7. lava
8. eruption
9. landslide
10. aftershock

Listening: Preserved in time (page 244)

Q17:

The once proud Roman town of Pompeii is now 1. **associated** with only one event, the 2. **catastrophic** eruption of the sleeping giant, Mount Vesuvius, in AD 79. Indeed, for the best part of two 3. **millennia**, Pompeii existed only in historical reference, the actual 4. **vicinity**being buried by the age old remnants of an event which was as devastating to mankind at that time as the Hiroshima bomb was in the twentieth century. A lethal 5. **ejection** of ash and fumes rocketed more than twenty miles into the air, dispersing grey cloud across the region and turning day into night.

And so Pompeii lay, untouched and 6. **undisturbed** for around eighteen hundred years. Records show that 7. **excavation** started in the 1860s, and archaeological teams since that date have unearthed not only the ruins of foundations of Roman buildings within Pompeii, buried under the 8. **crusted** layers left by the 9. **pyroclastic** flows, but some of the unsuspecting residents themselves, petrified in ash and forever preserved in an 10. **eerie**, but intriguingly lasting testament to the carnage caused by the power of the volcano.

These pyroclastic flows, the lava and lahars which ran down the mountainside at temperatures of 1300 degrees Fahrenheit, were the main killer. The vertical explosion and the resultant ash cloud added to the casualties, but the 11. **unerring** speed of the flows is what 12. **engulfed** the town and more than 15,000 of its inhabitants.

Today, the once lost town of Pompeii is a popular tourist attraction, with millions of visitors worldwide travelling to see the ruins and experience the 13. **legendary** tale first hand. Vesuvius has not erupted since 1944, and never with the same 14. **ferocity** as recorded in Roman times, but nevertheless, its silent threat looms large over the hordes of souvenir hunters, with experts theorising that the longer the volcano lies dormant, the greater the significance and 15. **magnitude** any future eruption will have.

Writing: Coping with disasters (page 245)

Model answer

Report for the attention of All Staff

Overview

Natural disasters often happen without warning and can catch ordinary citizens and workers unaware and unprepared. However, working in an area such as this near the coast in Scotland, we can put some plans in place to ensure we are ready for the possibility of flash flooding, should it happen again with the severity that it did a few years ago.

Physical preparations

There is not much we can do in terms of buying equipment to prevent floods but we should ensure we have a good alarm system in case of emergency and that our email correspondence has a protocol for such situations. This is a recommendation I have made to management that shall be implemented shortly. In addition, management will purchase sandbags which will be stored in the supplies cupboard near the front door should we need these in the event of a flood.

Training

First of all, we need to devise an escape plan. I suggest that if flooding looks likely, or is beginning nearby, that you act quickly and follow a route out of the office along the west corridor and down the south staircase where we can proceed to the hill at the car park and safer, higher ground. Secondly, ensure that any vulnerable persons are accompanied during a flood. These could be young children from the office nursery, elderly or disabled clients. Consider how you will ensure safe passage for such people whom you are responsible for, and take them out of the office to the meeting point.

General behaviour

It is important that we all evacuate the building quickly and calmly. If you have time and it is safe to do so, you may wish to place sandbags in front of office doors and windows. Stay upstairs in the office if the flood happens too quickly to evacuate the building. Take food and water and your mobile phone and call for assistance from your phone or from an upstairs window. Above all, remain calm and patient. Help will arrive, so do not take any unnecessary risks.

(Word count: 350 words)

Reading comprehension: The most destructive volcano (page 247)

Q18: False

Q19: False

Q20:

1. buoyed
2. cataclysmic
3. volatility

Q21: The team / Volcanologists

Q22: A: In a newspaper or magazine

Listening comprehension: Earthquakes (page 248)

Q23:

Perched upon a multitude of converging tectonic plates, or 'fault lines', Japan is perhaps the most **precariously** located country in the world when it comes to susceptibility from earthquakes. Over a thousand tremors are measured on mainland Japan and in the oceans nearby every year. The majority of these pass by unnoticed by the average Japanese commuter or tourist, as they are too far underground or too low on the Richter scale to be **detectable** at surface level. Nonetheless, the Japanese public are the most informed and prepared of any world nation for the possibility of a huge earthquake. Tokyo has been **uneasily** anticipating an overdue major quake for the last ninety years.

The Great Kanto Earthquake of 1923 claimed the lives of one hundred thousand citizens of Tokyo. Since that time, Japan's government has placed earthquake damage limitation and **evacuation** procedures high on its political agenda. Safety standards and building design are subject to rigorous **scrutiny** to ensure that they meet the required levels of earthquake proofing.

The focus on the capital city has itself been controversial and eye-opening for the people of Japan. The 2011 tsunami and the earthquake of 1995 in Kobe, in the west of Japan, served as a wake-up call to authorities whose efforts had arguably been too focussed on the most **populous** and economically important areas of their country. Both of these events, although not the strongest earthquakes recorded in or around Japanese shores, **wreaked** havoc and devastation on a **gargantuan** scale with tremendous loss of life. The lesson learned? An earthquake's magnitude is not the defining point in its ability to cause widespread destruction and despair. Indeed, regular earthquakes of 7 and 8 on the Richter scale are recorded in the seas surrounding Japan, but because the **epicentre** is deep underwater and because of their geographic location, these quakes tend to cause minor, if any, damage to small fishing villages in rural Japan. Move the source of the earthquake one hundred miles nearer the mainland and pointing towards Tokyo, and such **seismic** activity would have an altogether different level of impact. The Kobe earthquake's epicentre was so near to the city that the **carnage** it caused was enormous.

The avoidance of a repeat of the Kobe earthquake in other major **metropolises** is a conundrum for the Japanese government, as the number of variables when attempting to forecast earthquakes is enormous. Seismologists estimate a seventy-five per cent chance of a major earthquake occurring in the Tokyo vicinity within twenty-five years. Therefore the authorities have an obligation to do all that they can to prevent it.

Fire safety has been improved in most homes and offices in Tokyo. State of the art sprinkler systems are installed as a matter of course nowadays, and **inflammable** furniture is now illegal. Fires resulting from the aftermath of earthquakes are one of the biggest killers, and therefore reducing their likelihood is a controllable and measurable preventative action.

Computer aided design has enabled structural engineers to ensure that they are using the best resources when assembling new office blocks. New structures have to withstand the strongest of tremors, and not crumble or **buckle** under all but direct pressure. Of course, not all buildings in Tokyo are new - and many residents simply cannot afford the considerable expense needed to shore up their older homes structurally against the threat of earthquakes. It is these most vulnerable residents whom the Japanese authorities are racing against time to safeguard.

Answers to questions and activities for Unit 3

Topic 1: Learning skills in context

Book titles (page 255)

Q1:

A) History

B) Science Fiction

C) Children's

D) Business

E) Biography

F) Religion

G) Politics

H) Horror

I) Crime

J) Languages

The blurb (page 255)

Q2: b) Adolescents

Q3: a) Horror

Q4: b) Romance

Q5: a) Adults

Q6: c) Thriller

Q7: d) Drama

Extracts (page 257)

Q8: c) Space Exploration

Q9: a) Social Unrest

Q10: d) Market News

Q11: e) Unemployment Crisis

Q12: b) Education

Dictionary practice (page 259)

Q13: a) obliged

Q14: b) caused

Q15: b) quickly

Q16: a) levy

Q17: c) end

Q18: b) exceptional

British and American English (page 260)

Q19:

Henry strode out of his **apartment** and onto the **sidewalk**. After that long shift he was overcome with hunger, so he made his way as quickly as he could to the **diner**. "Two hot dogs and a **pitcher** of beer", he barked at the waitress. "We're all outta dogs, all we got left are some **cookies**. . . you want one with your beer?" Henry had always liked the waitress, she had cute **bangs** and a tempting smile, even if she managed to make serving drinks look like brain surgery. "Sure", he replied, ". . . and you got an **eraser**? I just started this crossword and I think I got one wrong. . . " "An **eraser**, Yeah, I'll have a look for you honey, why not? You want me to get you a **pacifier** and change your **diapers** while I'm back there?"

Henry was too focussed on the couple who'd just entered the diner to deliver one of his typically sharp ripostes. They'd parked their **station wagon** just by the other door, the one facing the busy **intersection**, before saddling in, arm in arm, the fresh faced girl chewing on a **granola** bar and carrying a **soda**. "Why am I not with this **granola** girl, or even the waitress?" Henry wondered to himself, as he took his diabetes **shot**. I need to get myself outta this job, this town, that **apartment** with that damn leaky **faucet** and that insufferable **boarder**. . . "**Check**, please!" he shouted through the back to the waitress, "But you've not even eaten yet!" came the puzzled reply. Henry had already left a ten dollar **bill** on the counter and made his way out, determined to kick start his day, maybe even his life. . .

Q20:

apartment	flat
sidewalk	pavement
pitcher	jug
cookies	biscuits
bangs	fringe
pacifier	dummy
diapers	nappies
station wagon	estate car
intersection	crossroads
granola	muesli
soda	drink
faucet	tap
check	bill
bill	note

Reading: How best to read (page 262)

Q21: b) To eliminate bad reading habits

Q22: a) True

Q23: a) True

Q24: a) True

Q25: devoured

Q26: counterproductive

Q27: phenomena

Pre-listening: Talking literature (page 263)

Q28:

1. Science Fiction / Love Story
   A man who can travel in time / The relationship between a married couple
2. Science Fiction / historical fiction
   The lives of three characters in the Baroque period in Europe
3. Classic Fiction (French)
   Character called Therese Raquin
4. Thriller
   The fate of a climatologist framed for murder

Listening: Talking literature (page 264)

Listening transcript

Martin: So did you finish the book then?

Janine: Yes I did. Oh it was fantastic! So moving. I cried!

Freya: What was it you were reading?

Janine: Oh it's a book called the Time Traveller's Wife have you read it?

Freya: No I haven't. What's it about? Would you recommend it?

Janine: Well I really enjoyed it. It has a kind of science fiction element to it but it is very much a romance as well. It's about a man, Henry, who has a genetic disorder which causes him to travel involuntarily in time. He is married to Clare, an artist and a lot of the novel focuses on how she deals with constantly losing him and then ultimately how she copes, or rather doesn't cope, with his death. There are lots of interesting shifts in time and perspective. At one point for example she meets him when she is very young and he tells her to write down the dates that she will see him throughout her life. There is also a very unsettling chapter in which he meets his daughter in the future when she is aged ten and he discovers that he has died when she was five, a fate which he can't alter. The end is really poignant. Clare had been unable to accept death and kept waiting for him. The wait seems futile until at the end of the novel he comes back to visit her and she does have a chance, aged 82, to hold him again. The language is very powerful and although yes it's science fiction, still when you read it's credible. Anyway in many ways it's a classic love story. It's a very pure love and the tragic impediment to their happiness is his disease. Oh they've made a film of the story. Anyway you might like it Freya but am not sure it's your cup of tea Martin.

Martin: No I'm not really into romantic novels though I do like science fiction. I think that literature really is gender related! I mean loads of women rave about Jane Austen and the Brontes but I'm afraid that type of literature is totally soporific for me!

Freya: What kind of books do you read?

Martin: Well recently I read a book called The Baroque Cycle by an American writer. It is in fact part of a trilogy and though in many ways it is historical fiction I think the writer prefers to describe it as science fiction. It places three main characters into the Baroque period, late 17th and early 18th centuries, describing the minutiae of life in the English and French courts through their experiences. In fact one character travels around the world, and because of that the writer has an extremely wide canvas to work with. What the characters have in common is their intelligence and this enables them to survive their often horrific destiny - one character for example, Eliza, is abducted into slavery. It's a fantastic romp through events of the time drawing on real life characters - of course the writer can't change any of the historical facts but the fictional characters are malleable. The level of detail is impressive and has to be attributed to the amount of research by the author. The language is extremely evocative. It's history, fiction and to some extent science fiction too. I really recommend it! Freya your turn what kind of books do you like to read?

Freya: At the moment I am re reading a French novel I read as a student at university, Therese Raquin, a classic French novel, and it's really amazing to compare my memory of it with the way I see it now.

Janine: What's the plot?

Freya: Well Therese is married to Camille who is her cousin and with whom she was brought up. He is quite odious and she doesn't care for him. Camille's friend Laurent and Therese become lovers and decide to kill Camille by drowning him. Having murdered Camille though, they are then haunted by visions of him between them in and around the house, to the extent that they are no longer able to sleep and it drives them insane. In the end they commit suicide but not before trying to kill each other. When I first read it, I was struck by the powerful descriptions of their descent into madness. It seemed to be a metaphorical haunting and I saw it as a moral tale in which the lovers were punished by guilt for their misdemeanours. However this time I am more aware of how unsympathetic the characters are. I mean they are all horrible! Laurent concedes no remorse in spite of the torment he endures following the murder. He says he would do it again! Apparently the book was condemned by many at the time of publishing because it fails to take a moral stance. It was seen as completely immoral. Fantastic book. Okay just you left Grace. What are you reading?

Grace: I've just finished Ordinary Thunderstorms. It was a really good read. It's essentially a contemporary thriller, with lots of twists and turns. It's set in London, which is where my family is from and perhaps why I was drawn to it in the first place. It's about a character Adam Kindred, a climatologist who because of a chance encounter, is framed for a murder he didn't commit. He is then forced to go underground, to disappear without trace in order to survive. Although obviously quite an unlikely turn of events, the story is so well written that it seems extremely plausible. The descriptions of the characters he encounters and their misfortunes are very disturbing. It's quite a cerebral novel with lots of witty references and allusions. The reason I liked it so much though I think is because it really calls into question what makes us who we are. What is our identity when we have been extracted from the life we know, stripped of all our worldly goods, contacts and points of reference? Hmm it really makes you think......I could talk about books all day but I guess we ought to get back to the grindstone.

Q29: b) Janine has just finished a book

Q30: Timing, the characters and the language

Q31: involuntary

Q32: malleable

Q33: descent into madness

Q34: Go underground and disappear without a trace

Q35: Therese Raquin/Freya and Ordinary Thunderstorms/Grace

Q36: The Time Traveler's Wife/Janine and The Baroque Cycle/ Martin

Q37: The Time Traveler's Wife/Janine and The Baroque Cycle/ Martin

Q38: The Time Traveler's Wife/Janine and The Baroque Cycle/ Martin

Q39: Ordinary Thunderstorms/Grace

Q40: Ordinary Thunderstorms/Grace

Genre analysis (page 265)

Q41: f) letter to a newspaper

Q42: e) theatre review

Q43: d) letter of complaint

Q44: a) magazine article

Q45: g) report

Q46: b) email to a friend

Q47: c) discursive essay

Identifying purpose (page 267)

Q48: 5

Q49: 2

Q50: 3

Q51: 6

Q52: 4

Q53: 1

Q54: 7

Features of language: Genre (page 269)

Q55:

A) 3, 4, 5, and 6

B) 2, 4 and 5

C) 1, 3, 6 and 7

D) 4 and 5

E) 4 and 5

F) 1, 3, 6 and 7

G) 4

H) 1, 3. 6 and 7

I) 4

J) 2

Features of language: Writing conventions (page 269)

Q56: The writer is likely to know the gender of the editor of the publication

Q57: metaphorical

Q58: not only am I disappointed

Q59: a magazine

Q60: was highlighted

Q61: I

Q62: nevertheless or at the same time

Features of language: Finding meaning in context (page 271)

Q63: intrinsic

Q64: fulfil

Q65: hierarchy

Q66: conducive

Q67: engage

Q68: relevance

Q69: facilitator

Q70: imposed

Generating ideas (page 272)

Possible answers

Here are some possible answers.

Food: badly cooked/ over-cooked/ tasteless/ cold when meant to be warm/ foreign body in it e.g. insect or hair Service: slow/rude/lazy/sloppy/not paying sufficient attention.

Atmosphere: too noisy/ rowdy customers/ loud music/ cold /empty.

Apologies: Offers of free meal, course or drinks.

Writing a letter of complaint (page 272)

Model answer

17
Anderson
Road
Glasgow
G12
9RS
21st
April
2017

Mr L
McGinley,
Pasta
Pasta
112
Beachwood
Road,
Glasgow

Dear Mr McGinley

I am writing to you to in order to convey my disappointment with both the food and standard of customer service to which I was subjected in your restaurant last night. I hope that by drawing your attention to this matter, I shall be offered appropriate compensation and at the same time protect others from a similar experience.

I have been a regular customer at PastaPasta for many years. For this reason I chose the restaurant as the venue for a special celebration with some classmates last night. My complaint is not essentially with the food, although what we received was disappointing, but with the quite bizarre approach to customer service adopted by the staff, notably the new manageress.

In the first place the waitress brought the wrong starters to the table, she then replaced mine with a stone cold version of the correct order. Finally following some prompting, she presented me with a lukewarm version of my choice, which naturally remained largely uneaten on my plate. When asked presently by another waitress if everything was all right, I said that I hadn't eaten the food because it was still cold. At this point the manageress came over and told me quite aggressively that if the food was still cold I shouldn't have touched it all.

Strangely enough, following this exchange, in which I had the temerity to suggest an apology would have helped, the manageress then said she was unwilling to serve us. Having reached this impasse, obviously we left and of course, are unlikely to return. I cannot believe that any restaurant owner would condone this approach to customer service.

It is very disappointing to find this change in a favourite haunt and as a hitherto loyal customer to be treated in this shoddy fashion. I have taken the time to write this letter because I feel very strongly that you have been let down by your staff. Nevertheless I expect that many others will simply choose other venues to frequent.

I expect a full apology and refund at the very least and look forward to an early response.

Yours sincerely

Q71: The appropriate sentences are 2, 5, 7, 8 and 9

The reasons why the other examples are inappropriate are:

1: informal
3: not a useful comment
4: irrelevant
6: informal
10: not helpful nor likely to have a positive effect on the reader

Listening comprehension: Giving feedback (page 273)

Listening transcript

Teacher: For the first part of today's session I would like you to get into groups of three or four and complete some feedback forms. This is one of the ways in which we are able to get information from students about what we are doing well and also get recommendations about ways in which we can improve. So have a chat with the people in your group first and then fill in the forms. It's totally confidential, so I'll leave you with this and come back in about half an hour.

Marie: Okay so let's have a look at some of the questions we have to answer, there are quite a lot. Will we start with section one and write each section up as soon as we've finished?

Thomas: Sounds like a good idea. Do you agree Anne?

Anne: Yes that's fine with me

Marie: Okay the first question is "what are you studying?" Well that's straightforward I'm doing Social Sciences, Thomas you're doing Multimedia Design and Anne you are doing Dance. Question two, "Why did you enrol on this particular course?" Thomas?

Thomas: Well. . . I've always been really into computers and have been working with computers for a few years. I had kind of moved into the field of design. The problem was I didn't have formal qualifications for the work I was actually doing. I felt that my promotion prospects were limited because of that. I started to look for courses and thought this one had the most to offer me. It's got the syllabus content I want and the qualification should help advance my career. Oh and I can get here easily by bike.

Anne: I've been dancing since I was about five! I love music and movement and I have never wanted to do anything else but be a dancer. My parents are really supportive, they are behind me 100% but they wanted me to get some qualifications because dance is so competitive. I really wanted to put their minds at rest. This course will qualify me to be a dance teaching assistant which would be a good fallback position, a security blanket if I didn't make it as a professional dancer. What about you Marie?

Marie: Well I never thought about studying when I was at school. No one in our family had been to university so I thought it was out of reach. Perhaps I could have got more qualifications, but at 16 I had no plans or ambitions. I got married and had children quite early. I really got inspired to learn when my kids were studying, when helping them. Suddenly university seemed feasible. Now I am here on the first rung of the ladder and I just want to see how far I can get.

Marie: Question 3 is "Are you satisfied with the course so far?"

Thomas: Yes I am really happy so far with the course I think that the teaching staff are really helpful and the course covers everything I wanted it to. The only small issue for me is that I could really do with a bit more access to the computer rooms. You know we get a lot of homework and from a financial point of view, I just can't invest in the necessary technology to do the work off campus. We could do with late access to the computer rooms, if only a couple of times a week.

Anne: I know what you mean Thomas I feel the same. The college seems to open till eight on a Tuesday but I'd love to get more practice time in the studio. Apart from that I am really positive about it all. The amount I'm learning is amazing and my teacher has great handouts for us to read at home with fabulous pictures.

Marie: Well I find the course I am doing extremely stimulating. My tutor is fantastic he has a breadth and depth of knowledge about his field that is really impressive. I couldn't fault the course! The next question is about what we plan to do on completion of our studies here. Well as I said I want to go as far as I can, university is the next step.

Thomas: To be more successful in my current field. That's my goal!

Anne: I want to dance, but I mean really dance not just as a spare time thing. I want to be earning a living doing the thing I love!

Marie: Right let me get some of this down on paper.

Q72: Social Sciences, Multimedia Design and Dance

Q73:

1. Promotion prospects /formal qualifications
2. Parental pressure
3. University entrance

Q74: Security blanket and fallback position

Q75: Suddenly university seemed feasible

Q76: Access to college computers

Q77: Breadth and depth of knowledge

Writing: Reports (page 274)

Model answer

Introduction

The following report is based on a survey of communications students. The students were invited to comment on a range of issues including their background and current experiences of college life. The report will focus on the following areas: reasons for study, aspirations, positive and negative comments.

Reasons for Study

The students surveyed were from the following programmes: Multimedia Design, Dance and Social Sciences. Respondents indicated a range of reasons for choice of college and course. Students had opted for further education for a variety of purposes including desire to enhance opportunities for promotion in current employment, ambition to embark on a university career and parental pressure. The choice of particular course tended to reflect personal ambition.

Positive Comments

The respondents indicated a high level of satisfaction with the quality of teaching which they had experience thus far. One student was particularly impressed with the erudition of her tutor whom she described as inspirational. In general students were happy with course content, materials and homework.

Negative Comments

Some students indicated that they would like to be able to use the college facilities in the evenings. There was some disappointment that the college was only open late on one evening each week. Students indicated that they sometimes found it difficult to keep up with homework as they lacked the facilities required such as computer technology or dance space at home.

Conclusion

The survey indicates a high level of satisfaction with college. Quality of teaching and learning and facilities were all rated highly. However students would like the college to increase the hours of access to college facilities to include more evenings.

Reading comprehension: Curriculum for Excellence (page 275)

Q78: C

Q79: A

Q80: Implementation
interpretation
lack of detail

Q81: Examples of good practice, culture of openness, potential of the new standard for challenge, meaningful learning and progress

Q82: It presents arguments for and against Curriculum for Excellence

Q83: encourage, enable and enhance

Topic 2: Further education opportunities

Vocabulary: Commonly confused words (page 280)

Q1: principal

Q2: lose

Q3: stationery

Q4: proceed

Q5: effect

Q6: advice

Q7: whether

Q8: morale

Q9: practice

Parts of speech: Definitions (page 281)

Q10: principal: noun

Q11: lose: verb

Q12: principle: noun

Q13: stationary: adjective

Q14: effect: noun

Q15: stationery: noun

Q16: precede: verb

Q17: proceed: verb

Q18: practise: verb

Q19: whether: conjunction

Q20: loose: adjective

Q21: moral: noun

Q22: affect: verb

Q23: expand: verb

Q24: advise: verb

Q25: weather: noun

Q26: advice: noun

Q27: morale: noun

Q28: practice: noun

Q29: expend: verb

Reading: University challenge (page 283)

Q30: c) Both of the above

Q31: c, e, f

Q32: insurmountable

Q33: concur

Q34: muster

Q35: b) false

Q36: a) true

Writing: Tuition fees (page 284)

Model answer

Gaining a university education is something to which most young people in secondary schools in the UK aspire. From the 1970s until the end of the 20th century, the number of students entering university had been increasing but, as can be observed from the table, as of 1998 there has been a steady but significant growth in the costs associated with attending university which may threaten the inclusivity of Higher Education institutions.

Students on university courses before 1998 had no mandatory fees. Student grants covered their fees and at that time students only needed to take out loans for extra costs such as accommodation and bills. Loans were optional and therefore many students graduated around this time with little or no debt.

1998 saw a dramatic change to the fees system and at this time students could expect to graduate from their four-year degrees owing a total of at least £4000. It could be argued that £4000 is not an unreasonable sum to expect students to repay when they enter the working world. However, this figure did not remain at such a level for very long. Indeed, the costs of degrees have drastically spiralled upward in the subsequent two decades, meaning the average student had debt of between £12000 to £15000 in 2009 and £20000 to £36000 for new graduates in 2017.

Over a twenty year time period, the cost of the journey through university has risen from being free to some students or affordable to others, to a level which will see many students repaying debt for several years after they graduate. It is difficult to say if the fee increases will directly affect the number of graduates or even applicants in the early part of the 21st century, but it is something that potential students need to consider much more carefully than those who studied a generation before them.

(311 words)

Correct word choice (page 285)

Q37: Constance's grades were disappointing, probably due to her illness prior to the exams. We will initiate an **appeal** on her behalf, as it would be an unfortunate outcome had she to **resit** this year.

Q38: I am sorry, but the conditions for attachment to the external Higher examination were made abundantly clear from the outset. The decision is based on both your **prelim** result and the successful completion of all **continuous assessments**.

Q39: Emily is investigating the possibility of a five-year course of study, with a **sandwich** placement in Russia prior to the **Honours** year.

Q40: That's right, yes. Our evening provision is primarily geared towards those without an academic background, and those who have been outside of academia for some time. We pride ourselves on our commitment to **vocational** courses, widening participation and **lifelong learning**.

Q41: Professor Wood, from the Social Science and Linguistics **faculty**, will be able to answer any questions you have about **postgraduate** study, and she will also be able to discuss the requirements of the dissertation.

Vocabulary: Academia (page 286)

Q42: resit

Q43: continuous assessment

Q44: prelim

Q45: appeal

Q46: faculty

Q47: honours

Q48: postgraduate

Q49: sandwich

Q50: vocational

Q51: lifelong learning

Listening comprehension: Robot teachers (page 287)

Q52: a) true

Q53: b) false

Q54: b) false

Q55: c) To act as a teaching assistant to a real teacher

Q56: c) There were financial implications

Q57: b) He does not care what the critics think

Q58: a) unclear

Writing: Technology in the classroom (page 289)

Model answer

The way that students learn is always changing, developing in line with advancements in technology which are utilised by schools, colleges and universities to improve the educational experience. This essay will examine both the positive effects and the drawbacks of new technology on students and teachers in modern society.

Teachers always want to provide the best resources and use the latest methods to get the best out of their students. New technology in the last couple of decades has helped them do this. For example, it is unlikely that you will find a chalkboard in any classroom these days. Interactive electronic boards have become standard. The ability to access webpages, graphics, animations and videos on these boards has meant that the standard board has suddenly become multi-faceted and encompasses a computer, a video and audio player, a projector and a standard board all in one. Even some textbooks are now produced electronically so the teacher can navigate them on screen. This has helped teachers save time preparing lessons and delivering them in class and makes the whole experience of learning more enjoyable for students. Similarly, students can use phone apps, blogs and virtual learning environments to enhance and extend the learning experience outside of the classroom.

All of these developments are potentially very positive, but what about teachers who do not understand or are not comfortable with using technology? Although some educational institutions will offer training, many teachers are left just to learn how to use the technology themselves, with varying results. Teachers need to acquire new skills and for some this is daunting, time consuming and worrying. This is a factor often overlooked in the adoption of new technology in the classroom.

The future looks likely to bring more technological advancements. The virtual or remote classroom is often talked about and to some extent, it already exists. This is a realm in which the teacher and student never meet and everything is conducted online. While an exciting prospect for future generations of learners, it raises more questions about what happens to the teachers who cannot keep up with technology.

(Word count: 350 words)

Listening comprehension: Scotland Street School (page 290)

Listening transcript

Contemporary Glasgow is home to a plethora of educational establishments; three universities, a prestigious art school, half a dozen Further Education colleges and a wealth of school provision. However, one of the most interesting facets of Scottish education is preserved in the Charles Rennie Mackintosh designed Scotland Street Museum, an everlasting monument to the school environment of bygone days in Scotland.

Now disused but far from derelict, walking around the school gives off the feeling of being inside at interval time, or on a free period, and you half expect to hear the teacher's ominous footsteps approaching outside as you survey the empty classrooms.

There are three painstakingly recreated classrooms reflecting the different eras that pupils here would have experienced, from the early Victorian period of the school's construction to the late sixties. Ink wells are a feature of the antique looking desks, and the schoolmaster's cane dominates the front wall next to the blackboard... which may explain the distinct lack of graffiti on the desks, as unruly pupils in those days would have been subject to a rap on the knuckles, at the very least, for any violation of school rules. The evolution of Scottish education is encapsulated in every brick, and the history of the public school is awakened through the implementation of audio visual presentations and displays of memorabilia from the annals.

The re-enactment of an historic, living breathing school does not begin and end with the classrooms, however. The restoration works have also brought the cloakrooms, hallways and corridors to life, as seen at least fifty to one hundred years past. Part of the appeal clearly lies in the distinctive and evocative stylistic features synonymous with Mackintosh, and his trademark motifs are evident throughout the building.

The last pupils put down their pencils in 1979, when the urban decay of the Tradeston area had become an insurmountable obstacle to pupil recruitment, the school roll dropped from its once lofty days of 1200 plus pupils to barely one hundred, and the construction of more modern secondary schools in the area meant that parents no longer saw Scotland Street as the place to enrol their children. The bell had rung for what seemed to be the last time.

The school building lay empty for some years, prior to the decision of the city council to invest in its preservation, in no small part again due to its architectural significance.

Nowadays, Scotland Street school museum hosts a variety of exhibitions and activities, all of which have an educational theme. The school is a popular location for visiting schoolchildren on class outings, and on occasion the staff organise an historical live classroom programme, which allows visitors an immersion experience through recreation of actual classes from yesteryear, taught by staff members who simulate school teaching practices of days gone by.

Q59: b) False

Q60: b) False

Q61: b) False

Q62: synonymous

Q63: immersion

Q64: a) True

Q65: c) To train staff about the museum's facilities

Reading Comprehension: Mind your language (page 292)

Q66: obstinate

Q67: c: Fear of the UK being left behind

Q68: 2: Apprehensive about the impact of some changes

Q69: allusion (s)

Q70: eradicate

Q71: supplant (ing)

Q72: 1: true